THE MOTH

THE

MOTH

Preface by
Adam Gopnik

Foreword by
George Dawes Green

Edited and with
an Introduction by
Catherine Burns

hachette
BOOKS

NEW YORK BOSTON

Hachette Books
Hachette Book Group
1290 Avenue of the Americas
New York, NY 10104

www.HachetteBookGroup.com

Printed in the United States of America

LSC-C

Originally published by Hyperion.
First Hachette Books trade edition: October 2014

15

Hachette Books is a division of Hachette Book Group, Inc.
The Hachette Books name and logo are trademarks of Hachette Book
Group, Inc.

The Hachette Speakers Bureau provides a wide range of authors for
speaking events. To find out more, go to www.hachettespeakersbureau.com
or call (866) 376-6591.

The publisher is not responsible for websites (or their content) that
are not owned by the publisher.

Library of Congress Cataloging-in-Publication Data

The moth / edited and with an introduction by Catherine Burns; preface
by Adam Gopnik; foreword by George Dawes Green.—First edition.
    pages   cm
  ISBN 978-1-4013-1111-7 (pbk.)
1. Moth radio hour (Radio program) 2. United States—Social life
and customs—1971—Anecdotes. 3. Popular culture—United States—
Anecdotes. 4. United States—Biography—Anecdotes. I. Burns,
Catherine, editor of compilation. II. Gopnik, Adam. III. Green,
George Dawes. IV. Moth radio hour (Radio program)
  PN1991.77.M675M68   2013
  791.44—dc23

                                                    2013014785

For Wanda

Contents

THE MOTH

Carpe Diem

Save Me

Preface

Who knew that what New York needed was a front porch? That the secret desire hidden in the hearts of hipsters and banksters alike was a chance to sit after dinner in a screened-in space, to escape—or maybe just enjoy—the summer heat, and there, in the dark, lit by a single lamp with its attendant insects, swap stories, tell tales? Who knew that what we really wanted was one shared place where everyone from a kid off the street to a cop just off the beat to Salman Rushdie could tell about this weird thing that happened: *Did I tell you this already? No? Well, you remember that time I went round on Christmas to Uncle Norm's . . .*

Storytelling, story-sharing, tale-bearing in the good sense, *yarn-spinning*—who knew that what New York (and now the nation; we'll get there) needed was . . . *that*?

Well, the men and mostly women of The Moth knew. This book relates what is itself an improbable story, a yarn spun about how The Moth sprang from a simple idea of George Green's, slowly grew, and then eventually became a national phenomenon.

But the deeper questions are: Why now? Why here? And, above all, why does it work? What is it about this improbable form that The Moth has made its own and shared with the world—the timed, short personal story, rooted in reminiscence and memoir, distinctly unprofessional even when offered by a pro—that vibrates with its era?

A lot of its success has to do, as always in life, with much preparation and calculation beneath the seeming spontaneity. For all their seeming inconsequence and improvisational air, a good Moth story is as carefully prepped and cultivated as a bonsai tree, with the same understanding that the miniature form, far more fragile than the bigger kind, needs more constant tending. You have a little stage space to waste in a two-hour play, but there's not a second that doesn't have to count in a ten-minute story. The producers and directors of Moth evenings—an astonishing array of those mostly female overseers, who somehow combine the role of effusive cheerleader and hard-headed theater critic—"run" the stories, *work* the stories, over and over, until that thing you hear, though never written down, is incised on the storyteller's consciousness for good, with all its inner twists and turns.

That relentless preparation may be, for the arrogant writer-type who thinks he already knows all there is to know about storytelling—i.e., me—the most difficult, and then in the end the most rewarding thing about the Moth process. A good story, we're reminded, is shaped, plotted, rehearsed. The best guy on the porch was planning his tale right through dinner. A good story needs an A plot and usually a B plot, and then, if it's to "levitate the room," to use the lovely expression the women of The Moth use themselves, it almost always needs some last rising touch, a note of pathos or self-recognition or poetic benediction, to lift the story, however briefly, into the realm of fable or symbol.

Three more C's spring to mind to encircle the mystery of The Moth. A lot of the magic of the Moth story is confessional: Everyone likes to talk about himself, to be sure, but the stories we like to hear most are the ones that you would think we would be most unwilling to tell. The human need for confession in the presence of others, left mostly untended by the churches these days, is fulfilled by the Moth occasion. An uncanny number of the best Moth stories are *admissions*, even apologies, frank, candid ("I spent Christmas in a transgender bar" or "When I was fourteen, I shot my friend by accident"). And the audience listening implies, by the perfect silence of their attention, that they are rapt—right there with you. Throughout even a self-humiliating Moth story, one hears the rarest thing: the sound of an audience keeping an open mind. Then often laughter—and always, applause—closes the circuit. The unspeakable or embarrassing thing admitted turns out to be . . . not so bad, maybe even surprisingly commonplace. We didn't all insult James Brown or get busted making hooch in Attica, but life presents relentless difficulties and complexities and humiliations even to the luckiest of us, and we applaud warmly as if to say, *I know.* The audience doesn't release its breath as it does at a high-tension tragedy, or applaud in culminated pleasure as at a good musical. No, the audience pauses, reflects for a bare half moment, and then erupts in the pleasure not of seeing a thing accomplished but of hearing a truth shared. Some ancient ritual of expiation seems to be taking place: that's okay, the exhalation says, what happened to you, however hair-raising, and the Moth stories that have been told about escapes from prison, accidental shootings, and near-death experiences are now part of what has happened to *us* all.

The second C is that of comedy. Perhaps the hardest thing those Moth story directors have to teach the storyteller is that the laughter will come only if there are no self-conscious jokes. *This isn't stand-up*, they say, in pleasant effect, to the guy who, with a microphone suddenly in his hands, wrongly thinks himself a second Seinfeld. (Me, again.) The laughter provoked by a Moth story has to be ethical laughter: not the laughter of a taboo transgressed, but the laughter of a truth revealed. And nothing is more *helpful* to a storyteller who may also be, in mufti, a pro writer than this reminder that the ethic of all storytelling is credibility, truth.

Much has been made of the human need for narrative, but, truth be told, stories don't make us better people. But they do make us truer writers.

My own Moth experience came along, for instance, at a moment when I often felt mired in the damp, soggy marsh of the four-thousand-word essay, with its exhausting, sapient certainties and predictable drop-cap caesuras ("Edmund Burke was born in . . ."). The pressure of Moth storytelling made me newly aware of what propulsion can do for a paragraph. It reminded me that drama and pacing and even suspense could be wooed from the slightest materials, and that the key to good writing (one key, anyway) is that the reader should never look back. (Even Proust, for all his elaborating, is a spiraling but not a circular writer. We may move round and round, but we press ahead.) Every essay is really a story, and every story, truth be told, shares the same ethic, the same motto. The great storyteller Frank O'Connor defined it best, saying once that every good story should end, in spirit, with the exact same words: "And everything that ever happened to me afterwards, I never felt the same about again." (He actually got to use that ending, once.) In this book of Moth stories, that test of significance, of meaning, is met again and again. There are very few of these well-told tales that don't have those words as an invisible addition. You can mouth them to yourself as the story ends: *Jesus, she could never have felt the same about* anything *after that . . .*

Confession, comedy, and then one last alliterative thing—connection. Poetry and philosophy may be there to teach us, in a sudden stunning lurch of perspective, the virtues of detachment, but storytelling, large and small, is there to teach us the beauties of attachment. The sweat and worry of a Moth evening nearly always ends with the sense of membership in a private club, but one shared by speakers and listeners. We wring each other's hands, not in sweaty acknowledgment, but in shared appreciation: Every story knits together with every other. It must: A small connection, a link in a chain, is always forged.

If "I'll never feel the same" is the moral of every good story, "We're all in this together" is the moral of every Moth occasion. Of all the alchemies of human connection—sex and childbirth and marriage and friendship—the strangest is this: You can stand up and tell a story that is made entirely, embarrassingly, of "I's," and a listening audience somehow turns each "I" into a "me." This alchemy, of self-absorption into shared experience, is the alchemy of all literature. No one will ever know exactly how it happens, but however it happens, it is what makes The Moth fly too.

Adam Gopnik

Foreword

Once on a porch on a Georgia island, while a troupe of moths staggered around the light, while cicadas kept time in the live oaks, Dayton Malone told us of the night he'd let 6,000 chickens escape from the shed he was supposed to be minding. I've forgotten the details (too much bourbon), but his easygoing frankness has stayed with me. He was simply unsuited for the job of chicken-minder. He'd left a door unlatched and gone to bed. In the morning, the girls were gone. He went out and searched the horizon, and saw a far-off smear of white—the last of them—receding.

I loved Dayton when he told that story. This feeling surprised me, because we'd never really gotten along—he was a true son of the South and was always needling me about my newfound Yankeeness, my *scalawaggery*—plus he was always trying to shake salt on my food (he was a pro-salt fanatic). But his saga of the lost chickens seemed so candid and clownish and human, and everything about it—the hill-country cadence, the trailing-off sweep of his hand as he muttered, "Gone—every last one of them," his sad whistle of defeat—struck me as . . .

well, not *honest* exactly (he was too much of a showman for that), but utterly revealing of the man.

We heard stories like that all night. If you were looking for literal truth, you wouldn't find it, but on Wanda's porch, you got such full doses of character and loss and destiny that you'd always come away reeling (of course the bourbon heightened this effect).

Years later I was living in New York, and one night I happened to be at some particularly dull and sing-songy poetry reading in the East Village, and I started missing Wanda's porch, and wishing that the poet would lower her aesthetic screen for a moment and just *tell us a story*.

That was it—that was the germ. An idea fluttered through my thoughts: that I might organize a night of storytelling in New York City in honor of those nights at Wanda's. I supposed it would be fairly easy: New York must be filled with frustrated raconteurs. And so several years later, after much fussing and feinting and overthinking, that idea finally launched. I hosted an evening at my loft in Manhattan. I hired a director, the brilliant and indefatigable Joey Xanders. We rented chairs. We served hors d'oeuvres. We called it The Moth, and it was a bomb.

The stories were all overcrafted, or too prettified, or too lugubriously confessional. And way too long. I didn't tell a story, but in saying "a few words," I managed to be as long-winded as any of them. My guests were polite afterward—someone even called the evening "noble." But I wanted to crawl into a hole. However, late that night, after many drinks, my friend Sheri Holman said, "Well, yeah, it was awful. Unquestionably. But there was still something moving about it. Just the idea of it. A night of stories!"

And the way she said, "A night of stories!"—it recalled

Wanda's porch so vividly, so romantically, that suddenly I was hell-bent to try again. I got many friends to pitch in, and Joey scoured the city for raconteurs. We set down some guiding principles. All stories would be rehearsed, shaped. We would demand freshness and the non-jokey kind of wit that bubbles up naturally from true human predicaments. We would insist on pithiness. Pithiness above all: we brought in a saxophonist to be a timekeeper.

We began to put on Moths all over town. And to discover, one by one, true raconteurs.

Jonathan Ames was our first star. His style was frenetic and disturbing. Standing before us, composing on his feet, he'd dip into his bank of memories and drag to the surface whatever hideous artifacts he happened upon. He would not censor them. Once he told us of his first discovery of masturbation, and how he'd gone running exultantly to his mother with the news of it. If he was ashamed of that episode, he shared it anyway. With such passion would he plunge in! He'd get wilder and wilder; he'd seem out of control; I'd imagine him as some crippled storm tossed ship bound for the rocks. Though the rudderlessness was all illusion: Jonathan was sitting calmly in the pilot-house and knew exactly where he was going. When he was ready, he would bring his story to a sudden, casual, shrugging close—and then stroll offstage while we caught our breaths.

Frank McCourt, author of *Angela's Ashes*, had a sweet voice and scapegrace cheekiness. A sense of great loss accompanied him always. He laughed at that loss and held it in contempt, yet it was so present to us that all hearts were broken the moment he began to speak.

Whereas George Plimpton seemed truly buoyed by his defeats. He'd tried his hand gamely at various sports, and failed spectacularly at all of them (except court tennis—he was a master of that one lovely oddball game). His pratfalls had inspired a half dozen great memoirs, and they were the source also of his power as a raconteur. We loved best the moments in his stories when his impostures would be revealed—when all pretension would be unmasked.

They were true raconteurs. Our Moth directors made them work, made them condense and tweak and reshape and condense some more, but those gentlemen never complained—because they truly *liked telling stories*. They liked telling them over and over.

Of course they all knew that the key to personal storytelling is owning up to one's foolishness. They had learned Orwell's famous lesson, "Autobiography is only to be trusted when it reveals something disgraceful. A man who gives a good account of himself is probably lying, since any life when viewed from the inside is simply a series of defeats." But beyond that—each knew how to expose his humiliations in his own way; each had his own squint or stutter or palms-up gesture of hopelessness, and could make himself into a singular, full-body work of art up on our stage.

It was something to behold.

So much so that some of us boldly predicted that this new thing (new in the sense that these nights of raw personal stories, porch stories, were coming out at last from the kitchen to the stage) might well become the art of the twenty-first century.

To nurture that dream has been an enormous labor, and many folks have given up huge chunks of their lives (please see my thank-yous at the back of this book). In the impossible early years, I had to beg fortunes from friends just to keep us alive.

And of course there have been insane fireball clashes of ego, which attend I suppose the birth of any creative enterprise. So many prima donnas! The famous acrobat who scorned direction with a volley of insults and had to be scratched. The famous French philosopher who could recount his dull successes untiringly but who could not, when pressed, recall a single thing that he had ever failed at. The comedian who would not shut up no matter how loudly the saxophone played. The self-obsessed movie star . . . well, I know Catherine is terrified as she reads this and I probably shouldn't tell you about the self-obsessed movie star.

But there are also nights when I'll walk to one of our slams and pass block after block of people who've been waiting in line for hours because our nights of shared stories are so compelling. Or I'll be at Cooper Union hearing Mike DeStefano's tale of giving his dying wife, Franny, one last Harley ride, and I'll look around and every man and woman within sight will be openly weeping. Or I'll be sitting in on a high school slam rehearsal in a suburb of Atlanta and a shy teenage girl will be relaying the smallest possible episode—her encounter with a buck deer on her way home from school one day—and all of us will be grinning from ear to ear because her little vignette is such an immense pleasure.

Or I'll be at the immortal Players Club in Manhattan, and the room will be dotted with my beloved friends, and one of our greats, Adam Gopnik or Juliet Hope Wayne or Joan Juliet Buck or Edgar Oliver, will be up on stage, approaching their tale's climax, and there will be not a sound in the room. Every spine in the house will be tuned to the soul standing before the microphone. Everyone awaiting the word, locked into the rhythm of the teller's breathing and waiting for whatever perfect confession of futility and foolishness and humanity is about to come rolling down upon us—and at those times that silly little notion that I had sixteen years ago will seem quite smart.

George Dawes Green
Founder

Introduction

In the early 1970s, my Mama heard that "a nice young woman novelist" was staying in a cabin down the lake from our house and called her up (having never met her before) and invited her over for lunch. One of my first memories is four-year-old me sitting down at our kitchen table to dine on mini pimento-cheese sandwiches and deviled eggs, and Mama introducing me to our guest, "Miss Harper Lee." She had come to my tiny hometown in Alabama to do research for what she thought might be her second book.

When I thought back on this as a teenager, I was kind of blown away by my Mama's kindness, but also her audacity. I said, "Mama, you just CALLED HER UP and invited her to lunch?!? She'd just won the *Pulitzer Prize!*"

But Mama just shrugged and said, "Well, I didn't know about that, but she was new in town, and living down the street, and I wanted to be neighborly. You gotta get to know your neighbors. You never know who is in line in front of you at the grocery store, and what's been going on with 'em."

Thirty years later I'm in New York City at The Moth,

meeting and getting to know people with astoundingly diverse backgrounds. Whether it's a grossly underprepared matador, a press secretary who overslept and missed Air Force One, or a grandmother of five who got up the guts to call our pitchline, our first conversation is always the same: "Tell me about yourself, tell me the story of how you became *you*."

We ask people to share the biggest moments of their lives— the moments that changed them for the better (or worse). And while many of our favorite stories are about moments of triumph, stories about our *mistakes* can often be even more revelatory. The number one quality of great storytellers is their willingness to be vulnerable, their ability to tell on themselves.

Few of us will go into outer space like Michael Massimino, but who can't relate to spending months preparing for a big event only to get there and be undermined by something as tiny as a stripped screw? We understand Alan Rabinowitz's need to save jaguars on a deeper level after we hear about his debilitating childhood stutter. It's hard for most of us to relate to their almost superhuman strengths, but their flaws help us slip into their shoes.

They share their stories; they don't read or perform them. We help them shape their stories, but when they take that stage, it's just them up there. That high-wire act is what makes The Moth so magical when it works. The audience's faith in the storytellers becomes a safety net that allows them to explore the most intense moments of their lives onstage in front of a room full of strangers.

We strive to make every Moth night feel like an intimate dinner party, each storyteller a guest holding the attention of the table for a moment while they relay a spellbinding tale.

Trying to capture that feeling on the page was, frankly, daunting. But as we began transcribing and reading sixteen years' worth of stories, we were astonished by their power in print. We considered more than three thousand stories, finally boiling down the list to these fifty.

As I sat down to edit them, there was not a story in the book that I hadn't heard at least a dozen times in audio. I was worried they would lose something on the page, but it was just the opposite. Even if you're a Moth fan who has heard many of these, we hope you'll find new things to love as you *read* them for the first time.

You will also find brand-new stories that you would never have encountered otherwise, like the one told by the beautiful Anoid Rakhmatyllaeva. Her story—of finding the courage to stand down a room full of machine gun–carrying soldiers who were destroying the pianos in her music school during a civil war—was told at a show we produced in Dushanbe, Tajikistan. The only surviving audio was captured in our rehearsal at the U.S. Embassy on a little handheld recorder that was set up in front of our interpreter, Anya, as she translated Anoid's story into English from her native Russian. But the audio is so muddy that it would never have made it onto our radio show or podcast.

(It's important to note that while these stories are among our all-time favorites, they should not be considered a definitive list—this isn't "*Billboard*'s Top Fifty Moth Stories." The idea of the book was that it would feature lightly edited transcripts of stories from the live recordings. Here we've chosen fifty that we felt worked best on the page.)

The world is becoming increasingly digitized: we sit in our

little boxes, staring at other boxes, communicating through our fingers on a keyboard. Human beings weren't meant to live this way. All our little devices and programs are supposed to connect us, but they really don't. They *kind of* connect us, but there's always a block there—an electronic wall that keeps us from really experiencing each other in a human way.

As a society, we have forgotten how to listen deeply. Each Moth evening is a chance to practice listening.

At The Moth, people tell intimate stories, stories that are sometimes so private you could have known a person for five years without hearing them. Your neighbor who you think you have nothing in common with gets onstage, and you discover that you actually share a great deal. When you see them on the street the next day, your perspective of them is changed because you know something important about them.

As we go to press, I'm working with an eighty-eight-year-old man named Hector Black. His story is about being consumed with hatred for the stranger who murdered his daughter, and deciding to find out more about "the monster" (as Hector thought of him) who had taken his child's life. He learned that the man was born in a mental hospital, and that when he was eleven years old, his mother took him and his brother and sister to a swimming pool and said that God was ordering her to destroy them. He and his brother escaped, but watched while his mother drowned his little sister.

Hector said to me, "I wondered what I would be like if this had happened to me—if the woman who had brought me into the world had tried to destroy me. He became human to me again in that moment. I was able to forgive him, and felt as though a tremendous weight had been lifted from me."

Hector's story speaks to how essential it is to open ourselves to others, even in the most extreme circumstances. And while that intimacy can feel terrifying at times, it's vital. It's what will save us.

Catherine Burns
Artistic Director

Innocents
Abroad

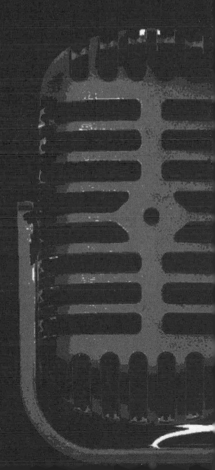

Life on a Möbius Strip

Einstein famously said, "Only two things are infinite: the universe and human stupidity." Then he added, "And I'm not so sure about the universe."

And it's true, there's a realistic possibility that the entire universe is finite; it's mathematically and physically possible. There was a period of time in my research when I was obsessed with this idea. I was fixated on the implication that you could leave the Earth and travel in a straight line to a planet in a distant galaxy on the edge of the observable universe and realize the galaxy was the Milky Way that you had left behind you, and the planet you had landed on was the Earth. There were also weirder possibilities that the Earth was reconnected like a Möbius strip—if you took a left-handed glove on that same trip, it would come back right-handed.

The hazard for a scientist working on something so esoteric is the possibility that it just might not be true or it might not be answerable. I felt myself kind of navigating this precipice between discovery on the one side and obscurity on the other side. At the time I was working at Berkeley, living in San Francisco. I would spend a lot of time in the coffee shop across the street from my apartment. I was trying to find some kind of tangible connection to a more earthbound reality. And it was there that I met this guy named Warren.

Warren came charging past me the first day I saw him and pinned me with his blue eyes and said, "*You're* the astrophysicist." Which I knew. And then he had so much momentum after having built up the nerve to say this to me that he kept walking; he didn't wait for my response. He went right out of the coffee shop and down the street.

And so it begins.

Warren is just everything I would never want in a man. He can't drive, he's never had his name on a lease, he's by his own confession completely uneducated, he's a self-professed obsessive-compulsive. He comes from a really tough part of working-class Manchester. He writes songs like

Daddy was a drunk, daddy was a singer,
daddy was a drunken singer.
Murdered in a flophouse, broke and drunk. . . .

You get the idea. It's not good. So naturally I'm completely smitten. And he is mesmerizing. He has all this intensity, all this energy. He's full of opinions. He was going to start his own music station called Shut the Folk Up.

I said, "The gag is going to be that nobody's going to understand his accent. Nobody will understand a word he says! He'll just rant." It was a Manchester accent, but it did seem even more tangled than one would expect. It was quite a brogue. He would talk so fast that the words would just slam together—it was really undecipherable. But when he sang, this big, beautiful, warm tone just lifted out of him; it was like this old-timey crooner, this rare crisp and clear sound. So I used to tell him, "If there's anything that's really urgent that you need me to understand, just, like, sing it to me, OK?"

So, Warren and I started seeing each other, and he never asked me about my work, which was quite a relief from my own sort of mental world. And it's like we were both in exile. Warren was in exile from his actual country, and I was in a kind of mental exile. And he would obsess all day about music and melody, and I would obsess all day about mathematics and numbers. And it was like we were pulling so hard in such opposite directions that the tension kept both of us from floating away.

After a few weeks of seeing each other, Warren decides we should live together, and he's going to convince me that I should let him move in. So he gives me this argument—some fairly inventive logic, which I'm a little suspicious of, and laden with all kinds of Manchester slang I don't really follow. But Warren can convince me of anything, just anything, so I relent, and he says, "I'll be right back!" He's so excited; he comes back in less than an hour, and he's moved in. He's carrying his guitar and whatever he can carry on his back, because he has this philosophy, "If you can't carry it, you can't own it." Right? So he moves in with me.

And my parents are thrilled. Their recently Ph.D.-confirmed daughter—I have a Ph.D. in theoretical physics from MIT—is living with an illegal immigrant who can't spell words like "non-viable," "unfeasible." Even our friends are full of doubt. Our good friend, the musician Sean Hayes, is writing lyrics like

We'll just play this one out until it explodes
Into a thousand tiny pieces
What's your story universe
You are melody, you are numbers
You are shapes, and you are rhythms

Warren and I hear this, and we're pretty sure it's about us. And I'm filled with doubt too. I mean, this is a crazy situation; it's totally improbable. And my fellowship's coming to an end, and the only other offers I have are in England. And Warren hates England. He slumps when he describes the low-hanging skies and the black mark of his accent there, and the inescapability of his class, but he says, "Baby, you know, I'll follow you anywhere. Even to England," as though I'm bringing him to the acid marshes of hell.

But he makes himself feel better by convincing me we have to sell all our stuff, because you can't own what you can't carry. So we're sitting on the steps of our apartment, and I watch stuff that I've been carting around my entire life just disappear.

People come in and out of the coffee shop and stop to talk to us and say, "So you're the astrologer?"

And I say, "Well, no, I'm more of an astronomer." And they ask me about how is it possible that the universe is finite. And I explain how Warren and I could go on this trip from San Francisco to London, and if we kept going in as straight a line as possible we'd eventually come back to San Francisco again, where we started. Because the Earth is compact and connected and finite, and maybe the whole universe is like that. And Warren and I make this leap, his left hand in my right hand, and we board a plane to the UK.

And it does suck. We have this very difficult wandering

path, but finally I land a fantastic fellowship at Cambridge. It's beautiful. But not before we spend a few weeks in a coin-operated bed-sit in Brighton. If you ran out of pound coins, your electricity went off and the lights went out. We often ran out of pound coins, and towards the end we were so despondent we would just sit in the dark. I could hear though not see Warren say things like "At least I don't have to look at the wood-chipped wallpaper," which for some reason really depressed him, this very English quality of the wood-chipped wallpaper.

But eventually we get to Cambridge, and my work takes a beautiful turn. I start working on black holes, these massive dead stars tens of kilometers across spinning hundreds of times a second ripping through space at the speed of light. This is very concrete compared to my previous research. So I'm excited about the direction my work's turning in. I'm in Hawking's group in Cambridge, which is very exciting, but he doesn't pay me any attention at all. But I'm invited by Nobel laureates to Trinity College for dinner, and I get to watch this ceremony of dinner at this old, beautiful college from the privileged perch of high table.

Meanwhile Warren's down the road in another college washing the dishes because it was the only job he could get. And as things go on, we both start to retreat into our mental worlds, me in my math and Warren in his melody, but it's like we're not really keeping each other from floating away so much anymore.

Eventually it starts to rain, and it rains forever. Woody Allen said, "Forever's a very long time, especially the bit towards the end." And a rainy winter in Cambridge is a *very* long time. Warren picks up a mandolin; he starts playing these Americana bluegrass tunes over and over again, you know, *na na na na na na na*. And it's this manic soundtrack to our mounting insanity, and eventually we explode. It takes about six months of that relentless rain, but we explode, and it's over. And all we see is how improbable we are; we see that we're nonviable and unfeasible. Which are words, by the way, that Warren can spell by then.

We both leave. We pack up everything we have, each of us just what we can carry. We end up in a bus terminal in London, clutching each other. I'm waiting for Warren to convince me, because he can always convince me, that we can do the impossible. But it's like the light's gone out in his eyes, and I disappear into London and he just . . . disappears. And the silence is total.

A graduate student of mine recently said to me, "The emotional dimension is the least interesting part of the human experience." And I know scientists are odd, but I agree. I was like, "Yeah, I know what you mean." So it's difficult for me to recount how dark those nights were. Even in my worst moments I knew that my despair was just sort of not interesting. I needed to get back to mathematics and the universe and this connection because in its sheer magnitude it would diminish the importance of my personal trials.

I searched all over London until I found a perfect warehouse to move into, because I wanted to connect with a more earthbound reality while I was doing my research. I found the perfect place. It had broken windows and shutters. It was dead empty—no bathroom, nothing. I had the windows replaced, and I had a bathroom installed, and my unit became a part of this artists' community building on the east end of London, along the canals.

So I had a great community around me, and I started a new life there, and I started to write. I got a book deal. It was a book about whether or not the universe was finite, and it was a diary about the terror of a scientist working on that really frightening divide between discovery and total oblivion. And it became a parallel story about Warren, about the unraveling of an obsessive-compulsive mind. I think if I'm honest it was also a way of still hanging on to him. This book kind of came out of me fully formed; it took one year.

When the book was finished, I delivered it to my publisher, and in part fueled by the London gloom and in part fueled by nostalgia, I decided I wanted to go back to San Francisco just to recuperate. To go back to where the book actually starts, when we sell all of our stuff on the steps in San Francisco.

I go back to California, and I take these beautiful walks in the city. San Francisco is so beautiful. And I find myself, despite myself—because I tell myself not to do it—walking past my old neighborhood. I end up going past my old coffee shop, and I'm going like three miles an hour, you know, there are like five thousand feet in a mile, and there's like three thousand, six hundred seconds in an hour, so I'm going about four and a half feet, I figure, per second. It takes me about two seconds to go past this coffee shop window.

In that time, because I'm looking at my building, my old apartment, full of sentiment, what I don't realize is that on the other side of that window, inside the coffee shop, is Warren, who, after I left him in the London bus terminal, went back to California, came back to London, went to France, came back to London, and just recently returned to San Francisco, and got a job in the coffee shop, where he regaled the patrons with stories about his travels. He was so uprooted. But the light was back on in his eyes. And as he's turning around to deliver a coffee, he lifts his head to see me, in those two seconds, walk past the frame of the window. And he shouts, "It's self-service!"

He stumbles out of the coffee shop. People are grabbing

muffins and coffees, they're like, "Warren! What's up?!" And he's trying to get out of the coffee shop, trying to grab on to the handle of the door. He keeps banging his head. It's like a bird trying to get out the window. And all of the sudden, the door swings open and deposits Warren in front of me.

You often think, *What am I going to say when I bump into my ex?* But, it's just this electric moment between us. There's this swell of warmth, and we laugh that we're back where we started on this very spot in San Francisco.

I try to give him the essential data. I'm living in London Fields, and he tells me I've moved onto the block he lived on when he was nineteen and squatting in London. Out of the whole city of London. And he recognizes the names of all the locals I can rattle off. And by the end of the conversation he's saying, "I'm coming with you back to London aren't I?"

And I'm thinking, *Are you out of your mind?* I mean, what woman in her right mind is going to let this lunatic come back to London with her? There is no way.

About a year later, we're married. Our rings, which were made by a friend of ours, are stamped with the lyrics "Melody and Number, Shapes and Rhythms" with no small dose of irony and defiance. About a year after that, we're having a baby, and we're laughing at how improbable this kid is.

We have no idea. When this kid is born, he is so beautiful, and afterwards a young medical resident comes charging into my hospital room, and he's so excited he's beaming. And I'm thinking, *He sees how beautiful this boy is.* But he's carrying an X-ray, which he slaps on the window of my hospital room so the light can come through, and I can see it better. But I still don't know what I'm looking at.

He says, "Your son's heart is on the right side." And he

doesn't mean the correct side, he doesn't mean the left side. He means my son's heart is on the *right* side.

And all I can think in this terrifying moment is *Get Warren*.

And the resident says, "Your son has dextrocardia with situs inversus; all his organs are on the opposite side."

And I say, "Get Warren."

And the resident tells me he's so excited, because he never thought he'd ever see anything like this. To his knowledge, nobody else in the hospital's seen it in real life. And he's describing studies for me that are made up of only twelve cases because the numbers are so rare.

And then Warren's there, and he's saying in that rough, raw, beautiful accent what only he can convince me of, the totally impossible. He's saying, "He's perfect."

And our now eight-year-old son is a perfectly formed mirror image of the more conventional human anatomy, a very rare and unlikely alignment. It's as though Warren and I took our left-handed code on a Möbius strip around the universe and brought back this right-handed boy. And that boy, as intense and spirited as his father, is like a living testament to the incredibly improbable trip that we're on.

Janna Levin is an astrophysicist and writer. She has contributed to an understanding of black holes, the cosmology of extra dimensions, and chaotic spacetimes. Her second book, a novel, *A Madman Dreams of Turing Machines*, won the PEN/Bingham prize and was runner-up for the PEN/Hemingway. She is the author of the popular science book *How the Universe Got Its Spots*. Janna is a professor at Barnard College of Columbia University and was recently named a Guggenheim Fellow (2012).

Mission to India

It was a Saturday afternoon in September 1989, and I was home alone unpacking boxes when the phone rang, and a woman that I did not know started to interrogate me.

"Are you Dr. Lombardi? Are you Dr. George Lombardi? Are you an infectious disease specialist? Did you live and work and do research in East Africa? Are you considered to be an expert in tropical infections? Would you consider yourself to be an expert in viral hemorrhagic fevers?"

At this point I paused, gathered myself, and asked the obvious question, "Who are you?"

She introduced herself and said she was the representative of a world figure and Nobel laureate, someone who was suspected of having a viral hemorrhagic fever, and she was calling to ask if I would consult on the case.

Now I found this highly improbable. I was thirty-two years old. I had just opened my office. The phone never rang. I had no patients. In fact I remember staring at the phone trying to will it to ring. But she persisted, and she mentioned that she had gotten my name from a colleague of mine who had told her to "call Dr. Lombardi. He knows a lot about very weird things." She arranged a conference call, and in ten minutes I was transported through the telephone wires to a small hospital in Calcutta, India, where I found out for the first time that the patient was Mother Teresa.

On the line were her two main Indian doctors. We chatted and discussed the details of the case for about an hour, and though those details are now hazy to me, what came through the staticky wires was their deep abiding concern for their patient—these guys were worried.

I wished them well as I got off the line, and I went back to unpack some boxes. She called again an hour later. She said, "They were very impressed by what you had to say, and they'd like you to go to Calcutta. I'm making the arrangements. I can get you out tomorrow afternoon on the Concorde for the first leg."

I said, "This is impossible," as I had just found my passport in one of these boxes, and I told her it expired three months before.

She said, "That's a minor detail. Meet me in front of your building tomorrow morning, Sunday, at 7 A.M."

Well as you can probably surmise, I'm somebody who pretty much does what he's told. So seven o'clock the next morning she comes careening down the block in a wood-paneled station wagon with bad shock absorbers. I jump in. The next stop's the passport office at Rockefeller Center, where on a Sunday morning a State Department official came, let us in, took my picture, and in fifteen minutes handed me a brand-new passport. The next stop was the Indian Consulate, where, again on a Sunday morning, the entire staff came in full dress uniform to give me an honor guard procession, which I walked past as they ushered me in to the consulate general himself, who affixed the visa to my passport.

He leaned in towards me and said, "We bestow our blessings on you. The eyes of the world are upon you."

Now I knew who Mother Teresa was, of course, but this was the first moment I realized what she meant, not just to the Indian people, but to the world.

I get back in the car. I'm getting into this.

"Where next?"

She says, "We're ahead of schedule. I'm going to drop you off at your home; I'll be back at 11 A.M. I'll meet you downstairs." Sure enough, 11 A.M., tires squealing, she pulls up with one addition: in the backseat of this station wagon are wedged five Sisters of Charity—five nuns—as if sitting on a perch. They start handing me letters in envelopes and small packages wrapped in burlap and tied with twine, saying, "Well if you see Sister Narita and Sister Rafael, please give them this from me." I'm a courier. This is all before Homeland Security.

We barrel off to JFK, and when we get there I ask, sotto voce, "Why are they here? They could have just given you these things. I don't understand why they had to come to the airport."

And I was told, "Well, I didn't know how to tell you this, but you don't have a confirmed seat on the Concorde—you're flying standby." My eyes widened. "Well, the sisters are going to go up and down the line of ticketed passengers and beg until someone gives up their seat." I stood off to the side, just out of earshot, as I watched the scene unfold.

The five nuns surround this first New York City businessman. He's listening to them, he's looking over at me, he's looking back at them, he shakes his head no, he's sorry, he can't help. They move on to the next one. And now I can hear their voices, which obviously have been raised, and in about fifteen seconds this businessman realizes that resistance is futile, and he hands over his ticket. The sisters come towards me, and they hand me this ticket as an offering, and there is a small triumphal grin on each of their faces—the nun equivalent of a high five.

I wag my finger at them. I say, "You sisters are little devils! I'm going to tell Mother Teresa what you just did!" And they laugh, and that breaks the tension.

Next stop Calcutta, after twenty-four hours in flight. One hundred degrees, one hundred percent humidity. I get off the plane, and I'm met by my own personal private security detail of nuns. They whisk me through customs and deliver me directly to the hospital where the doctors are waiting for me, and the doctors intone, "She's deteriorating."

I go directly to her room. I'm meeting Mother Teresa for the first time. She's clearly very weak, and she beckons me towards her, and I feel as if I'm about to get a blessing.

She says the following: "Thank you for coming. I will never leave Calcutta. Do not ever disagree with my Indian doctors. I need them. They run my hospitals and clinics, and I will not have them embarrassed." And with that she dismisses me with a wave of her hand.

I go and wash my hands, and I come back to examine her. As I go to pull her gown down to listen to her heart and lungs, the nuns who surround her lift the gown up. I pull the gown down; they pull the gown up. This Kabuki dance goes on for several minutes until, from sheer exhaustion, I just banish them from the room. After I perform my examination, I still don't know what's wrong with her. So I do what an infectious disease doctor does: I do my cultures and my Gram stains and my buffy coat smears and my Tzanck prep. And we agree we'll meet the next morning at 9 A.M.

As I leave the hospital, I set upon five thousand pilgrims who are holding a candlelit prayer vigil. I escape back to the hotel, where I pour myself a stiff drink, order room service for dinner, and turn on the local news hoping it will serve as a distraction.

And there I am.

The lead story on the evening news, that night and every night, footage of "Dr. Lombardi entering and leaving the hospital," with the reporters saying, "Dr. Lombardi's come from the United States to attend to Mother Teresa as she inches closer towards death." The drumbeat of the death watch had begun.

She deteriorates over the next forty-eight hours; she's in septic shock. *The rude unhinging of the machinery of life* as it was described 150 years ago, as apt a description now. And on the third day, two propitious events collide. The first is the most beautiful sight I've ever seen: small, tiny translucent dew drops on the blood culture plate. This is important. This could be a bacterial infection. This is an important clue. The second is one of the pope's cardiologists flies in from Rome. He's an impressive man, straight from central casting: a head of silver hair, a Brioni suit, Hermès tie, Gucci loafers. And at our first meeting, when I tell the group of doctors excitedly that the cultures are turning positive, and we may have an answer here, and my concern is that a pacemaker that was put in several months before could be the cause of the infection, he erupts Vesuvius-ly.

"Out of the question!" he bellows. "This is a clear case of malaria." Well if they could diagnose malaria anywhere, it would be on the subcontinent of India, and this wasn't the case.

She worsens over the next couple of days, and I'm having dreams where she's actually falling just beyond my outstretched hand. And I change my routine; rather than fleeing the hospital at the end of the day through the side exit, I go out through the front, and I walk through the pilgrims, and I'm bolstered by their love and their devotion.

On the fifth day I make my most impassioned plea. I stand before the group, and I tell them that this is septic shock. It has a bacterial cause, and it's due to the pacemaker. This pacemaker must be removed. Dr. Brioni (as I've come to call him) stands at the lectern carrying his copy of *The Merck Manual*. It's a small book that many doctors carry; he has the Italian version [*in an Italian accent*] *Merka Manuale*. And in a scene right out of Shakespeare, as he talks he's pounding the lectern with his book, "If you listen" *Boom! Boom! Boom!* "to this American upstart," *Boom!* "I will not be held responsible!" *BOOM!*

The sounds ricocheted through the somber conference room like gunshots, and in that moment I looked into the eyes of the courtly, elegant Indian doctors, and they had lost respect for him. They asked us to wait outside as they considered their options. I sat there with my vinyl knapsack and my socks with sandals. He sat next to me elegantly attired with two equally elegantly attired attachées from the Italian Consulate. They called us back in and said, "We've decided to go with Dr. Lombardi." The pope's doctor silently packed his bag, left the hospital, went directly to the airport, and flew out of the country.

I said, "Let's get that pacemaker out."

And they looked at me and said, "You want it out, you have to take it out."

I said, "I've never done that before." They gave me this wonderful nonverbal Bengali head waddle.

So I went down to her room. I banished the nuns. I got a charge nurse and a basic tray, and I prepared the patient. The pacemaker box came out readily, but the wire, the wire that had been sitting in her right ventricle for several months, was tethered into place, and it would not budge. I twisted and turned and did all kinds of little body English. This thing was stuck. I started to sweat, my glasses fogged over. There had been stories that if you pull hard enough you can put a hole in the ventricle, and she could bleed into her chest and die within a matter of minutes.

So in the most surreal moment, I said a prayer *to* Mother Teresa *for* Mother Teresa, and the catheter came loose.

I took it out, I cultured the tip, and I proved that this pacemaker was the cause of her infection. She got better. Her fever broke. She woke up. A couple of days later she was sitting in a chair eating.

My work was done, but they wouldn't let me leave. I stayed another two weeks as I was the only doctor who could start her IVs, who could thread those catheters into those tiny, fragile elderly woman's veins. It's a skill I had picked up in the mid-1970s as a medical student at NYU Bellevue Hospital, where I learned to start IVs in the hardened veins of IV drug addicts. It's a skill I honestly thought I would never ever need again. When it was my time to leave, they held a press conference and they publicly thanked me, and that's why I'm able to tell this story. I flew back to my life and to my two sons.

She lived another eight years, and I saw her periodically. But the best part of this for me is that I have an ongoing relationship with the Sisters. They're a wonderful group of women;

they truly do God's work, however you may want to define that. And I take care of whatever their medical problems are.

Several months ago, the mother superior came in. I had to fill out some paperwork, and she brought two young novitiates with her, and she asked me, "Dr. Lombardi, can we go to the back? Can they see the pictures?" I have some pictures on the wall that memorialize this trip, and they like to see the faces of the other sisters when they were so young.

I said, "Of course."

And we go to the back, and they're oohing and ahhing, and one young novitiate squeezes my arm, and she says, "Dr. Lombardi, you represent a link to our past."

And I say, "I'm deeply honored by that."

And the other sister says to me, "Dr. Lombardi, in the convent we think of you as a rock star."

Dr. George Lombardi is a lifelong New Yorker and a graduate of City College of New York and New York University School of Medicine. He is in private practice in New York and his practice consists of saints and sinners. He has two sons, of whom he is enormously proud, and a fabulous Czech girlfriend. He credits his love of stories to his father, who raised his gift for lamentation to an art form.

ANDREW SOLOMON

Notes on an Exorcism

'm not depressed now—but I was depressed for a long time. I lived with blinding depression and had long stretches when everything seemed hopeless and pointless—when returning calls from friends seemed like more than I could do, when getting up and going out into the world seemed painful, when I was completely crippled by anxiety.

When I finally got better and started writing about the process of recovery, I became very interested in all the different kinds of treatment that there were for depression. And having started as a kind of medical conservative, thinking that there were only a couple of things that worked—medication and certain talking therapies—and that that was really it, I very gradually began to change my mind. Because I realized that if you have brain cancer and you decide that standing on your head and gargling for half an hour every day makes you feel better, it may make you feel better, but the likelihood is that you still have brain cancer, and you're still going to die from it; but if you have depression and you say that standing on your head and gargling for half an hour makes you feel better, then you are actually cured, because depression is an illness of how you feel. And if you feel really great after you do that, then you're not depressed anymore. So I began to think all kinds of things could work.

I researched everything from experimental brain surgeries to hypnotic regimens of various kinds. I had people writing to me because I had been publishing on this subject. There was one woman who wrote to me that she had tried medication, therapy, electroshock treatments, and a variety of other approaches to depression, and she had finally found the thing that worked for her, and she wanted me to tell the world about it. And that was "making little things from yarn" ... some of which she sent me. In any event, I had that rich engagement.

As I was doing this work, I also became interested in the idea that depression exists not only in the civilized West, as people tended to assume, but also across cultures, and across time.

And so when one of my dearest friends, David, who was living for a little while in Senegal, said to me, "Do you know about the tribal rituals that are used for the treatment of depression here?" I said, "No, I don't know about them. But I would like to know about them."

And he said, "Well, if you come for a visit, we could try to do some research on this topic."

And so I set off for Senegal, and I met David. And I was introduced to David's then-girlfriend, now ex-wife, Helene. And it turned out that Helene had a cousin whose mother was a friend of someone who went to school with the daughter of a person who actually practiced the *ndeup*, the ritual David had mentioned, and that I could therefore go and interview this woman who had practiced the *ndeup*.

And so we went off to a small town about two hours outside of Dakar. And I was introduced to this extraordinary, old, large woman wrapped in miles and miles of African fabric printed with figures of eyes, and she was Madame Diouf. And we did an interview for about an hour, and she told me all about the *ndeup*. At the end of it, feeling rather daring, I said, "Listen, I don't know whether this is something you would even consider, but would it be possible for me to attend an *ndeup*?"

And she said, "Well, I've never had a *toubab* attend one of these before [the local word for foreigner was *toubab*], but you've come through friends. Yes, the next time I perform an *ndeup*, you may be present."

And I said, "That's fantastic. When are you next going to be doing an *ndeup*?"

And she said, "Oh, it'll be sometime in the next six months."

I said, "Six months is quite a long time for me to stay here in this town, waiting for you to do one. Maybe we could expedite one for somebody, move it forward? I'll pitch in."

She said, "No, it really doesn't work that way. I'm sorry, but that's how it is."

I said, "Well, I guess I won't be able to see an *ndeup* then, but even so this conversation has been so interesting and so helpful to me. And I'm a little sad about leaving here not actually getting to see one, but I thank you."

And she said, "Well, I'm glad that you could come. I'm glad it was helpful . . . but there is one other thing. I hope you don't mind my saying this."

And I said, "No, what? What is it?"

She said, "You don't look that great yourself. Are you suffering from depression?"

And I said, "Well, yes. It was very acute. It's a little better now, but I still do actually suffer from depression."

She said, "Well, I've certainly never done this for a *toubab* before, but I could actually do an *ndeup* for you."

And I said, "Oh! What an interesting idea. Well, um, yes, sure. Yeah, absolutely, yes, let's do that. I'll have an *ndeup*."

"Oh, well, that's great," she said. And she gave us some fairly basic instructions, and then we left.

And my translator, the aforementioned then-girlfriend, now ex-wife of my friend, turned to me, and she said, "Are you completely crazy? Do you have any idea what you're getting yourself into? You're crazy. You're totally crazy, but I'll help you if you want."

So we left. And the first thing we had was a shopping list. We had to buy seven yards of African fabric. We had to get a calabash, which was a large bowl fashioned from a gourd. We had to get three kilos of millet. We had to get sugar and kola beans. And then we had to get two live cockerels, two roosters, and a ram.

So Helene and I went to the market with David and we got most of the things, and I said, "But what about the ram?"

And Helene said, "We can't buy the ram today. What are we going to do with it overnight?" I saw the sense of that.

So we got into a taxi for the two-hour drive to the *ndeup*, and I said, "What about the ram?"

And Helene said, "Oh, we'll see a ram along the way." So we were going along and going along, and there was a Senegalese shepherd by the side of the road with his flock. And we stopped the cab, and we got out, and we bought a ram for $7. And then we had a little bit of a struggle getting the live ram into the trunk of the taxicab. But the cabdriver seemed not at all worried, even by the fact that the ram kept relieving himself in the trunk.

So then we got there, and I said, "Well, here I am. I'm ready for my close-up."

And the thing about the *ndeup* is that it varies enormously depending on a whole variety of signals and symbols that come from above. So we had to go through this whole shamanistic process. And I still didn't know really very much of what was going to happen.

First I had to change out of my jeans and my T-shirt and put on a loincloth. And then I sat down, and I had my chest and my arms rubbed with millet.

And then someone said, "Oh, we really should have music for this."

I said, "Oh great." And I thought, you know, drumming, some atmospheric thing.

And Madame Diouf came out with her very prized possession, which was a battery-operated tape player, for which she had one tape, which was *Chariots of Fire*.

So we started listening to *Chariots of Fire*. And in the meanwhile, I was given various shamanistic objects I had to hold with my hands and drop. I then had to hold them with my feet and drop them.

And they would say, "Oh, this augurs well. This augurs badly." There were five assistants to Madame Diouf who had all gathered around.

And we spent the morning like this. We'd started at about eight o'clock, and at maybe about eleven, eleven-thirty, they said, "Well, now it's actually time for the central part of the ritual."

And I said, "Oh, okay." And the sound of drumming began— the drumming I had been hoping for. And so there was all of this drumming, and it was very exciting. And we went to the central square of the village, where there was a small makeshift wedding bed that I had to get into with the ram. I had been told it would be very, very bad luck if the ram escaped, and that I had to hold on to him, and that the reason we had to be in this wedding bed was that all my depression and all my problems were caused by the fact that I had spirits. In Senegal you have spirits all over you, the way here you have microbes. Some are good for you. Some are bad for you. Some are neutral. My bad spirits were extremely jealous of my real-life sexual partners— some of whom are here tonight. And we had to mollify the anger of the spirits.

So I had to get into this wedding bed with the ram, and I had to hold the ram very tightly. He, of course, immediately relieved himself on my leg.

The entire village had taken the day off from their work in the fields, and they were dancing around us in concentric circles. And as they danced, they were throwing blankets and sheets of cloth over us, and so we were gradually being buried.

It was unbelievably hot, and it was completely stifling. And there was the sound of these stamping feet as everyone danced around us, and then these drums, which were getting louder and louder and more and more ecstatic.

And I was just about at the point at which I thought I was going to faint or pass out. At that key moment suddenly all of the cloths were pulled off. I was yanked to my feet. The loincloth that was all I was wearing was pulled from me. The poor old ram's throat was slit, as were the throats of the two cockerels. And I was covered in the blood of the freshly slaughtered ram and cockerels.

So there I was, naked, totally covered in blood, and they said, "Okay, that's the end of this part of it. The next piece comes now." And I said, "Okay," and we went back over to the area where we had done the morning preparations.

And one of them said, "Look, it's lunchtime. Why don't we just take a break for a minute? Would you like a Coke?" I don't drink Coke that much, but at that moment it seemed like a really, really good idea, and I said yes.

And so I sat there, naked and completely covered in animal blood, with flies kind of gathering, as they will when you're naked and covered in animal blood. And I drank this Coke.

And then when I had finished the Coke, they said, "Okay, now we have the final parts of the ritual. First you have to put your hands by your sides and stand very straight and very erect."

And I said, "Okay," and then they tied me up with the intestines of the ram. In the meanwhile its body was hanging from a nearby tree, and someone was doing some butchering of it, and they took various little bits of it out. And then I had to kind of shuffle over, all tied up in intestines, which most of you probably haven't done, but it's hard.

I had to shuffle over and take these little pieces of the ram and dig holes, and put the pieces of the ram in the holes.

And I had to say something. And what I had to say was actually incredibly, strangely touching in the middle of this weird experience. I had to say, "Spirits, leave me alone to complete the business of my life and know that I will never forget you." And I thought, *What a kind thing to say to the evil spirits you're exorcising: "I'll never forget you."* And I haven't.

So anyway, there were various other little bits and pieces that followed. I was given a piece of paper in which all of the millet from the morning had been gathered. I was told that I should sleep with it under my pillow and in the morning get up and give it to a beggar who had good hearing and no deformities, and that when I gave it to him that would be the end of my troubles.

And then the women all filled their mouths with water and began spitting water all over me—it was a surround-shower effect—rinsing the blood away from me. It gradually came off, and when I was clean, they gave me back my jeans. And everyone danced, and they barbecued the ram, and we had this dinner.

And I felt so up. I felt so up! It had been quite an astonishing experience. Even though I didn't believe in the animist principles behind it, all of these people had been gathered together, cheering for me, and it was very exhilarating.

And I had a very odd experience five years later, when I was working on my current book, and I was in Rwanda doing something else altogether. I got into a conversation with someone there, and I described the experience I had had in Senegal, and he said, "Oh, you know, we have something that's a little like that. That's West Africa. This is East Africa. It's quite different, but there are some similarities to rituals here."

He said, "You know, we had a lot of trouble with Western mental health workers who came here immediately after the genocide, and we had to ask some of them to leave."

I said, "What was the problem?"

And he said, "Their practice did not involve being outside in the sun, like you're describing, which is, after all, where you begin to feel better. There was no music or drumming to get your blood flowing again when you're depressed, and you're low, and you need to have your blood flowing. There was no sense that everyone had taken the day off so that the entire community could come together to try to lift you up and bring you back to joy. There was no acknowledgment that the depression is something invasive and external that could actually be cast out of you again.

"Instead, they would take people one at a time into these dingy little rooms and have them sit around for an hour or so and talk about bad things that had happened to them. We had to get them to leave the country."

Andrew Solomon is the author of the *New York Times* best sellers *Far from the Tree: Parents, Children, and the Search for Identity* (winner of the National Book Critics Circle Award and many other awards) and *The Noonday Demon: An Atlas of Depression*, a Pulitzer Prize finalist and winner of fourteen awards, including the 2001 National Book Award. His first novel, *A Stone Boat*, which was a finalist for the *Los Angeles Times* First Fiction Award, has recently been reissued. Solomon's work is published in twenty-two languages. He is a lecturer in psychiatry at Cornell University and special adviser on LGBT affairs to Yale University's Department of Psychiatry.

Man and Beast

I was five years old, standing in the old, great cat house at the Bronx Zoo, staring into the face of an old female jaguar. I remember looking at the bare walls and at the bare ceiling, wondering what the animal had done to get itself there. I leaned in a little towards the cage and started whispering something to the jaguar. But my father came over quickly and asked, "What are you doing?" I turned to him to try to explain, but my mouth froze, as I knew it would, because everything about my young childhood at that time was characterized by the inability to speak.

From the earliest time that I tried to speak, I was handicapped with a severe, severe stutter. Not the normal kind of repetitious "bububub" kind of stutter that many stutterers have or many children go through. But the complete blockage of airflow, where if I tried to push words out, my head would spasm and my body would spasm. Nobody knew what to do with me. At the time there were very few books written about stuttering. There was no computer, no Internet. The reaction of the New York City public school system was to put me in a class for disturbed children. I remember my parents trying to fight it, telling them, "He's not disturbed." But the teachers said, "We're sorry, whenever he tries to speak, it disrupts everything and everybody." So I spent my youth wondering why adults couldn't see into me, why they couldn't see I was normal, and that all the words were inside of me, but they just wouldn't come out.

Fortunately, at a very young age I learned what most stutterers learn at some point. You can do two things without stuttering. One of them is sing, and I couldn't sing. The other is you can talk to animals and not stutter.

So every day I would come home from the special class, which all the other kids called the retarded class, and I'd go straight to a closet in my room. I had a little dark corner of that closet. And I'd go into the closet, and I'd close the door, and I'd bring my pets—New York–style pets (hamster, gerbil, green turtle, a chameleon, occasionally a garter snake), and I would talk to them. I would talk fluently to them, and I'd tell them my hopes and my dreams. I would tell them how people were stupid because they thought I was stupid.

And the animals listened. They felt it. And I realized very early that they felt it because they were like me. The animals, they had feelings too, they were trying to transmit things also. But they had no human voice, so people ignored them, or they misunderstood them, or they hurt them, or sometimes they killed them.

I swore to the animals when I was young that if I could ever find my voice, I would try to be their voice. But I didn't know if that would happen, because I realized that I lived in two worlds. One world was the world where I was normal, with animals, where I could speak, but the other world was the world of human beings, where I couldn't.

My parents didn't know what to do, but they did everything. They tried hypnotherapy, they tried drug therapy, they sent me to many kinds of psychologists, but nothing really worked. I got through grade school, junior high school, high school, and eventually college by learning tricks stutterers learn. Learning when to not speak, learning to avoid situations, learning just to not be around people. When I did have to speak, then I would prove to people that I was not only like them, but I was better than they were. In academics, I excelled. I got straight A's in everything. In sports, I joined the wrestling team and the boxing team, and I helped take all my teams to the state championships. Everybody always said I was an up-and-coming athlete, but I wasn't. I didn't even like it. I was just a very, very frustrated young man who had to find an outlet for his anger.

By the time I was a senior in college, I had never been out on a date, I had never kissed a girl, except for my mother, and I had never spoken a completely fluent sentence out loud to another human being.

About midway through my senior year in college, my parents learned of an experimental new program in Upstate New York, in Geneseo. It was very intense. They had to send me away, and I was essentially locked away for two months. The program was for severe, severe stutters, and it was very expensive. But they would do anything for me. So my father sold something very dear to him in order to send me there.

That clinic changed my life. It taught me two very important things. One of them was that I was a stutterer, and I was always going to be a stutterer. There was no magic pill, and I was not going to wake up one morning as I had always dreamt and be a fluent speaker. But the other thing it taught me, the more important thing, was that if I did what they were teaching me at this clinic—which was to mechanically control my mouth, the air-flow—if I worked hard, I could be a completely fluent stutterer.

I worked hard, and it was unbelievable. For the first time in twenty years, I could speak. I could speak! In twenty years I had never been able to voice everything inside of me. Now I could. It took a lot of work, because while I was speaking I had to be thinking about hard contacts, airflow, this and that, but it didn't matter—none of it mattered. I was a fluent speaker now. Life would be different. I would go back to school, and they would accept me.

I returned to finish the last half of my senior year, and things were different—on the outside. I could speak. But nothing had changed on the inside. Too much had happened for that. I was still the stuttering broken child inside.

Throughout my academic years I had focused on science. I loved science because science to me was the study of truths apart from the world of human beings. And when I got to college, I decided to channel that science into medicine, thinking maybe if I became a doctor people would like me, people would accept me. But I never liked working with people. And when I got back from the clinic, I realized I couldn't be doing this. I hated being in labs, and worse than that, I was tortured feeling the frustration and the pain of the lab animals in the little cages, spinning in those little wheels.

So I applied to graduate school at the University of Tennessee in wildlife biology and zoology. I got accepted. And that first year I was down in Tennessee in the Great Smoky Mountains studying black bears. When I was in the forest with the animals, I was at home. This was what I was meant to be doing. Being in the forest alone with the animals was my real-world closet. This was what made me feel good. And I came to realize what I'd always known in my heart but had never been able to put into words, and that's that the truth of the world, the reality, is not defined by the spoken word. In fact it's not even speakable. And I knew that this was how I had to live my life, somehow.

Fortunately, right before I got my Ph.D., I met the preeminent wildlife biologist in my field, Dr. George Schaller. He and I spent the day together following bears in the Smoky Mountains, and at the end of the day George said to me, "Alan, how would you like to go to Belize and be the first one to try to study jaguars in the jungle?" The very first thought in my mind, and I remember it so clearly, was *Where the hell is Belize?* But the very first words out of my mouth, not thirty seconds after he had asked me that, were "Of course I'll go. Of course."

Within two months I had bought an old Ford pickup truck, packed everything I owned in the back—which didn't even take up half of it—and driven from New York to Central America. Those last few miles of driving into that jungle, where I would set up base camp for the next two years, were just unbelievable to me. Driving by the Mayan Indians gawking at me, I was entering the jungle to catch jaguars, which nobody knew how to do, and put radio collars on them and get data that nobody had ever gotten before. This was what my life was all about. This was where it had to take me.

For the next year I did just what I had set out to do. I learned from hunters. I learned how to capture jaguars. I captured them. I followed them. Many things almost stopped me from achieving my goal. There was a plane crash where I almost died; one of my men got bitten by a fer-de-lance, a poisonous snake, and unfortunately he died. Those things changed me. I had to really look upon things differently. But this was my life, this was where I knew I could stay forever and be happy and be comfortable.

But I couldn't. Because I also realized that as fast as I was catching jaguars and gathering information about them, they were being killed in front of me. My jaguars were being killed. The jaguars outside of my study area were being killed; they were all being wiped out. Yes, I could sit in that jungle, but then I wouldn't be true to myself. And more important, I wouldn't be true to the promise I had made to the animals in the closet, that I would be their voice. And I had the voice now, if I wanted to use it. So I realized I had to come back into the world of people and try to fight with that world to save the animals, and these jaguars in particular.

But, ironically, I realized that if I was going to save these jaguars, not only did I have to enter the world of people again, but I had to go to the highest levels of government. I had to talk to the prime minister of Belize. Well it took some doing, but within six months I was standing in the capital city, outside the office of the prime minister. He had given me an appointment with the cabinet. They had given me fifteen minutes. They had no idea what I was going to say to them. Frankly I'm sure they gave me the appointment because they just wanted to meet this crazy foreigner who was in the jungle catching jaguars.

I had fifteen minutes. I couldn't stutter. I couldn't stutter. I couldn't distract them from the point of trying to save jaguars. I had to use everything I had learned and be a completely fluent speaker and convince one of the poorest countries in Central America—no protected areas in the entire country at that time, a place where tourism wasn't even of economic benefit, ecotourism wasn't even a term at the time—that they had to save jaguars.

An hour and a half later I came out of there, amidst laughter, backslaps. The prime minister and the cabinet had voted to set up the world's first and only jaguar preserve. And I promised them I would make it work. I promised them I could show them it would be of economic benefit.

A month later, I was in the jungle following my jaguars. You never see jaguars. If they can be seen, they'll be killed, so the most prominent evidence of jaguars is their tracks. I knew all my jaguars in the study area from their tracks. But this one day when I was in there, trying to see where they were all going and what they were all doing, I crossed a completely new track. It was the biggest male jaguar I had ever seen in my life, the biggest track. I knew I had to follow him, hoping I could catch a glimpse, but at least find out what he was doing in here, whether he had come in from the outside. Was he passing through? I followed him for hours, glued on those tracks, until I realized it was getting dark, and I didn't want to be caught in the jungle at night without a flashlight. So I turned around to go back to camp.

As soon as I turned around, there he was, not fifteen feet behind me. That jaguar, which I had been following, had circled around and was following me as I was following him. He could have killed me at any time. I didn't even hear him.

I knew I should feel frightened, but I didn't. Instinctively I just squatted down, and the jaguar sat. And I looked into this jaguar's eyes, and I was so clearly reminded of the little boy looking into the face of that sad old jaguar at the Bronx Zoo. But this animal wasn't sad. In this animal's eyes there was strength. And power. And sureness of purpose. I also realized, as I was looking into his eyes, that what I was seeing was a reflection of the way I was feeling too. That little broken boy and that old broken jaguar were now this. Hah.

Suddenly I felt scared. I knew I should be scared. And I stood up and took a step back. The jaguar stood up too, turned, and started to walk off into the forest. After about ten feet, it stopped, and turned to look back at me. I looked at the jaguar. And I leaned a little towards it, the way I had at the Bronx Zoo so many years before, and I whispered to it: "It's OK now. It's all going to be OK."

And the jaguar turned and was gone. Thank you.

Dr. Alan Rabinowitz is the CEO of Panthera, a nonprofit dedicated to saving the world's wild cat species. Dr. Rabinowitz is one of the world's leading big cat experts and has been called the "Indiana Jones of Wildlife Conservation" by *TIME*. He has authored over one hundred scientific and popular articles and six books, including *Jaguar: One Man's Struggle to Establish the First Jaguar Preserve*; *Chasing the Dragon's Tail: The Struggle to Save Thailand's Wild Cats*; *Beyond the Last Village: A Journey of Discovery in Asia's Forbidden Wilderness*; and, most recently, *Life in the Valley of Death: The Fight to Save Tigers in a Land of Guns, Gold, and Greed*. He has been profiled in *The New York Times*, *Scientific American*, *Audubon*, *Men's Journal*, *Newsweek*, *Outside*, *Explorer*, *The Jerusalem Report*, and *National Geographic Adventure Magazine*, and has been featured in numerous documentaries, including BBC's *Lost Land of the Tiger* and *National Geographic's In Search of the Jaguar*; and on TV shows including *The Colbert Report*, *60 Minutes*, and CNN. Dr. Rabinowitz has dedicated his life to surveying the world's last wild places, with the goal of preserving wild habitats and securing homes, on a large scale, for some of the world's most endangered mammals. His focus on cats is based on conserving top predators, which affect entire ecosystems. His most recent endeavors include creating and securing biological and genetic corridors for jaguars across their entire range, from Mexico to Argentina, and for tigers in the Indo-Himalayan region of Asia. To learn more, please visit www.panthera.org.

The Prince and I

I was an eighteen-year-old NYU dropout struggling to pay my rent in New York by dancing at the Kit-Kat Club on 56th and Broadway, when a friend of mine approached me about a casting call. This casting call was supposedly to entertain rich businessmen in Singapore. It didn't seem all that different from what I was already doing, so I went.

But when I got the job, they told me that it wasn't in Singapore at all. In fact, I was being invited to be the personal guest of the Prince of Brunei.

Now, Brunei is a sultanate in Southeast Asia. It was a country I had only recently even heard of, and at the time the Sultan of Brunei was the richest man in the world. I was being hired to work for his youngest brother, who is Prince Jefri Bolkiah, also known in the media as the Playboy Prince.

My job description was elusive, at best. But I fantasized that I might get to Brunei and find a wild adventure, a pile of money, and an employer who was nothing less than Prince Charming. I suspected more realistically that I had signed on to be some sort of international quasi-prostitute. But even that seemed like a wild and exotic transformation for a Jewish girl from the burbs of Jersey.

And honestly, I wanted nothing less than transformation. I wanted so badly for my life to be something more exceptional than just going to usually fruitless B-movie auditions during the day and squeaking around a brass pole at night. I thought maybe this was it, and it seemed like it would be worth the risk.

When I was sixteen, and I first heard Patti Smith's album *Easter*, I decided that Patti Smith was the absolute barometer of all things cool and right. And ever since, I would ask myself when faced with tough decisions, *What would Patti Smith do?*

So I weighed my options. Should I stay? Should I go?

What would Patti Smith do?

And I decided Patti Smith would go. She would get on a plane and go to exotic lands, and she would never once look back. And that's what I did.

When I arrived at the airport in Bandar Seri Begawan, I was greeted by two Secret Service agents who immediately took my passport, supposedly to update my visa or something. I had the first flicker of a thought that maybe I had not completely understood the implications of the decision that I had made to come here.

But all of these apprehensions were overshadowed when I saw the royal compound. It was immense. It looked like a resort in Fort Lauderdale, if it had been imagined by Aladdin. There were gold domes, swimming pools, and tennis courts. I saw all of this, and my head raced with plans.

I thought, *Is it that far out of the realm of possibility that maybe I could make a prince fall in love with me, and my life will change in dazzling and unexpected ways?*

Inside, the palace was just as impressive. It was cavernous, and in the entryway there was a big fountain, and the carpets glowed because they were *actually woven with real gold*. On the walls there were Picassos and Pollocks.

This wasn't even where the prince lived. There were other palaces where he lived. There were still other palaces where his three wives lived. This was strictly his play palace. And at this palace, every night, he threw parties.

And at the parties there was alcohol although—strictly speaking—it was illegal in Brunci. There was music. There was dancing. And above all there were women—beautiful women from all over the world. There were women from Thailand, Malaysia, the Philippines, Singapore, Indonesia, Hong Kong, a handful of us from the US, and *all of us* were vying for the attention of the prince. It was like the original *Bachelor*.

We would go to these parties every night, and then we would stumble home drunkenly at five in the morning, and we'd sleep all day. And the days tumbled into nights, tumbled into days, tumbled into nights.

After two weeks there, contrary to all my big plans, I had not made a prince fall in love with me. Rather, I had sat there and watched from across the room as all the other women flirted with him, and he ignored me. I wondered what they had that I didn't. I figured I just didn't know how to play that game. I didn't rate. And I thought that was gonna be it; I was going to be going home just like that.

But one morning I was spirited away from the palace, and I was taken to an office building in the capital city. I was locked in an office there, and it was freezing cold, and it was stuffed with all this tacky furniture and what seemed like a hundred pictures of the prince's three wives. I tried one door, and it was locked. I tried the other door; it was locked. There was no bathroom.

I waited there for four hours, until I was trembling from hunger, from cold, from nerves. I considered peeing in a trash can.

I hoped that I was waiting there for the prince, and not for some other mysterious, unthinkable fate, because they had taken my passport. And these were people who were way more powerful than me. Very few people even knew where I really was. I could vanish at that moment and there would be no culpability. And there was nothing I could do about it. So I closed my eyes, and I tried to imagine I was somewhere warm, and I fell asleep.

When I woke up, it was to the sound of the door opening. Standing in front of me was the prince. Until that moment, I had only seen him in casual clothes, but he looked—that day— like a prince. He was dressed in this snazzy uniform, and he had medals on his chest. I sat up way too quickly.

I wouldn't say what I felt for him at that minute was love, exactly, but I felt this very deep sense of gratitude for the fact that he had rescued me from this freezing cold, locked room. I also felt a profound desire to be valued by this person.

And I think in extreme circumstances, the combination of these two things can look very much like love. The prince kissed me, and that was how our romance started. I got to know him a little bit, and as I did, I found out that the prince was not only handsome, he was also bright, educated, and, yes, charming. In spite of the totally bizarre circumstances, I liked him. And for whatever reason, he liked me too.

I rose very quickly through the ranks of the women, and I became his second favorite girlfriend. I know. You're probably thinking, *His second favorite girlfriend, is that good?*

It was. In the context, under the circumstances, it was good enough. And the prince at this time was looking for a fourth wife.

Now, for a fourth wife, it would not be inconceivable for him to choose from amongst the women at the parties. And honestly, I thought about it. I did. I imagined what it would be like to marry him. What Disney-brainwashed American girl would *not* think about it?

But I really tried not to add self-delusion to my growing list of character flaws at this point, because I realized that we were prostitutes. I mean, if you go to the same party every night, wind up making out with the guy throwing the parties, and walk home with a handful of cash, you are a hooker. And at first this didn't really bother me. But eventually all of the locked doors and the constant surveillance we were under started to wear on my nerves.

So one day when I was with the prince on a business trip in Malaysia, a guard came to fetch me. He told me to put on an evening gown in the middle of the afternoon. This was not all that unusual, but what *was* unusual was, when we got in the elevator, he did not press the button for the penthouse where the prince was staying. He pressed the button for the roof.

I panicked. I thought, *What could be on the roof? Oh my God, what have I done? I know too much, and they're trying to get rid of me. They're gonna pitch me off the edge. They're gonna fabricate the headlines. They're gonna say, you know, "American teenager dies in a drug deal gone wrong at the Kuala Lumpur Hilton."*

But when we got to the roof, there was a helicopter there. That was a relief. I got in the helicopter, it hopped over to the next building, and I was escorted to a suite.

The suite looked like . . . if a wedding cake was dipped in

gold, that was what this hotel room looked like. And at the other end of the suite, a football field away it seemed, sat the Sultan of Brunei, the richest man in the world. I recognized him because in Brunei his face was everywhere. It was on the billboards. It was on the television. It was on the money. And the Sultan of Brunei asked me to come over and sit down next to him, and I did. I poured us a cup of tea, and he introduced himself as Martin.

Now, all of the royal brothers had Western nicknames from their schooldays in England. But I was a little disappointed by "Martin." It did not seem very sultan-y to me. It seemed more like one of my Jewish uncles [*with a Jersey accent*]—*Uncle Marty.*

Martin and I chatted, and he was lovely. He was so different from the prince. The prince was moody and demanding. He was very hard to please. The Sultan was cheerful and breezy, and he was easy to please. He just wanted me to do a little dance (which, by the way, is a terrifically awkward thing to do with no music), and then he wanted some oral sex, and then he very definitely wanted me to leave, which I did.

I had been in Brunei for long enough to know that I was not meant to be insulted by the fact that the prince had passed me off to his brother. I was meant to be honored that I had been this gift.

But as I walked away from the Sultan that day, this trickle of truth started to work its way into my brain. I had come there really wanting an adventure. I had started out wanting to be free, and I had wound up a piece of property.

And I asked myself, *What would Patti Smith do?*

And the answer was: She wouldn't be there, really. She wouldn't.

I would like to tell you that this stunning little gem of

self-knowledge instantly transformed me into a person who made wiser and more self-loving choices, but that's not the case. Although eventually, I'd like to think that is what happened.

I stayed in Brunei for a while after that, until I really figured out that numbness is its own kind of misery, and that freedom from caring what happens to you is not freedom. And when I figured that out, I walked away from the prince, and I never went back.

And so now when I ask myself, *What would Patti Smith do?* I can usually say that I think she would like where I wound up.

I think she would stay right here.

Jillian Lauren is the author of the memoir *Some Girls: My Life in a Harem* and the novel *Pretty*. Her writing has appeared in *The Paris Review Daily*, *The New York Times*, *Los Angeles Magazine*, and *Vanity Fair*, among others. She has performed at spoken word and storytelling events across the country. She lives in Los Angeles with her husband and son.

The Day I Became a Matador

I'm going to take you back to Spain in the summer of 1959, when the big event was a mano a mano bullfight between the two great matadors of that era—Luis Miguel Dominguín and Antonio Ordóñez. There hadn't been such a bullfight, a mano a mano, in thirty years, and there hasn't been one since then. So it was a great event.

And my longtime friend, Ernest Hemingway, called me and said, "I'm going to go there and cover it for *LIFE* magazine. Why don't you come on over, and we'll have another adventure?"

I had met Ernest when I edited his novel *Across the River and into the Trees*, and afterwards I had adapted many of his short stories and novels for television and for the movies. We'd had some great adventures together.

So I went to Valencia where the first mano a mano was held, and both bullfighters were marvelous. The second mano a mano was in Malaga, where they were even better. And afterwards we all adjourned to the Miramar terrace, where we had a great deal of red wine and tapas and had a good time.

And during the course of it, Antonio, who was Ernest's favorite bullfighter of all time, said, "You know something, Pecas, I think you should be in the ring. What do you think, Ernest?"

He called me Pecas, that was his nickname for me. Pecas means "the freckled one," which I was at that time.

Ernest said, "That's fine. Hotch, you should be a matador, and I'll be your manager!"

And we drank a lot of red wine, and we're having a great time. I'm extrapolating over where I'll fight, and I know that's just red wine talking and nothing is going to happen. And before we leave, Antonio says, "Tell you what, the next mano a mano is in Ciudad Real. You can be the *sobresaliente*, and I'll put you in one of my suits."

I didn't think anything more of this.

When we got to Ciudad Real to see the mano a mano, we went up to the hotel room where Antonio was, to wish him *suerte* ("good luck"), and on the bed there was a bullfight suit, and it was Antonio's.

He came over and said, "I thought you'd like the colors. They're ivory and black with a touch of red. I think it goes with your complexion."

I said, "My complexion right now is white and getting whiter."

So they proceeded to dress me.

Now, I want to tell you, a bullfighter's costume is no laughing matter. The undergarment is pulled on you, and it's like new skin. Then they give you your *traje de luces*, which is your outer garment. It's like an anvil being put on your back. So I was dressed up in my suit. There was no way really to move in any direction—I was mummified! You have to be suited like this because if you go in a ring and there's a breeze, a little wind, and you're wearing anything that moves, the bull is going to go for you instead of the cloth that you're waving at him. So I am now put together, and I thought: *Well, you know, this is one of those bibulous jokes. They've got me dressed up and then "ha ha" they go to the ring. And they leave me here in the room in this ridiculous costume. I'm not going to be in a bullring.*

As the hour approaches for the fight, everybody leaves except Antonio and me. We're alone in the room. Antonio goes over to a table where he has some religious objects, and he starts to pray over them. I'm in my corner wishing to hell I had something to pray over.

I am now in the van, we're on our way to the bullfight, and I'm sitting next to my manager, Mr. Señor Ernest Hemingway.

And he says to me, "You know, this is my first time as a matador manager, and I'm rather nervous. How about you?" At that moment the van is going by the bullring, and outside the edges of the bullring is a poster bigger than this room. At the top it says "Mano a mano Dominguín versus Ordóñez" and underneath, "Sobresaliente, El Pecas."

Now, I want to tell you what a *sobresaliente* is. It's a substitute sword, and this matador, who's the third matador, only goes in the ring if the other two have been blasted off the face of the sand, either by a goring or some other calamity.

We go under the stands now. We're prepared for the *pasello*. You've all seen in the movies the *pasello*, where everybody goes across the sand—the horses and the matadors and everybody else. I'm standing there with these two great matadors. They have fixed my ceremonial cape so it's exactly right.

And Antonio says to me, "Listen, be careful when we walk the *pasello* over to the judges' stand where the *presidente* is, follow me exactly because of what happened when the matador, Letri, took young Count Teba in as his *sobresaliente* as a joke.

But Count Teba was a little bit wobbly, and the warden spotted him. They arrested him, and he spent a week in jail."

And I thought, *Now's the time to run.*

But off we went. The horses first, then the two matadors, then El Pecas, and then the rest of them. Walking from there over to the president's box felt like four miles. I did everything I could to be just like Antonio, and I guess I pulled it off. I didn't wind up in jail. We doffed our hats to the president. I went into the *callejon*, which is the little alley between the wooden *barrera* and the first row of seats.

My manager is standing there. He says, "You know, there's something I forgot to tell you."

By the way, I'll tell you one thing he told me in that wagon, that I glossed over, but you should know.

I said to him, "When I get to the ring, I'm not conversant with what a matador does. Give me some advice, you're my manager!"

He says, "You only have to do three things. Number one: look tragic. The bullfighters are very serious, so you should look like you're serious."

I said, "Have you looked at me?"

He says, "Number two: when you get to the ring, people are watching you. Don't lean on anything; it's ugly for the suit. And number three: if the photographers come towards you, put your right foot forward—it's sexier."

So there's my manager, who now says to me, "There's something I forgot to tell you. There's a fourth thing, and that is that you have to show yourself to this crowd. The *sobresaliente* always must make his presence known."

Whatever blood was left unfrozen, froze.

At this point Dominguín had already fought the first bull.

Ordóñez got the second bull. He did a couple of cape works with him, and then he fixed him, so the bull was motionless. Then Antonio walked over to the *barrera* and motioned to me.

I came out. I doffed my hat to the crowd, and I was ready to leave, my cape was over my arm.

The fixed bull decided not to be fixed. If you can imagine yourself on a railroad track, and there's a locomotive coming right at you, that was that bull.

Ordóñez said to me, "Pecas, don't move!"

Don't move? I was frozen stiff.

As the bull approached us and got within striking distance, Ordóñez, who was to my right, swiped his cape, pulled him away, and did a *faena*. And the *sobresaliente*, whose cape had slipped down, pulled it up. I guess the crowd thought I was making a pass. At any rate, I stiff-legged out of there, and that was my only experience in the ring.

Antonio was terrific with the last bull, his third bull. It was a *faena* like nobody had ever seen. The crowd went crazy. They waved their white handkerchiefs to influence the judges. And the judges gave him the ultimate award—both ears of the bull, the tail, and a hoof. And they also demanded a tour.

So now we do a tour of the ring, and Antonio comes out and brings me with him. So El Pecas, the *sobresaliente*, is now going to make a triumphal tour of the ring with this great matador. The aficionados in Spain are very appreciative of a great performance, and they throw all manner of things to the matador—cigars, bottles full of wine, tiaras, shoes, hats, money, shawls, decorated fans, and so forth.

So this cornucopia is falling down on us, and Antonio says, "Pecas, pick up the ladies' shoes, nothing else. My men will get the rest."

So I'm following him, and I'm picking up ladies' shoes. Now, if you've got a tight jacket on, and you can't really get your arms around, and your pants are so tight they feel like you're going to fall over every time you bend down, picking up ladies' shoes is not easy. And also, it's not very fulfilling. Not for a matador. So we circle the ring, and my arms are full of ladies' shoes.

We finish, and as is often customary, a group of men came out and they lifted Antonio up onto their shoulders, and they paraded him out to the streets to the hotel, and the band followed them. And left alone, in the center of the ring, was the *sobresaliente* with his arms full of shoes. I didn't know I could move as fast as I did to get back to that van as it was pulling out.

I got back to the hotel, and I went to Antonio's suite, and Antonio said, "Hey, Pecas! You were wonderful. Just throw them on the bed." So I dump the shoes on the bed.

He said, "Come on, the wine is flowing, and we've got tapas!"

I went over. I had a glass of wine. Ernest was enjoying himself.

There was a knock on the door, and Antonio said, "Pecas, you get that."

I open it up and there is the most gorgeous señorita you've ever seen. She's in stocking feet; she's holding one shoe.

She says, "I come for my other shoe." She selects her shoe, and I put it on her dainty foot. And Antonio and Ernest come over and invite her for wine.

So we were all having wine and tapas, when there's another knock on the door, and another knock on the door, and another knock on the door. And in they came. They reclaimed their shoes; they joined the party. It was wonderful. It was a marvelous party. They stayed until the wee hours.

And the next day, the photographer for *LIFE* magazine who

had been with us and taken pictures of the day before, he came with his prints. And there was a big eight-by-ten of a beaming El Pecas with the two great matadors of the world on his right and left.

And Ernest came over and said, "Ah, that's wonderful, Hotch, you found your true profession."

I said, "Just a minute, it may be wonderful to you, but look at the front of their pants, those significant humps, and then look at the insignificant thing that I have!"

He said, "How many handkerchiefs did you use?"

I said, "Handkerchiefs! You're my manager, you didn't tell me to use handkerchiefs."

He said, "Well you've been to a lot of bullfights with me, didn't you see that all these matadors have nice humps in the front of their pants?"

And I said, "The subject never interested me until now!"

He said, "All right, look, I can make it up. Antonio has his next fight in Ronda. He wants you to be there as his *sobresaliente* again. And this time, we'll make a level playing field out of it."

I said, "How?"

He said, "I'll tell you what we're going to do."

And then he paid me one of the greatest compliments I ever got, he said, "While they're dressing, they'll be using two handkerchiefs, but Pecas, you only need one."

¡Olé!

A. E. Hotchner is the author of nineteen books and numerous plays for Broadway and television. He became a close friend of Paul Newman's after Paul starred in Hotchner's film, *Adventures of a Young Man*. As a lark, with a bottle of Newman's salad dressing, they co-founded Newman's Own, Inc., which has donated close to $400 million to charity, all the profits from its line of foods. Aaron Edward Hotchner was born and raised in St. Louis, where he earned a law degree from Washington University. In 1942, he left the practice of law to enter the Air Force, where he attained the rank of major. After the war, he became an editor and writer in New York, where he edited a novel written by Ernest Hemingway. For the next fourteen years, until Hemingway's death, they remained solid friends. Hotchner's memoir *Papa Hemingway*, an international best seller, is an account of that friendship. Hotchner also adapted many of Hemingway's stories and novels for the theater, film, and television. In addition to their food business, Hotchner and Newman founded the Hole in the Wall Gang Camp for children with cancer and other life-threatening diseases; there are now sister camps throughout the United States and the rest of the world. Hotchner's evocative memoir about growing up in St. Louis during the Great Depression, *King of the Hill*, was made into a movie in 1993, the screenplay adapted and directed by Steven Soderbergh.

In the
Trenches

Life After Death

When I first arrived on death row, the guards decided they were gonna welcome me to the neighborhood. So they took me to the part of the prison they call "the Hole." It's a very small, very dark, filthy part of the prison that's in complete isolation. And for the next eighteen days they beat the hell out of me. They used to come in at about twelve, one o'clock in the morning, and they would chain me to the bars of the cell and beat me with nightsticks. They beat me so bad at one point that I started to piss blood. I still wake up at night sometimes now dreaming that I'm pissing blood again.

They starved me. They tortured me.

Eventually word of what they were doing started to leak out into the rest of the prison. Other prisoners started to hear about it. So they went to a deacon from the Catholic Church, who used to come to prison to bring Catholic inmates Communion, and they told him what was going on. And he went to the warden's office, and he told the warden, "I know what you're doing to this guy. I know you're killing him. And if it doesn't stop, I'm going to go public."

So that night they took me out of the Hole and put me back in a regular prison cell. The other prisoners told me later that they had expected to see me carried out in a body bag any day. And I think the only reason they didn't murder me is because they realized they were being watched.

When I was a kid, my family was incredibly poor, beyond dirt-poor. When we did finally move into a trailer park with running water and electricity, we thought we were really moving up in the world. I used to take refuge in books and music. Reading became a sanctuary for me. It allowed me to escape the world I lived in for a little while. I'd read Stephen King novels over and over, listen to music like Iron Maiden. I started dressing in black all the time because it was like a security blanket for me. It made me feel a little safer in an unsafe and scary world. I didn't have many friends; in fact, my only real friend was this skinny blond kid with a mullet named Jason Baldwin, and Jason was with me the night I was arrested.

It was me, Jason, my sister, and my girlfriend sitting in the house, in the living room watching movies, when the cops started beating on the door. Hammering on it. And when I opened the door, they were pointing guns at me. They swarmed into the house like ants. They stampeded over everything and pawed through every single possession my family owned. They put me and Jason in handcuffs, threw us into the backs of cop cars, and took us to jail.

I spent all night in a cell about the size of a closet. I wasn't allowed to go to the bathroom, wasn't given so much as a drink of water. Every so often a cop would come in and ask me if I had anything to tell him, or if I was ready to make my confession yet. This went on all night, until the next day, when we were given an arraignment hearing. At this hearing the judge tells me that I'm being charged with three counts of capital murder. That I'm being accused of killing three children as part of a satanic sacrifice. He says someone has confessed, but he refuses to read the confession in the courtroom. Instead, I am put in a broom closet somewhere in the back of the jail and given a transcript of this confession.

I'm only eighteen years old, and I'm in complete and absolute shock and trauma. I'm suffering from sleep deprivation. My life has just been destroyed. But even reading this thing, I could see that there was something wrong with it. It made no sense. It was like some sort of bizarre patchwork Frankenstein thing that they had stitched together. Turns out that they had picked up a mentally handicapped kid in our neighborhood and coerced him into making a confession, and then he was led to implicate Jason and me. Nothing in this confession made any sense whatsoever, but it didn't matter to them. I was put in a cell, and I kept thinking, *Surely someone's gonna step in and put a stop to this. Surely, someone is gonna rectify the situation. They can't put you on trial and prove you've done something you haven't done.* It seemed to me that science would say that's impossible.

But they did.

They took us to trial, and the evidence was the Stephen King novels that I read, the music I listened to, the clothes that I wore. And they found us guilty. I was sentenced to death. Not once, not twice, but three times. The judge read these death sentences in this really bored, monotone voice, like it was just another day at the office for him.

People asked me later, "What were you feeling when he was sentencing you to die?" It's almost impossible to articulate. If you've ever been beaten, a lot of times, you know, when you're punched in the head, you don't register pain. You see a bright

flash of light, hear a loud noise, and you're completely disori-
ented, you have no idea where you even are for a few minutes.
That's what it was like when he was reading those death sentences; it was like being repeatedly punched in the head.

They sent me to death row. I was in a cell for about a week
before I noticed a shadow on the wall. It was from the man who
had already been executed, who was in the cell before I got
there. He had stood against the wall and traced around himself
with a pencil really, really lightly, and then very subtly shaded it
in. I mean it was so subtle I didn't even see it for about the first
week. And then after I saw it, I couldn't un-see it. So for years I
slept on a dead man's mattress, stared at a dead man's shadow,
and lived in the cell with ghosts.

They filed appeal after appeal on my behalf, all before the
same judge who sentenced me to death. He denied them all.
Even when new DNA evidence came in that excluded me and
the other two guys from the crime scene, and instead pointed
the finger at one of the victims' stepfathers and the man who
was providing the stepfather with an alibi, the judge still said,
"This is not enough."

Then we were allowed to appeal to the Arkansas Supreme
Court, and by this time awareness of what's going on, public interest in the case, had been building. There'd been documentaries, there'd been books, countless newspaper articles and
magazine stories and TV shows. So the Arkansas Supreme Court
knew they were being watched. And in the end that was the only
thing they really cared about, winning the next election. So they
ruled that all of this new evidence would be heard, and the pros-
ecutors realized that meant there was gonna be another trial.

So a deal was hammered out—an Alford plea. What an

Alford plea means is that I plead guilty, and I walk out of the courtroom, and I can still publicly maintain my innocence, but I can't sue the state.

And people have asked me what I was thinking about the day that I went into court knowing that I could very well go home that day? And the truth is, I wasn't thinking anything. By that time I was so tired and beat down that all I wanted to do was rest. I was dying. My health was deteriorating very rapidly. I was losing my eyesight. I knew I wasn't gonna make it much longer.

The prosecutor said that one of the factors for him making this deal was the fact that the three of us together could've collectively sued the state for $60 million. I knew they could've had me stabbed to death for $50 any day of the week. Happens in prison all the time. So I knew if I didn't take that deal, one way or another I would never live to see the outside of those prison walls. So I took it.

I've been out of prison now for a little over ten months, and I live in terror every single day. I'm scared of everything, all the time. But I'm trying to fight my way through it. I have to force myself to every day that I get up. And I know that I will eventually. I'll do it, and I'll be free of it, because if there's one thing that I learned from eighteen years in prison, it was how to fight.

Born in 1974, **Damien Echols** grew up in Mississippi, Tennessee, Maryland, Oregon, Texas, Louisiana, and Arkansas. At the age of eighteen, he was wrongfully convicted of murder, along with Jason Baldwin and Jesse Misskelley Jr., thereafter known as the West Memphis Three. Echols received a death sentence and spent almost eighteen years on death row until he, Baldwin, and Misskelley were released in 2011. The WM3 have been the subject of

Paradise Lost, a three-part documentary series produced by HBO, and *West of Memphis*, a documentary produced by Peter Jackson and Fran Walsh. Echols is the author of the *New York Times* bestselling memoir *Life After Death* (2012), and a self-published memoir, *Almost Home* (2005).

ARI HANDEL

Don't Fall in Love with Your Monkey

"Don't fall in love with your monkey." My advisor warned me, but I didn't listen. There are some things you have to learn for yourself.

It was 1992, and I was a young graduate student getting ready to take Santiago out of his cage for the first time. So, I put on these bouffant boots and a little blue cap and a big pair of welders' gloves, and I turned to my advisor. And my advisor gave me this one last piece of advice, "Be as inevitable as the tide." And he sent me up to the monkey room.

So I go upstairs, and I unlocked the door, and a waft of warm air comes whooshing out at me, and it smells like a combination of Purina monkey chow, monkey feces, and just plain monkey. And I walk in, and it's a small room. It's cinder block, and it's just big enough for eight cages, four on the top, four on the bottom. Santiago's cage is in the bottom right-hand corner.

I lean down and unlock the door, and I try to go and take Santiago out of the cage. I stick my hand in, and it's a little scary.

Santiago is a wild animal. He does not want to be taken out of his cage. He keeps batting at me and trying to hit my hand when I reach for him, and he's big, and he's fast, and he's nimble. And I'm slow, I'm in bulky clothing, and I'm starting to get hot. I'm starting to sweat. And the monkeys in the room can sense that there's a conflict going on. They're starting to hoot and holler and screech.

Finally I get one hand around Santiago's bicep, and Santiago does exactly what you would do if some blue ogre reached into your house and grabbed you by the arm and tried to take you out. He bites me as hard as he possibly can right here in the soft part of my hand. And it hurts. It really hurts. It hurts a lot. And every nerve in my hand is screaming to me, *Drop the monkey.*

But I am as inevitable as the tide, so I do not drop the monkey. Instead, I reach my other hand in, grab his other bicep, and pull his arms behind his back, and I take him out, and I stick him into his monkey chair and bring him down to the lab.

Down in the lab, Santiago is now the one who is frightened. He is quaking, he is shivering in his chair. So I take a bottle, and I fill it with juice, and he starts to suck on the juice. It's Hawaiian punch. He starts to suck the juice, and I can see his little mouth around the edge of the bottle, and the juice is dripping down his chin, and he is so cute. I'm looking at him, his little eyes, and I see this look in his eyes, and it is joy. And I know what that joy is—it is the fake fruit flavoring in the bottle. But I can't help feeling that some of that joy is for me.

Now, I think that I became a neurobiologist in fourth grade when my mom gave me this coloring book of the human brain for a book report, and it said that this part of the brain back here is for seeing things, and this part up here, that's for thinking about stuff, like when you have to do your math homework, and there's a part in the middle that's for feeling things, that's like when you get scared of the dark, and you don't want to go downstairs into the basement. And that meant to me that when we see, perceive, think, and feel about the world, we are using this [*points to his head*], so if we want to know how to understand the world, what it's like to live inside the human mind, then we just have to understand this [*points to his head again*].

When neurobiologists want to study the human mind, they look at the brains of monkeys. And I wanted to ask complex questions about mental functioning, which meant that I had to use a complex behavioral task, and that meant that Santiago had to learn to play a video game.

So I would put him in a room facing a giant screen with a tube connected to his mouth that contained juice, and I would go into the next room, where I had a computer and could control all these lights that would flash on that screen. And Santiago's job was to look at the lights in the right order and with the right timing, and if he did it right, he would get some juice.

Now, this was not actually a very complicated game, but it was very hard to teach Santiago how to play. And the reason was that I could not just tell him how to play. Santiago could not speak English. In fact, Santiago lacked the capacity to speak any human language whatsoever, so we had to invent our own language.

And I would watch Santiago's eye movements, and I would see that if they were drifting slowly, that meant that he was very frustrated, but if they were shimmering very fast, that meant he was excited. So I would watch his eye movements, and I would adjust the difficulty of the task accordingly, to cajole him forward or to calm him down, so that slowly and surely, the teacher and the student, we learned this task together.

And when we did, Santiago got very, very happy. He was like a gambler who had just cracked the code of the blackjack tables, because now he could just get juice, juice, juice, as much as he wanted, and he would sit in that room, and he would play that game all day long. And he would drink tremendous, tremendous volumes of juice, and that made me happy too, because I could do the thing I wanted to do, which was to lower a probe down into Santiago's brain.

And I would listen to the activity of individual neurons while he performed this task. And what I found was that there were neurons in Santiago's brain that would become activated every time he made an eye movement. But the thing that was cool, so cool, so cool it was mind-blowing, was that these neurons did not get activated just when he made a movement; they got activated as soon as I gave him enough information that he could choose which eye movement to make.

Listening to these neurons, I could predict in advance what he was going to do even before he did it. That meant I was eavesdropping on him while he was making a decision. I was inside that coloring book. I was reading my monkey's mind.

We did this for quite some time. Santiago would get juice, and I would get data out of his brain, and we would do this for days and days and days. And at night I would go up to the monkey room, and I would give all the monkeys treats. I would give them apples and oranges and grapes and bananas. And I would also give an extra big handful to Santiago because he was my boy, and I wanted him to know that. We went on like this for some time. And then something happened that had not happened in a long time.

I went upstairs to get Santiago, and he tried to bite me. And when I brought him downstairs to the game room, he just would not work, he just banged and banged and aborted every trial. *Bang, bang, bang!*

I couldn't figure it out at first, and then it slowly dawned on me that Santiago was a smart animal. I mean, he was smarter than a dog or a cat. He was primate smart. And I realized he must have figured out sometime during the night that I was not bringing him down to that room so that he could play games, so that he could have fun. I was bringing him down there for my benefit. He was my servant. He realized that, I think, and that realization made the juice taste bitter, and he didn't want to do it anymore. He was having no part. And I had a monkey who was on strike.

So I did the thing you do when that happens. I turned off the water in Santiago's cage. Now, the idea is that he's only going to get *enough* water, and anything extra, he's going to have to earn.

The problem with this plan was that every night I would go up to the monkey room, I would give Santiago his little supplement of water, and he would drink it right down in front of my face, and then he would have nothing. And I would go home and get a glass of iced tea, and I would drink it, and I would think about Santiago living in his cage with no water. And the iced tea would turn into a beer, which would turn into a bourbon. And I would wake up in the morning, and I would be filled with guilt over what was happening to Santiago, what I was doing to him.

But when I got up in the morning, when I put him in that booth, and he still wouldn't work, that guilt turned to anger, because whose fault was it really that Santiago was not drinking?

Whose fault was it that I felt guilty every day that I was forced to be the asshole? It was Santiago's fault. I mean, he was sitting with the juice tube in his mouth, there was a game he knew how to play, and he wasn't playing. And I would get so angry with him. I would get so frustrated, I would storm into that room and I would scream at him, "Santiago, why don't you just work already? The game is here and you know how to play. Why don't you just go back to the way it used to be? You were getting the juice. I was getting the data. We were so happy!"

But he wouldn't listen. And I would get so angry sometimes, I would pull on his little monkey ear and he would go "EEEH."

And then the anger would turn back to guilt. And I would run into the other room, and I would find the button that controls the juice. And I would just press it *shsh, shsh, shsh*, giving Santiago juice until the guilt disappeared.

And this went on day after day after day after day. And I got so frustrated that eventually, I walked into the room one day and said, "I know you're thirsty. I'll show you how thirsty you are."

I poured myself a huge glass of Hawaiian punch. I took my mask off. I made eye contact with Santiago. And I drank that juice down, taunting him. And he just looked at me. And I realized that I had long ago left scientific objectivity behind. I needed help. This was not working.

So I went to my advisor, and he said to me, "Stop playing 'Who's the Monkey.'" And what he meant was, I was engaged in a battle of wills and a battle of wits with an animal whose brain was the size of my fist, and I was losing. I was supposed to be training him, and he was training me. And what he was training me to do was to get guilty, get angry, cross the line, get guilty again, and give free juice. And believe me, free juice is the sweetest-tasting juice there is. But now, no more. I was going to be hard. I was going to be serious.

And when it was treat time, I went up to the room, and every monkey in that room got treats. They all got nice juice treats, cucumbers and apples and grapes. But not Santiago. For Santiago, it was cashews and peanuts and crackers. And it took a long, long time, because I had really done a very good job of training Santiago that I was really a pushover.

But eventually, eventually, *eventually* there came a day, after months and months of suffering on his part and mine, when I walked up to the monkey cage and Santiago just did this [*extends one arm*]. And when I took his hand in my hand, Santiago did this [*places his other arm behind his back*]. And I grabbed him, and I brought him downstairs to work. And he started to play the game. But he didn't play with the exceptional enthusiasm he had played it with before. He wasn't like, *Wow, this is the greatest thing*. He sat there and just played the game like a factory worker on an assembly line—*whish, whish, whish.*

And that should have been a good day for me, because I was getting back to the science now. I would get my data, Santiago would get his juice. The suffering for us was over.

But it wasn't a good day, because with all that stuff that had come before, the competition and the cooperation between, I had gotten to know Santiago. And now *that* Santiago wasn't there anymore. I was sitting here with just another monkey with a broken will. And I was the one who had broken it.

Something snapped a little for me too that day because I was going to finish my thesis, but the mystique of being a scientist—of finding out all this stuff about the mind—just didn't seem so magical anymore.

There were other monkeys. I didn't need to be told not to fall in love with them. Instinctively, I held myself aloof from them, and because of that, I had no mercy on them. And when they went on strike, when they got upset and it was time to break them, I broke them like that [*snaps fingers*], and that was good, because they didn't suffer very much and neither did I. But I also didn't go up to the monkey room anymore, because I didn't want to see those monkeys while they were still a little bit wild. I didn't want to be reminded of that part of them, and what I was going to do to that part of them.

It took me eight years, but I got all the data I needed, piece by piece by piece. And I put my brick in the edifice of human knowledge, and I got my Ph.D.

And then I quit.

I wrote a thesis, and the thesis is 364 pages long and is filled with facts and data and graphs and theories. But the most significant page for me is the first one, which says simply: "Dedicated to the memory of Santiago."

After receiving a Ph.D. in neuroscience in 2000, **Ari Handel** turned to filmmaking, where he has worked as both a writer (Darren Aronofsky's *The Fountain* and the upcoming *Noah*) and a producer (*The Fountain*, *The Wrestler*, *Black Swan*, and *Noah*). He is currently president of Protozoa Pictures and has served on The Moth's Board of Directors since 2005.

Tajik Sonata

It's half past five in the morning. I get up, and I don't feel rested because I have been walking and walking in my dreams all night.

I look around to see what I have left over from yesterday's meal. There's no bread, no sugar (I can't remember when I last saw sugar). So I drink some tea with herbs.

I look outside to see which flag is out. Our city is at war, and what dress I should wear today will be influenced by which side holds the city as of this morning.

Today it is a red flag, so I can wear European clothes and leave off my head handkerchief. But in the back of my mind, I think that I should take the dress and the handkerchief with me in case the regime changes while I'm at work.

I close my door, locking my two children in for the day. I'm going to my job as a piano teacher at the university.

I walk, and it usually takes me two hours each way. I don't want to think about bad things, but they keep entering my mind.

THE MOTH

It's the middle of November, and I still have no news from my husband. He left for work on the first of November, and he disappeared. I called his brothers, but his brothers are now missing as well. People keep disappearing from their homes. I can't leave the city, because if I do, he'll have no way to find me if he *is* able to get back. So me and my children stay in the city and wait and hope for his return.

I keep walking, and more thoughts come. My teenage daughter came home yesterday crying, with her eyes big. She was attacked for the second time in a row. In the middle of the day at a bus stop, two guys got out of their car and tried to drag her into the car, but there happened to be another woman standing there, and she and my daughter held on to each other and wouldn't let themselves be pulled into the car. So they were beaten and got large bruises, but they managed to get away. This time. I will probably have to send her to Moscow in the end, because I can no longer protect her here.

I keep going, and I reach the Hotel Dushanbe. This is the spot where the teachers usually meet, and we go to the university together. I'm waiting, but nobody comes today. So I continue alone.

At the first square, city residents are gathering, quietly protesting for the streets to be cleaned up and for the fighting to stop, so the people can get to work safely. The center of the city is currently in ruins.

For some reason people are very aggressive today. I notice these small sculptures in the square—my favorites—and I can see that some of them have been damaged, which makes me sad. If they were lighter I would probably try to bring some of them home to keep them safe.

Today arms are being given out in the square. And I notice

that the soldiers are not writing down who they give the arms to. It's scary.

I'm so frightened, but I keep going and enter the next square. There are cannons there that have appeared overnight. And then I come to Baghdad Square, and I fear it the most because there are often people screaming into microphones there, and they sometimes scream at me as I pass.

Finally I reach the university. I get to the sixth floor. It's still very early in the morning.

But as I step in, I see the deputy chief of the department running towards me, and he's screaming, *"Teacher, Teacher, there are soldiers! Soldiers in the music room! And they're smashing the instruments!"*

I don't quite understand what is happening, but I hear the sounds of instruments being destroyed, and I run towards the sound. The deputy chief stays behind on purpose, afraid to go in.

But I run into the room, and I see about ten soldiers kicking and hitting the instruments lying around the room. Their armor and machine guns are lying on top of the grand piano. I've seen soldiers in the street before, but they were dressed in green with turbans and Arabic script on their sashes. I was used to them.

These soldiers are different. They are so tall, and they're wearing all black, with black wraps around their faces—you can only see their eyes. I have no idea which army they come from. I've never seen them before.

I am in shock.

And I don't know what I was thinking, but I think I had just had it with this war that was destroying my city and my family.

And I walked right in and walked up to the first one, who was beating on a piano, and in a loud voice begged him to *stop smashing the instruments.*

I said, "The instruments are very expensive, and these instruments will serve your children and your grandchildren in the future. If you want, I can play the piano for you."

And they got very quiet and stared at me.

So I sat down, and I started playing the *Moonlight* Sonata. A few of them sat down too. Others came closer to see how my fingers moved across the keys.

And then one of them came even closer and asked me to play a Tajik folk song. When I had first walked in, they were all speaking Russian, but when he asked me to play, he asked in our native Tajik. So I played it, and all of them started singing along. They were like a choir.

And then out of nowhere, a man came to the door, and he said something to them, and they stood up quickly, took their armor and guns, and left, shutting the door behind them.

So I'm standing in the middle of the room, stunned. When suddenly the door opens just a tiny crack, and the deputy chief is peering in nervously.

He asks, "They left? Weren't you scared?"

And I actually got scared only when I saw *him*, because I suddenly remembered that I have two children locked in the house at home, and I instructed them not to open the doors to anybody, and I thought: *What would have happened if I had been hurt?* I didn't have any family staying in the city anymore.

In the evening I'm on the long, long road back home. And I'm walking, and I'm very tired. And I'm remembering that we didn't have any bread given out at work today, and what can I feed my children with? So I have to come home and stand in line for five hours to get bread. But my children are going to be happy about the hot bread, and that keeps me going.

And I'm sure that my husband will come back (and this is

what happened, a year later he did come back to us, and he's here with us tonight!).

And yet still even today so many women are waiting for their husbands to return to them. They *have* to believe they will come back.

And still they wait.

Anoid Latipovna Rakhmatyllaeva was born on October 31, 1955, in Stalinabad (present-day Dushanbe), Tajik SSR. From 1961 to 1972, she attended the Republican Music Boarding School, where she was in the piano department. In 1972 Anoid entered Tajikistan State Art Institute, the department of musicology. After graduating, Anoid taught in several music schools in Dushanbe, and in 1982 she was assigned to work at the central music school in the city of Kurgan-Tube. From 1992 to 1995, Anoid taught at Tajikistan Pedagogical University in the department of musicology. In 1995, Anoid opened a branch of the school, Music School #6, at the Russian division based in Dushanbe. From 2002 to 2012, Anoid worked as a teacher and concertmaster at Music School #6. She is happily married and has two children and one granddaughter. Anoid travels a lot between Moscow, where both of her children live, and Dushanbe. The Moth's artistic director, Catherine Burns, met Anoid when The Moth was invited by the U.S. State Department to direct a show at the Padida Theater in Dushanbe, Tajikistan. The show was co-directed and hosted by the monologist Mike Daisey and featured locals who had been affected in some way by the region's civil war, which had recently ended.

Impeachment Day

My story starts in late July in Washington, DC. It was a typical hot summer day. I found myself in the Oval Office by myself, and in walked the President of the United States, William Jefferson Clinton.

He said to me, "I hear you want to be my next press secretary."

And I said, "Yes sir, I think I do." And it happened.

Now, there should have been some warning signs for me. Some were obvious, like the Lewinsky investigation. But a couple were not so obvious.

The first was, the guy who I was replacing, Mike McCurry, started smiling as soon as he heard I got the job. And for six weeks the smile didn't come off his face.

The second, which was weird, was I was the only applicant for the job. There was no interview process. Nobody else applied. I was the only one in America who seemed to want the job.

But I had this thing about challenging myself personally, and I thought, *You know, I can do this, so I'm gonna try to do it.*

I didn't have to wait long for the challenge. My very first day, walking out to the podium in the White House Press Room, simultaneously—to the moment—the House Judiciary Committee was gathering for the third impeachment hearings in the history of the country. So I had a few things on my mind.

And I would love to say that I got off to a good start. But I can't.

Just after I started, we went on a trip. We went off to Russia, and then we were going to Ireland, doing big foreign policy stuff. The trip was going pretty well, but the last night, in Moscow, I was coming into the hotel, and I ran into an old friend of mine, the godfather to my daughter, who I hadn't seen in a couple years.

And he said, "Come on, we've gotta go out." And he convinced me, so we went to—I'll never forget—a place called the Hungry Duck. And they were doing things there that I couldn't take my eyes off, so I had to stay till five in the morning.

Which was okay, because we weren't leaving until six.

So I got back to my hotel and made one mistake, which was to sit down on the bed, and I obviously fell asleep.

And I'm telling you, you don't know anxiety until you've woken up as the White House Press Secretary on your first foreign trip, at six-fifteen in Moscow, without a passport, knowing you've missed Air Force One.

The only good thing that I could think of was the day couldn't get worse. I was wrong.

When I finally caught up with the traveling party, I was immediately surrounded by reporters who said, "How do you feel about being the first White House press secretary to ever miss Air Force One on a foreign trip?" And a strange phrase caught in my head, and I couldn't lose it.

About a week earlier, the President had been at a prayer breakfast, talking about his affair with Monica Lewinsky, and he said, "I'm really sorry for what I did. And I'm working very hard to make up for it, particularly to those I've hurt the most."

So when I got the question "How do you feel?" I said, "I'm really sorry for what I've done wrong, and I'm working hard to fix it, particularly to those who I've hurt the most."

Now, mocking the President of the United States when you make a mistake isn't always the best idea, but it came to my head, and I said it.

But the day went on, and we finally had a little break where the President had some private meetings, and I went to the back of the Irish ambassador's residence to go to sleep.

I hadn't been asleep for more than five minutes, and was actually pretty hungover, which is why I needed the sleep, when the President's personal aide came back and said, "The President's in a meeting right now, and he needs you to come into it."

Now, I'm not the smartest guy in the world, but this had practical joke written all over it, and I said, "Get lost."

About three minutes later, he came in again and said, "Hey, the President's in with the band U2, he's with Bono, and they want to talk to you."

I said, "Well, if the President wants to see me, he can walk his presidential ass right back to this room and ask me himself."

Well, about sixty seconds later, the presidential ass showed up and said, "What is your problem? These guys want to meet you."

So I walked into the meeting, and this guy, this rock star, Bono, comes up and gives me this big hug and says, "I really wanted to meet you."

And I said, "Well, that's great, Mr. Bono, but, um, why?"

And he said, "Anyone who can handle world affairs, and

Monica Lewinsky and all that, and still has time to stay out all night drinking is my kind of guy."

Now, most people would think, you know, Bono, U2, telling you that they like your work, that'd be great. Only problem, I'd spent most of the day making sure the President *didn't know* I'd missed Air Force One, and Bono busted me.

But after that inauspicious start, things started going pretty well. We reached a historic budget deal, and I got to talk about that. We made peace in the Middle East temporarily, and I got to talk about that.

But still looming above everything was this unresolved Monica Lewinsky investigation and what was going on in Iraq. And I'll always remember a very bizarre plane ride on Air Force One.

We're coming back from the Middle East, having done some peace talks, and the plane is divided into three sections. In the middle section, the President's political advisors were all gathered. We were getting near the impeachment vote, and we were very aware of who we needed with us to avoid being impeached. And it struck me as sort of a game of political Bingo, because people were calling members of Congress from the plane, and people kept shouting out, "Congressman Quinn, we lost him!" And people would write it down—*Quinn, yes on impeachment.* And we figured out in this meeting that we didn't have the votes, and we were going to lose.

Now, up in the front of the plane, where the President had his office, there was a meeting going on with the national security team, going through war plans for launching an attack on Iraq.

I was the only one going between the two meetings, and I do remember, in both meetings, sort of looking up at one point and saying, "Think things are going bad in *this* meeting? You should see what's going on in the *other* meeting."

But when we landed that night at Andrews Air Force Base, I realized three things. One was the President was going to be impeached, and soon. Two was we were going to start a war with Iraq, and soon. And three, I was the one who was going to have to convince the public that one and two had nothing to do with each other.

About ten days later the President of the United States was facing an impeachment vote. Now, we had a pretty simple strategy for dealing with this. We said that this was all about politics—it's partisan, the President's gonna stay focused on the people's business. It was simple, and people believed it—our ratings were up.

But at about eleven-thirty, the speaker of the House, Bob Livingston, went to the floor and said something to the effect of "Larry Flynt caught me, I had an affair, and the only honorable thing to do is to resign." And he resigned on the floor, during the impeachment debate.

Now, we had a simple message, but all of a sudden, they had one that was even simpler: do something wrong, get caught, resign.

I figured we had about fifteen minutes before everyone figured that out, and a drumbeat of TV pundits would start saying the President should resign.

So I ran down to the Oval Office. The President was there with the chief of staff, John Podesta. We were waiting for a couple of people to arrive to figure out what to do.

I said to the President, "What do you think? How do you feel about this?"

And he started talking, and I realized that what he was

saying was making a lot of sense, so I started scribbling it down, and when the rest of the team arrived, I said, "We don't need to have a meeting. This is what we're going to say." And as some of you may remember, the President said that it was a real shame that the congressman was resigning. That the cycle of the politics of personal destruction had to end and should end today. And that he was going to call Livingston and say, "Don't resign."

And, oddly, the fever that I was worried about, about the President being forced to resign, broke in that very moment. Which was good for me, because I was late for another meeting.

I had to go to a meeting where we were working on writing the State of the Union speech, and I do remember sitting in that meeting and thinking, *You know, we're sitting here discussing health care and education—this is why we're going to survive this. We're actually doing the people's business.*

Unfortunately, at that moment, someone came and tapped me on the shoulder and said, "We need you out here."

It was my deputy, and I remember looking at her and saying, "You know, if one more thing happens today, my head's going to explode."

And she said, "Well then, you don't want to go into your office right now."

In my office were some members of the President's national security team. They had been meeting, unbeknownst to me, talking about the military action that had been going on now for about ten days.

And I went in, and they said, "We've completed this military action, we've hit everything we can, and we're about to go to the President to recommend he make a statement calling off the military action and claiming victory."

And I looked at them and said, "You've gotta be fucking

kidding me. A week ago, you had me go out and say, 'We found out today we're gonna be impeached, and we're launching a war,' and today you want me to go out and say, 'Yeah, we got impeached, but guess what? We won the war!'"

They said yeah.

I said, "Well isn't there anything we can hit again? Can we go back and hit some buildings a second time?"

The military guy didn't think that was very funny.

I then had what we call in the business a "communications challenge," because we had two things that we had to do in the same time space. We tried to figure out what to do, and I thought, *You know what? Sometimes the best thing to do is not worry very much about it—just go out and do it.*

So first we had a hundred and fifty members of Congress— all Democrats—down on the South Lawn to stand with the President and say, "This impeachment was all partisan; it's all politics." It was a very simple message: this is partisan politics, Republicans suck. It all went well.

But then we had to talk about the war.

So we went inside and only ten minutes apart—same podium, just a different room—said, "There are no Republicans in this country, there are no Democrats, there are just Americans, and we have won the war."

Then the President left, leaving me to explain to fifty waiting reporters how the two things fit together. And I think it was so audacious that we took the breath away from even the press, and they seemed to let us get away with it.

And I remember at the end of this long day, walking across the hall to my office. One of my closest friends in the White House, one of the President's top aides, saw me come in, and I sat down, and he went over to the little bar in the office, and he got two beers and opened them up, sat down, and put his feet up.

And I'll never forget what he said to me.

He said, "You know, except for getting impeached, we had a pretty good day."

Joe Lockhart served as White House press secretary for President Bill Clinton during his second term in office. Joe currently is a communications strategist at the Glover Park Group, a leading communications organization he co-founded in 2001 in Washington, DC.

WAYNE REECE

Easter in a Texas Roadhouse

Travel with me if you will to a space called the Panhandle in North Texas. Travel with me to the year 1960, fifty years ago, specifically the Saturday before Easter.

I was in my last year in seminary at Southern Methodist University in Dallas, Texas, and I was also pastoring four rural churches. And on that Saturday I was agonizing to finish my sermon that I had worked on all week long, trying to get it down to the perfection that Christian preachers aspire to on Easter.

I had put in some of my own experiences and my reflections. I had also dropped in some wonderful quotations from the theologians of the day. And I was ready to preach *that* day, but I had to wait another day.

Now, that Saturday, in the evening some of the kids from the four churches that I was serving came over to prepare for an Easter sunrise service. At about nine o'clock they all went home, but one guy was left. His friend had left him behind—had forgotten him—and Brian asked me if I could take him home to Tioga.

I said, "Sure." I told my wife where I was going and what I was doing, and Brian and I jumped into my station wagon and we headed off.

But for me, this was virgin territory. Uncharted. I had driven these roads in the past two months, during the day, on the major thoroughfares, but I had not traveled those country roads in the dark. I got Brian to his home, dropped him, and headed back. It was about ten o'clock at night, and I was needing to get home and get to bed so I could be prepared for the four sermons the next morning.

And then it happened! I had forgotten to fill up my gas tank that day. My car started to sputter and spit, and then it died.

What do I do? I'm out here in the middle of nowhere. I can't see anything. I wondered, *Where do I go? Who can I find?* There were no houses around. There were no gas stations.

And so, apprehensively, I got out of my car, locked it up, and started going someplace, not knowing where I was going, or when I was going to get there, and what I would find when I got there. So, I had walked almost two hours, or at least it seemed two hours. Actually I found out, when I got to the place, I'd only been gone thirty-five minutes. But I saw, in the distance, a gleaming light. And like a moth being drawn to the flame, I went to that glow. And as I neared it, I heard twanging, blaring music, and I found myself at a country roadhouse, surrounded by pickup trucks and motorcycles.

Now, I had never been in one of these, and I didn't know what to expect. But I knew that I had to have somebody try to help me, and I wondered if I would find anybody like that here.

So I apprehensively went into the roadhouse, and over on the side there was a little room, and there were three guys, and they were playing pool. And so I thought, *Well, maybe they could help me, or at least they could tell someone who could help me.*

Just as I walked in one guy came up to me, and he said, "Hey, I'm Eric, and do you want to play pool?"

I thought maybe they thought I could be hustled, because I had—well, I *looked* like I had money.

I said, "Well, I used to play pool when I was in high school." And then I thought to myself, *and I had done pretty well.* But I hadn't played for six years.

He said, "Well, would you break on a game of Stripes and Solids?"

And I said, "Sure."

So I racked them up, went to get the cue stick, chalked it up, put talc on my hands, and stroked and cracked the rack, meaning the balls scattered. One ball went in. I stroked and hit again. A second ball went in. And then a third ball went in. And I realized that I had amazingly gotten back my youthful talent of pool!

Well, to make a long story short, I put in four more balls. There was only one ball left—the eight ball. This is the pièce de résistance in Stripes and Solids. I called it for the left corner pocket. I stroked, hit, and it went in.

And immediately, Eric said, "Oh, we've got a pool shark in our midst!" He was kinder than another guy, who said, "Okay, are you a pool hustler in the neighborhood?"

Well, huh, I thought to myself, *What do I say?*

And Eric said, "Okay, come and sit down." We sat down, and a couple of other guys joined us at the table, and he said, "I want you to tell us why you are in our neighborhood." Ah, man, what could I say to these guys?

I said, "Okay, I'm the new preacher of the Tioga Methodist Church. I'm on my way back home to Sadler," which was about thirty miles away. "I ran out of gas. I've got to get home because I'm preaching at four churches in the morning, and because it's Easter."

Roy said, "What's Easter?" Two of the guys chided Roy, because of what he had said, but he said, "Honestly, I've never been to church before, and I want to know the story about Easter."

So I thought to myself, *What do I tell Roy? Do I give him the sermon that I have prepared that was filled with illustrations from Paul Tillich's* The New Being? *Or do I try to find new ways to tell the story, the old, old story, to the new ears of Roy?*

So I thought for a moment, and then I swallowed, and started in. "Now, there was this guy named Jesus. He was born to an unwed teenage mother, and when he grew up he gathered around him twelve guys—his friends—and they were his gang, and they roamed the countryside together, and they talked about peace and justice and love and God. And they did great things. But the authorities wanted to get him, and so they tried to find ways of either capturing him or killing him."

Well, I told a little bit more of the story, until I came down to the end, and I said, "One night, one of the gang ratted on him to the authorities. And so they caught Jesus, and the next day they hanged him on a tree, and they killed him. Two days later, some of the gang went to try to find him in the tomb where they had laid him, and he wasn't there. And they searched around, and asked around, and finally someone said, 'God has raised Jesus from the dead, and has given him new life.' Now, Roy, that's the story of Jesus, and that's the story of Easter."

And Roy blurted out, "Man, that's an awesome story!"

And I said, "You know, I believe in an awesome God."

After a brief period of silence, Eric seemed to be the leader, and he got up, and he said, "Let's go get the Shark some gas." I had a new name, "the Shark"! And I had a bunch of new guys as my friends. We went outside, and they siphoned some gas from someplace. I don't know where, and I didn't ask. They put it in a can.

Eric said, "Hey, sit on the back with me." And so I got on the motorcycle with him, and this was another first. I'd never been on a motorcycle before! So we traveled three miles down the dusty road. I got off, poured the gas in the car, gave the can back to Eric, and they took off without saying a word. I was sorry to see my new friends go.

Well, I finally got home about twelve-thirty, and my wife was frantic, because she didn't know what had happened to me. You see, that was BC—before cell phones.

She said, "Why don't you come to bed?"

And I said, "I can't come to bed. I had a great experience tonight. I got stranded. I made friends. I played pool. I told the story of Easter to new people. I have got to rewrite my sermon, because the intellectual sermon that I have prepared for my people tomorrow is not their story."

And so she went up to bed, and I hurriedly wrote down the new message that had come to me as I was driving back on that awesome travel from the roadhouse. I went to bed. I felt great, and spent, and excited. This was going to be a chance to tell the story of the faith that had meant so much to me and had called me into ministry.

I woke up the next morning. I headed off to the first three churches on the circuit, and after each church I felt more confident, and more expectant, and I realized that if at all possible, I would never preach sermons the old way again.

I got to Tioga at one o'clock, and I walked in, and there the people were—eighty wonderful people, dressed in their Easter finery. As we were beginning to sing the first hymn, what did I hear outside but a roar of motorcycles coming up.

And in walked seven guys, dressed in their black leather jackets and their black leather pants—their uniform that they'd had on last night. And the usher looked at me and wondered what he was supposed to say, and on his own he said, "Could I help you?"

And Eric, in his great basso voice, said, "Hey, we're here to hear the Shark tell the story of Easter . . . again!"

Reverend Wayne Reece has been a United Methodist pastor for more than five decades. He has served congregations in Texas, Indiana, and Michigan, and has written three books in the *Becoming People of God* series as well as numerous religious articles and biblical lessons. Rev. Reece developed Project HOMES, which renovated low-income houses; spent two years as the president of a housing commission; and was a delegate to the World Methodist Conference. He did missionary work in Sierra Leone and Ganta Mission, Liberia, and is the recipient of the Amy Crotts Award for Humanitarian Service by *The Tennessean* newspaper. Rev. Reece spent fifteen years writing the Bible column for the *Michigan Christian Advocate*. He lives in Nashville, Tennessee, with his wife, and has four daughters, fourteen grandchildren, and nine great-grandchildren.

Bicycle Safety on Essex

Three of my favorite sayings are "God is a first-rate novelist, God is a second-rate novelist, and the fact that something really happened is the defense of the mediocre novelist."

In the last novel I wrote I spent a lot of time on the Lower East Side. And as is my wont, I wound up in the back of police cars a lot. The Lower East Side is a very low-crime area right now. It used to be the worst, but Giuliani and real estate pressure took care of that. Now the police basically have nothing to do down there in terms of crime. So what they do is they sit in fake taxis, you know—four beefy white guys in a fake taxi by the side of the Williamsburg Bridge—and they eyeball what's coming over from Brooklyn. If the car looks like a $200 shit-box or somebody's got an afro or a ponytail, they pull in behind the car, and they wait to see if the guy's going to go all polite in his driving, like put on lane-change signals, and then they know he's dirty.

It's fishing, really. It's a big fishing hole, Delancey Street. And I'd spent all night in this bogus taxi with about 850 pounds of white beef. And, at this point, it's the end of the night, and they made their collars, and there are two cops up front, and I'm sitting in the back.

When I ride with these guys, I don't really comment on what they do; I don't engage them in any kind of debate. I'm there to bear witness, and then see what I can do with it in my work.

They're riding up Essex Street, it's kind of Miller time, and as they're going uptown they pass a black guy on a bicycle. He's about thirty years old with dreads. And on the crossbars, he's got a white kid about nine, ten years old. The black guy and the white kid, they're kind of chatting, the kid's looking up at the guy. They look like they're familiar with each other.

And the cops drive by, and they're dead silent, and after about a block, one guy says to the other, "Hey, big guy. Does that look fishy to you? It's fucking midnight, what's going on here?"

And the other one says, "Well, what do you want to do, big guy?"

He says, "Well, I'll tell you, big guy. Make the light, pull over. Let's see what's what."

So they pull over, bike's coming up Essex, one of the cops steps in the road, puts his hand out, and says, "Hey, how you doing? Get off the bike, please?"

The black guy gets off the bike, and he goes, "Hey, officers!" You know, like it's an unexpected treat.

And the cop says, "Did you ever hear of helmets?"

"Oh! Yeah, gee. I'm really sorry."

At which point the other cop says to the little white kid, "Hey, big guy, what's your name?"

The kid goes, "Um, Noah Rosenberg?" You know, like he's not sure.

And one cop says, "Hey Noah, come here, buddy. Come on over here." And he separates the two, and I'm sort of hopping in between the two conversations at this point.

The black guy tries to follow the white kid, and the other cop puts his hand on his chest and says, "No, you stay over here. Let me see some ID."

The guy says, "What?"

"Some ID. Don't look at him, look at me."

"I was just picking him up from a playdate."

The cop says, "Did I ask you that?"

"No, no. You don't understand, I-I work the bar at Schillers—"

"Again, did I ask you that?!"

"Well, no."

"Why you trying to divert me?!"

"I'm not."

"Go down the same road as me."

"OK, OK."

And he gives the cop the ID, at which point the guy sort of waves to the kid, and the cop says, "What did I just say to you?"

"No, no. I'm really sorry. It's just Noah, he's kind of wound a little tight."

"Oh really? Have a seat." And he points to the curb, and he makes the guy sit on the curb with his feet in the gutter, and he says, "So where are you going? It's kind of late to be driving around with a kid on a bike, isn't it?"

"Well, I had the late shift."

At which point I leave those two, and I go over to Noah and the other cop, and that cop says, "So, your name's Noah, huh?"

And the kid says, "Yes, and for the millionth time, I don't have an ark!"

"You must get that a lot."

"Oh my God, you have no idea."

And the cop says, "So Noah, how old are you?"

"Well, next week I'll be one decade old."

"Well, that's great. And where do you live?"

"333 Avenue B."

"And you go to school around here?"

"Yes, I go to the Earth School."

"Oh cool, and who do you live with?"

"I live with my mom."

"Who's that over there?"

Noah says, "Well, I don't know who your friend is, but my friend is Cleve."

And the cop says, "OK, do you know what Cleve's last name is?"

"Yeah, Carter. Cleve Carter. Sometimes I call him Coca-Cola, sometimes I call him Carbon Copy."

"OK . . . Have you known him for long?"

"Well, yeah, like one and a quarter years? He's kind of like my godfather since my other godfather died."

"OK. And what do you guys do?"

"Well, he was taking me home from a playdate to my mom's."

"So he knows your mom?"

"Well, yeah, he and my mom are kind of like friends."

And the cop says, "Kind of like?"

Noah says, "Well they have, like, sleepover dates."

"So your mom knows that you're with him now?"

"Well, my mom sent him to pick me up because my dad lives in Woodstock." At which point, I'm going, *OK, let's see what's happening over with Cleve.*

I walk over there, and Cleve's sitting on the curb, and he's got his feet out there, and he's trying to make it look like it's natural. So he's deep massaging his thigh muscles, like he's limbering up for the marathon or something, you know. It's just humiliating as shit, and he's kind of smiling because he can't win, you got to play it through.

And he's sitting there, and the other cop is hitting his driver's license with a Maglite, one of those big, powerful flashlights, and he goes, "So, Cleveland, I see you're from Ohio."

"Yeah," he says.

"Cleveland from Cleveland, huh?"

"Well, actually, Oxford."

And the cop goes, "Oh! Miami College!"

And Cleveland goes, "Yeah, yeah, that's where I went."

"Oh! Wally Szczerbiak!" who's this big basketball player.

"Well, yeah, Wally was a little before my time."

"Oh, did you play ball for them too?"

"Well, not basketball, I played soccer."

The cop goes, "Oh, that's amazing, because I coach soccer out on the Island, the kids' league. And I keep waiting for that sport to blow up."

And Cleveland's going, "Yeah, yeah. That's amazing." He's sitting, you know, just wiping the street crap off his pants.

At which point a Mustang comes by with two black guys in it, and the guy in the shotgun seat looks out the window, and he sees Cleveland sitting on a curb, and he starts yelling out, "Homeboy to base! Homeboy to base! We got a black man down! I repeat, a black man down!" And he's laughing his ass off, and the Mustang floors it. Cleveland's squinting, and he's looking the other way. He's just mortified.

And then I'm hopping back to the other cop with the kid. "So Noah, does Cleveland live with you?"

"No. Cleveland lives at 444 Avenue D. We live at 333 Avenue B."

"Well, you ever been over to his house?"

"Only about a million times."

"Mostly with your mom, I guess, huh?"

He says, "*And* by myself."

"Oh, really? What do you do there?"

He says, "Well, you know, sometimes we walk his dog. It's a Rhodesian ridgeback named Mars. And one time he tried to teach me how to make scrambled eggs, but I don't really like his oven because you light the pilot match, and it goes *pshhhhht*, you know, and it scares me. One time, my mom had to go to court in Woodstock, and I stayed with Cleveland for three days."

The cop says, "Court, huh?"

"Yeah."

"Three days?"

"Yeah," he says, "but mostly, I'd say eighty-two and a half percent of the time, we watched television."

"You and Cleveland."

"Yeah, me and Cleve."

And the cop says to him, "Do you ever do anything else with him?"

"What do you mean?"

"Do you do anything else with him?"

And all of a sudden, the kid's eyes get really big and wet like steel. And the kid starts breathing heavy, starts shaking a little bit.

And the cop says to him, "Hey, Noah, look at this," and he pulls his jacket back, and he shows him his detective shield, and he says, "You know what that is?"

"It's a police badge."

"You know what this means?"

"What."

"That means that you can tell me anything you want, and you'll be perfectly safe. Do you understand that?"

And the kid looks at him, "Oh my God! Are you going to arrest him?"

And the cop, his heart's pumping in Kool-Aid, and he starts moving over, and he says, "Why?"

And the kid says, "If you *fucking* assholes arrest him again one more time just because he's black and I'm not, I'm going to kill myself! You came into my apartment and dragged him out because the crazy lady next door said he was a rapist, you put him in handcuffs when he came to pick me up at school, you pulled him away from me at the street fair and made me wait for my mom! I swear to God, I'm going to lose my *mind*!"

And the cops go, "Whoa! Easy, easy, easy!" At which point they're looking at each other like, *What's going on?*

And all of a sudden Cleveland sees the kid's losing it, and he goes, "Hey, Noah, buddy."

And the cop says, "What did I just say to you?! Stop talking to the kid!"

At which point Cleveland says, "Officer, you want to put this to rest? I tell you what, I'm going to reach for my cell phone in here. Why don't you call the kid's mom and just see what's going on?"

The cop says, "*I'll* call the kid's mom. What's her name?"

"Dana."

And he calls across to the other cop, "Get the kid's mother's name."

And the kid through sobs is going, "Dana," and Cleveland gives the cop the mother's number.

The cop calls, and he says, "Hey, how you doing? This is Sergeant Kelley from the eighth precinct. Who am I speaking to?"

"Oh my God, Dana Rosenberg. What happened?"

He goes, "Nothing happened. I just need to know, do you know where your son is right now?"

At which point she freaks: "Where is he? What happened? He's supposed to be with Cleveland, he's supposed to be taking him home from a playdate. What happened? What happened? WHAT HAPPENED?"

"Well, no, no, no, he's fine, OK?"

At which point the kid says to the one cop, "My mom says that if I get any more nervous I'm going to have to live with my father in Woodstock, you *fuck*!"

"No, no, no, the kid's great, the kid's fine. The only thing is they were riding without helmets, and it's a serious safety violation."

And she's going, "Oh my God, oh Jesus!"

"OK, don't worry about it, all right? Have a good night," and he hangs up, and they bring Cleveland and Noah together again, and they give them this half-ass lecture on bicycle safety.

The cop says, "I'm supposed to write you up. But I'm going to give you a pass this time." And Cleveland's still kind of smiling, but the smile doesn't go past here, you know, it never reaches his eyes. And he gets back on the bike, and the kid gets on the handlebars, and the kid's going through that post-crying jag, you know, shudder withdrawal, and Cleveland's kind of talking him down as he pushes off, and they disappear up Essex.

We get back in the police car, and I'm sitting in the back, and I'm not saying a fucking thing. And we go in dead silence for about two blocks, and one cop finally says to the other, "You know something, big guy?"

And the other guy says, "What's that, big guy?"

He says, "It still feels fishy to me."

And the other cop says, "Hey, we gave it a shot, man. That's all we can do."

Richard Price, who was born in the Bronx in 1949, is the author of seven novels. His first, *The Wanderers* (1974), which he wrote while enrolled as a graduate writing student at Columbia University, and his second, *Bloodbrothers* (1976), both became the basis of feature films. Following the publication of his fourth novel, *The Breaks* (1983), Price began writing for film, and his screenplay for *The Color of Money* (1986) was nominated for an Oscar. Price has continued to write for television and film, adapting three of his own recent novels, *Clockers* (1992), *Freedomland* (1998), and *Samaritan* (2003). He won an Edgar Award for his writing on the HBO series *The Wire* in 2007, and he was elected to the American Academy of Arts and Letters in 2009. His most recent book, *Lush Life*, was published in 2008.

JON LEVIN

Elevator ER

When I was young, I was a bright, happy, enthusiastic kid. So some people may have been a little surprised when years later I had become an angry, sullen, disaffected high school dropout.

It was perfectly logical to me. But life as a high school dropout quickly proved even more depressing than life as a high school student. So I tested my way into Boston University. But then dropped outta that.

If I could've signed a form to officially drop out of American society or the human race, that would've been next. So believe me when I tell you that when I was twenty-one in 1990, and I applied for a job working the night shift in the OR at Massachusetts General Hospital, it was not out of a great desire to help my fellow man. I was only doing it because the job paid really well— $9 an hour, which was $3 an hour more than the job I had been doing, working in a supermarket pushing carts of meat around.

The fact that the hospital hired me at that time in my life should be sufficient to scare all of you into taking excellent care of yourselves from now on. But hire me they did, and my actual job title was OR nursing assistant, night shift. I was basically an orderly with a few additional responsibilities.

The most fundamental part of the job was transporting patients to surgery, which I was trained to do during the day shift for two weeks, when everything is regularly scheduled; the patients are all in stable condition, usually awake but mildly sedated, and it's pretty simple.

On the night shift nothing is scheduled of course—it's the middle of the night. Patients are usually kinda bloody. Sometimes they're highly agitated and need to be restrained. But for the most part they were either heavily sedated or completely unconscious—there wasn't much interaction with me—so transporting them to surgery felt eerily reminiscent of my previous job: pushing carts of meat around.

I didn't see them as human beings at a time of great need so much as packages that needed to be delivered to a specific room as efficiently as possible.

You know: "Burst appendix to OR 22," "Coked up scumbag with multiple stab wounds to OR 27," "Pregnant woman hit by a drunk driver to OR 24," "Guy who shot his face off to OR 33." All manner of human suffering, but to me, it was all the same.

Every once in a while there would be a patient who'd be awake and wanting to chat. And in those circumstances, I was encouraged to talk in a soothing manner as I wheeled them through the halls, because it's been clinically proven that a freaked-out patient won't do as well under the knife.

Like this one guy, Alexander. He was a high school teacher who'd fallen a great distance in a rock climbing accident and injured his spine. He was afraid that he was gonna be paralyzed, and would he be able to teach? And what would his students do? He was really worried about his students.

And so I said to him, "Well, look, anyone who's only concerned about his students at a time like this is probably so dedicated to teaching that nothing will stand in his way." And then, for effect, I added, "I only wish I'd had a teacher like you when I was in school. Maybe I would've graduated."

Okay, I admit I was laying it on a little thick. But he seemed to genuinely appreciate that.

And, all right, he was sedated, but he responded by saying, "Well, you really helped me, so I'm gonna help you. I want you to promise me that you're gonna go back to school and finish your education."

I immediately thought, *Well, that's not gonna happen.* But, you know, what was I gonna say to this man—*no*?

So I tried not to roll my eyes as I made him this "promise." I got him to surgery, and I never saw him again, 'cause, you know, you deliver a package, and you don't stand around waiting to see what the guy does with the box. It was not my job to care or to follow up.

So maybe three months later, it's like three in the morning, and there's a call from the ICU. They have a patient named Mr. Williams who had had surgery the previous day and apparently had sprung a little leak and needed to come back down. So I go up to get him, and the nurses are disconnecting him from his respirator and his EKG and attaching a portable heart monitor to the rolling ICU bed and an air bag to his breathing tube, which I'm going to have to squeeze to breathe for him during the trip. This means that someone's gonna have to come with me, because you can't really steer an ICU bed and squeeze an air bag at the same time.

Unfortunately the nurses in the ICU were already overtaxed and couldn't spare anyone except for a young woman named Melissa, who I believe was a nursing student. She was very nervous because she'd never been anywhere else in the hospital before and had never really been given much responsibility.

But the nurses assured us that, despite appearances, Mr. Williams was pretty much okay and this would be totally routine.

I told Melissa, "Yeah I've done this dozens of times. It'll be a piece of cake."

So I'm pushing from the back and squeezing the air bag with my free hand, and I have Melissa steering from the front as I direct her on the shortest route to the OR. The entire trip would only take a few minutes, most of which would be spent waiting for an old, crappy elevator. So we're waiting for this elevator, and I briefly consider maybe going out of our way to another building connected by a ramp where there's a faster, more modern elevator, but I figure it's actually pretty far, and by the time we get there, the time savings will be nullified.

The elevator arrives. We get in. The doors close. I push the button. And nothing happens.

And then the lights go out.

And I'm about to say, *What the fuck?* when we start to move.

But it's not right, and we're moving too fast, and the elevator's not making its normal sound.

And my stomach is in my throat, and we're *falling*, and WE'RE FALLING!

And if I had had time for a thought process, it probably would've been like, *What the fuck? I'm not ready to die. I didn't sign up for this.* And then I would've shit myself.

But before any of that can take place, the elevator's emergency brake kicks in and slams us to a stop so violently that I'm thrown to my knees, and Melissa is thrown to the floor, and Mr. Williams is bouncing in his bed, his equipment jostling around.

So now we're stopped somewhere, in this tiny, dark box, and there's three sounds I can hear: the elevator's emergency signal buzzing, Melissa screaming, and Mr. Williams's heart monitor indicating that, like our elevator, his heart has stopped.

So I get to my feet, and for a brief moment I think, *No, no, no, no, NO!*

But denial and anger quickly give way to, in this case, bargaining: *Well, Melissa's got some actual medical education, so she should be in charge.*

But then reality sets in, and it was like: *Okay, Melissa's in a bad way right now. She's cowering in the corner, wondering if we're still all gonna die. But if we don't do something right away, ONE of us is DEFINITELY gonna die.*

So I then hit acceptance and begrudgingly admitted to myself that I had to get in the game here.

Fortunately, in a sense, our situation didn't really leave us with many options. And also fortunately the hospital had trained me to do CPR when they hired me. So I had Melissa stand up, and by the dim lights of the LEDs on the heart monitor, I could sorta see her hand.

I grabbed it and put it on the air bag, and I said, "Okay, you do the air bagging. I'm going to do chest compressions."

I moved around to the side, but Mr. Williams was a big guy, and I couldn't get good leverage, and unfortunately it was too dark to see the controls of the ICU bed underneath it to lower it. So in desperation I did something I had seen one of the emergency ward doctors do one time. I went to the foot of the bed and climbed up onto it, sort of mounting Mr. Williams, and, kneeling over him, did chest compressions from above. And it seemed to work okay as far as I could tell.

I have no idea how long we were like that in the dark, but it felt like hours, until the lights flickered and came back on, and the buzzing emergency thing stopped. And then a garbled voice came over the intercom saying, "Stand by."

And I was like, "Fuck you!"

But then we were moving again, only this time in a controlled manner, until we finally arrived at the third-floor OR and the doors opened. And Melissa was so overjoyed and eager to get us out of there that she started pushing us forward.

And that's when something *bad* happened.

The wheels on the front of the ICU bed swiveled around ninety degrees, right as they were situated over the gap between the elevator and the floor, and slid down into the gap like slices of bread going into a toaster.

I was nearly thrown off of the bed by our sudden change in momentum and had to grab on to the side rails just to stay in place. And then, of course, the elevator doors started slamming on us over and over again. Melissa stopped air bagging and ran to the front and was battling the elevator doors as she tried to lift us out of the gap. Of course it was no use, so she stopped and went back to air bagging. And I was still doing chest compressions, now slightly more difficult due to the incline.

I made eye contact with her, and without actually exchanging words, we both just started screaming for help. It was kind of a busy moment in the OR right then, and no one responded for a while. Finally someone showed up, a wonderful older gentleman named Mr. Selwin, who was one of the night cleaning crew guys.

He comes running in, and in his thick island accent says,

"What's all the commotion?" And then he sees us, and he's like, "Oh my God!" And he tries to pull us free, but it doesn't work, even though he's a strong guy.

So he's like, "Okay, you just keep doing what you're doing. I'll go get more help." And he runs out.

Within a few moments, he comes back with "reinforcements" in the person of Mr. Guppy, the surgical instrument technician. The two of them are now trying to lift us free, and they're struggling and struggling. And finally, with a horrible metal scraping sound, they wrench us free.

And now we're off!

And suddenly all the panic and confusion recede, and we are in motion.

They say, "Okay, where you going?"

"OR 29."

"Fine, okay."

And then the double doors just open, and we're whipping around the corners and everything's very effortless, and we're flying now—Melissa is running trying to keep up while still doing the air bagging.

And of course, I'm still on top of Mr. Williams, still pumping away at his chest, and there's a breeze in my face from our newfound velocity. And I have to say, it was absolutely exhilarating—to the point where I had to actively stifle the urge to laugh out loud.

So I screw my face up into a mask of seriousness because it would be a tad unseemly to appear to be enjoying riding a patient down the hall. And we get to OR 29, and the entire surgical team is there, of course, waiting for us like, *Where the hell have you been?* But as soon as they see us, they know the situation is not normal.

They fly into action and seamlessly take over for everybody, and I can now hop off because, obviously, Mr. Williams is in far more capable hands. So I grab the paperwork that was at the foot of the bed that I had to process for him, and they get to work on him.

They save him, and he lives.

And in this case, for the first time ever, I did follow up, and I found out that not only did he live through the night, but he recovered and left the hospital.

I processed the paperwork and found Melissa in the hall, and we breathed this collective sigh of relief. Then I escorted her back up to the ICU, taking a different route so that she wouldn't have to take the bad elevators. She gave me a hug, and I never saw her again.

I came back down to the OR, and there was my boss behind the main desk, and he said, "Hey Jon, I heard what you did. Nice job."

And part of me was really hoping that that would be the extent of the praise that I would receive . . . but another part of me was disappointed that that was the extent of the praise I received.

And of course in that setting, it was nothing special, but the thing that surprised me was that I cared. Like, since when did I give a shit about receiving recognition for anything, but specifically job performance?

So then my boss asked me a few questions about the particulars of what happened, and I told him, and he was like, "Oh yeah, I hate those elevators. Don't take those. Take the ones in the White Building instead."

Thanks.

That exhilarating feeling didn't go away. It stayed with me

for the rest of my shift, all the way home, and actually prevented me from getting to sleep that morning. It seems kind of obvious in retrospect, but at the time I was so unaccustomed to feeling anything positive, especially related to work, that it took me a really long time to recognize that I enjoyed what I did, and I enjoyed caring about it. I enjoyed caring about Mr. Williams and myself.

But about six months later, I found myself mentioning the incident in a personal essay that was part of an application to get back into college.

Jon Levin's latest project is a twisted sci-fi comedy about a postapocalyptic rock band in outer space. He chose this subject matter because it came to him in an ayahuasca vision and because his actual life is just too weird. He lives and writes in New York City.

The Big Things You Don't Do

It's 2004, and I'm playing in a $2 million winner-take-all poker tournament called the Tournament of Champions, and I have two tens, and I have to decide whether to put the last of my remaining chips into the pot and risk getting knocked out. And I've already taken fifteen seconds with this decision, and it's just way too long.

See in poker you make these very complex mathematic calculations, these very deep reads of your opponents, and you have to do it all very quickly because there are ten people at this table, and the action needs to keep moving along, so fifteen seconds in poker is an *eternity*. But I am having tremendous difficulty with this decision, and there are a few reasons why.

The first is that $2 million is just by far the largest amount of money that I have ever played for. And in fact, earlier in the year, in 2004, I won a World Series of Poker Championship, and I had only won about $150,000, so $2 million was putting a lot of pressure on me. But the second reason, and the more important reason for me, was that this was the first time I was playing on television with these new little lipstick cameras that they were putting in the rail of the table that could see your cards and expose them to the world. And this was causing me a lot of difficulty in thinking about this hand.

ESPN and Harrah's World Series of Poker had invited ten players—who they said were the ten best in the world—to come together and play this winner-take-all $2 million championship against each other on television. And I was there among these nine great players, five of whom were Hall of Famers. And the knock on me was that I was only there because I was a woman— that while I was *good*, I wasn't actually one of the best players in the world. ESPN had just decided that since women were a novelty in poker, it would be really good to have a woman at the table. And in 2004 I was, in fact, the winning-est woman in the history of the World Series at that time. So I was just the logical choice if they were going to put a woman in, but I didn't actually deserve to be there. The problem for me was that I actually believed them.

And so for the first time, as I'm sitting here trying to decide whether to put my money in this pot with these two tens and risk getting knocked out, I realize that my mistakes might be exposed to the world, and I might prove all of my critics right. And as thirty seconds pass I look over at my brother Howard. My brother at that time was, and he still is actually, one of the best players in the world, and he too had been invited to this table to play this big tournament.

About a decade before, when I was still in graduate school and living on a graduate student's stipend, and I couldn't really afford to go on a vacation, my brother had offered to fly me out to Las Vegas while he was playing in the World Series of Poker and put me up at the Golden Nugget for two weeks, which was the most luxurious place I had ever been at the time. And he brought me out for this vacation, and we're sitting there after midnight in the basement coffee shop of Binion's Horseshoe Casino, kind of a run-down casino on Fremont Street with this faux-Western decor. And you might say, *Well why were you there after midnight eating?* And the reason is that after midnight they had a $1.99 steak special. So for $1.99 you got a steak, a salad, a vegetable, and a roll, and this was really awesome for someone who was living on a graduate student's stipend.

My brother asked me how my vacation was going, if I was having any fun.

And I said to him, "Actually I'm kind of bored." My brother was playing poker all day at the World Series, because at the time he was already one of the best players in the world. And you couldn't really watch poker back then; there was a rail and you couldn't see the cards, and it was just hard to watch, so that wasn't any fun for me. And I really don't enjoy gambling, which I know, because I'm a poker player, sounds kind of crazy. But actually poker is very different from gambling since it's a skill game, and I didn't enjoy things like baccarat or craps or anything like that. And one night my brother's friends had kindly offered to kind of take on the burden of his sister's entertainment and taken me over to Glitter Gulch, which was the seediest strip club you've ever seen, down on Fremont Street. Somehow seeing naked women grind their breasts against my brother's friends was not only not fun, but slightly uncomfortable and unnerving, so I really didn't want to repeat that experience.

So I said to him, "I really don't have anything to do."

And he said, "Well, why aren't you playing poker? You've watched me play so much poker!"

I said, "Well, I don't really know if I know what to do, Howard."

And he took one of those little black Keno crayons out of the Keno well on the table, and he took his napkin from the table, and he wrote down all the two-card starting hands I was allowed to enter the pot with in Texas hold 'em.

He said, "As long as you just play these hands, I promise you you'll do OK." And he handed me this napkin and $100. And he sent me across the street, clutching this napkin, to the Fremont Casino, which, if anybody's been there, makes Binion's look like the Taj Mahal. At that time the nicest restaurant in the Fremont was a Carl's Jr.

So I went in there, and I played a dollar-to-three game, and I actually won $300 that trip, which was like, a lot of money. And very soon after that I kind of caught the poker bug, and I left graduate school to pursue a life as a professional poker player. And I just loved the life because it was so anonymous.

People would ask me, "Well, what do you do for a living?"

And I'd say, "Well, I play poker for a living."

And they'd say, "Oh! Where do you deal?"

I'd say, "No, no. I don't deal cards to people. I actually play."

And they'd say, "Oh! Well, what does your husband do?"

And I'd say, "Well, actually he stays at home, I support the family." And usually the conversation would devolve into something about the merits of Gamblers Anonymous, which has a lot of merits, but I don't think for me. But I loved that. I loved that people didn't understand what I did, and that I was eccentric, because I valued eccentricity so much. And I loved that nobody was going to know who I was. I was doing this in private on the margins of society, because at that time, nobody in poker could have imagined that ESPN would be airing this big thing that three million people might watch.

But the other thing that was so great about what I did was that I wasn't the only one who was anonymous; my cards were anonymous. So I was the only one who could see them, because they were facedown, which meant that when I made mistakes, I was the only one who knew.

As I started to find success, people would say, "She seems to be pretty good. She seems to have a lot of talent." And that felt really good. But all I saw while I was playing were my own mistakes. And so I started to feel just a little bit like a fraud. In fact, I started to feel a lot like a fraud.

So now here I am with these two tens at this table, and forty-five seconds has passed, and I am so afraid that the world is going to find out what I already know about myself, which is that I'm a fraud. And I am trying to make this really difficult and complex poker decision, and I am paralyzed.

I am up against this guy named Greg Raymer. I had opened the pot with these two tens, and he had pushed all his chips in, and he has more than I do, so I am trying to make this decision whether to risk all my chips against this guy. And I really don't know anything about him, because he's just come on the scene a few months before. Nobody had ever heard of him, and all of a sudden he won the Main Event of the World Series of Poker in July of that year. So I've never actually played a hand of poker with him.

The only thing I really know about him is that his nickname is the FossilMan, because he uses fossils as his card protectors—he sticks them on top of his cards—and if you manage to knock him out, which would be completely impossible on this hand, because I have fewer chips than he has, but if at some point during the tournament I could knock him out, I knew that he'd give me one of those fossils, which, you know, in comparison to the $2 million prize, is not really what I am trying to win, but I guess it would be something.

I really just have no idea how to figure out what he has, and the poker decision itself should actually be quite easy. I've got two tens, and if he has a hand like aces or kings, I'm actually just supposed to fold because those are much better than my hand. But if he has a hand like an ace and a king, I am supposed to call. But I am having trouble focusing on the poker, and as sixty seconds has passed at this table, I hear myself, as if it's someone else outside of my body, apologizing to this table of great players, these Hall of Famers, my brother, saying, "I'm so sorry. I know I'm taking too long, but this is just a really hard decision."

And they think that the hard decision is the poker decision. But I am so afraid of making a mistake, and what I really can't decide is whether I'm playing to win or just trying not to be the first one out.

And as I'm trying to figure this out, I look over at my brother, my mentor, trying to find some sort of solace, some way out of what was going on in my head. And in that moment I remember that we had watched Raymer playing on TV that week. And my brother had pointed out that there was something Greg did called a *tell*—that telegraphed the strength of his hand. And as I was looking at my brother, I suddenly remembered this, and I looked back over at Raymer, and I saw him do that thing that my brother had pointed out when he had watched him on television. And I knew in that moment that he had to have a really good hand. He had to have that pair of aces or kings, and that I could easily fold my tens because it was the right poker choice. And I did it confidently.

But the problem was that this was the hand right before dinner, which meant that we were now going to have to get up from the table. And as we were walking out the door to go take our hour break, Phil Hellmuth, twelve-time World Champion, "the poker brat," six feet, five inches towering over me, "reader of souls," says to me, "Annie, I know you had to have jacks or tens on that hand. Don't you know Raymer had to have ace king? It was totally obvious to me." And all the confidence that I had found in that hand just seconds before went out of me, and I was left for an hour in my room at the Rio, ruminating, filled with self-doubt, thinking that while I might have fooled myself into thinking I was good, clearly I had just made a decision to try not to lose so I wouldn't prove anybody right.

So I came back to the table after what seemed like an eternity, and clearly with no focus, no ability to really feel like I could play well. But the great thing in poker is that sometimes the cards save you from your own self-doubt, and you just get really good cards that aren't hard to play, and you win every hand.

And that's actually what happened to me. I came back, and I had two queens against Johnny Chan's two eights, and I won this really big pot. And then I actually had a really big hand against Greg Raymer, where I took a lot of his chips. And I wasn't the first one out of the tournament, or the second one out of the tournament, or the third one out, or even the fourth or the fifth. And now all of a sudden we're five, and I get into this huge pot against Greg Raymer, the FossilMan, the person who had put me to such a difficult decision earlier. And this time I have more chips than he does, and we get all the money in, and I actually knock Greg Raymer out. And he picks up his fossil, and he brings it around to me, my gift for knocking him out of the tournament, and he whispers in my ear, "Annie, I know the hand you had earlier was really hard for you, and I want you to know that I had two kings, and you made a really good fold."

So, in that moment, Greg Raymer gave me not just the gift of the fossil, but the gift of my confidence. And I realized that I could start playing to win again.

Now we were four people left, and I had the most chips, and the next one out was Johnny Chan. And then actually it was just three: me, my brother, and Phil Hellmuth. And I got a huge hand against my brother, and I actually knocked my own brother out of the tournament.

My brother wasn't happy for himself, but he was happy for me because he taught me how to play, and he taught me how to play hard. And he would have expected me to play just as hard against him as anybody else. And I suppose if he was going to lose all his chips, he probably was happy he lost them to me. And as he was getting up to go out of the room, he came around, gave me a big hug, and said, "Annie, you're really playing great, now just beat Phil."

So now I was heads-up against Phil Hellmuth, the thief of my confidence. And I got in a big pot with him when I had more chips, and I had king ten and he had ten eight, and I won the hand, and I actually beat Phil to collect the $2 million prize and win the tournament that no one thought I even deserved to be at.

And now when people ask me what the most important hand of poker I ever played in my life was, I don't say it was the king ten that I beat Phil Hellmuth with to win that big prize. I say it was the two tens that I found such a difficult fold with, because sometimes it's not the really big things that you do that get you the win, it's the really big things that you don't do.

Annie Duke has succeeded as a poker player, teacher, reality television star, business consultant, charity fund-raiser, and a co-author of *Decide to Play Great Poker* (2011). Through March 2012, Annie has earned over $4.2 million in live poker tournaments. At the World Series of Poker alone, she has cashed on thirty-nine occasions, made fifteen final tables, and won a gold bracelet in 2004. In 2010, Duke won the NBC National Heads-Up Championship, one of the most coveted titles in poker. Duke founded Ante Up For Africa and regularly runs fund-raising poker tournaments, raising millions of dollars for charities. In 2009, she raised $730,000 on *Celebrity Apprentice* for Refugees International. Annie is currently using her years of good decision-making at the table to help others become better thinkers through consulting and speaking on decision bias and critical thinking.

Coming Home

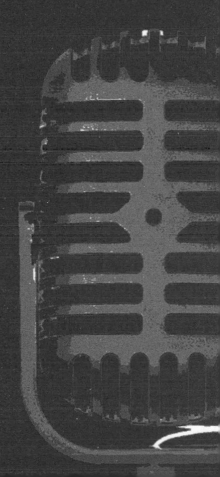

A View of the Earth

In 1984 I was a senior in college, and I went to see the movie *The Right Stuff.* And a couple of things really struck me in that movie. The first was the view out the window of John Glenn's spaceship—the view of the Earth, how beautiful it was on the big screen. I wanted to see that view. And secondly, the camaraderie between the original seven astronauts depicted in that movie how they were good friends, how they stuck up for each other, how they would never let each other down. I wanted to be part of an organization like that.

And it rekindled a boyhood dream that had gone dormant over the years. That dream was to grow up to be an astronaut. And I just could not ignore this dream. I had to pursue it. So I decided I wanted to go to graduate school, and I was lucky enough to get accepted to MIT.

While I was at MIT, I started applying to NASA to become an astronaut. I filled out my application, and I received a letter that said they weren't quite interested. So I waited a couple years, and I sent in another application. They sent me back pretty much the same letter. So I applied a *third* time, and this time I got an interview, so they got to know who I was. And then they told me no.

So I applied a fourth time. And on April 22, 1996, I knew the call was coming, good or bad. I picked up the phone, and it was Dave Leestma, the head of flight crew operations at the Johnson Space Center in Houston.

He said, "Hey, Mike. This is Dave Leestma. How you doing this morning?"

And I said, "I really don't know, Dave. You're gonna have to tell me."

And he said, "Well, I think you're gonna be pretty good after this phone call, 'cause we wanna make you an astronaut."

Thirteen years after that, it's May 17, 2009, and I'm on space shuttle *Atlantis*, about to go out and do a spacewalk on the Hubble Space Telescope. And our task that day was to repair an instrument that had failed. This instrument was used by scientists to detect the atmospheres of far-off planets. Planets in other solar systems could be analyzed using this spectrograph to see if we might find a planet that was Earth-like, or a planet that could support life. And just when they got good at doing this, the power supply on this instrument failed. It blew. So the instrument could no longer be used.

And there was no way really to replace this unit or to repair the instrument, because when they launched this thing, and they got it ready for space flight, they really buttoned it up. They didn't want anybody to screw with this thing. It was buttoned up with an access panel that blocked the power supply that had failed. This access panel had 117 small screws with washers, and just to play it safe, they put glue on the screw threads so they would never come apart. You know, it could withstand a space launch, and there was no way we could get in to fix this thing.

But we really wanted the Hubble's capability back, so we started working. And for five years, we designed a spacewalk. We designed over one hundred new space tools to be used—at great taxpayers' expense, millions of dollars, thousands of people worked on this. And my buddy Mike Good (who we call Bueno)—he and I were gonna go out to do this spacewalk. I was gonna be the guy actually doing the repair.

And inside was Drew Feustel, one of my best friends. He was gonna read me the checklist. And we had practiced for years and years for this. They built us our own practice instrument and gave us our own set of tools so we could practice in our office, in our free time, during lunch, after work, on the weekends. We became like one mind. He would say it, I would do it. We had our own language. And now was the day to go out and do this task.

The thing I was most worried about when leaving the airlock that day was my path to get to the telescope, because it was along the side of the space shuttle. And if you look over the edge of the shuttle, it's like looking over a cliff, with 350 miles to go down to the planet. And there are no good handrails.

When we're spacewalking, we like to grab on to things with our space gloves and be nice and steady. But I got to this one area along the side of the shuttle, and there was nothing good to grab. I had to grab a wire or a hose or a knob or a screw. And I'm kind of a big goon. And when there's no gravity, you can get a lot of momentum built up, and I could go spinning off into space. I knew I had a safety tether that would probably hold, but I also had a heart that I wasn't so sure about. I knew they would get me back, I just wasn't sure what they would get back on the end of the tether when they reeled me in. So I was really concerned about this. I took my time, and I got through the treacherous path and out to the telescope.

The first thing I had to do was to remove a handrail from the telescope that was blocking the access panel. There were two screws on the top, and they came off easily. And there was one screw on the bottom right and that came out easily. The fourth screw is not moving. My tool is moving, but the screw is not. I look close and it's stripped. And I realize that that handrail's not coming off, which means I can't get to the access panel with these 117 screws that I've been worrying about for five years, which means I can't get to the power supply that failed, which means we're not gonna be able to fix this instrument today, which means all these smart scientists can't find life on other planets.

And I'm to blame for this.

And I could see what they would be saying in the science books of the future. This was gonna be my legacy. My children and my grandchildren would read in their classrooms:

We would know if there was life on other planets . . . but Gabby and Daniel's dad . . . My children would suffer from this.

Gabby and Daniel's dad broke the Hubble Space Telescope, and we'll never know.

And through this nightmare that had just begun, I looked at my buddy Bueno, next to me in his space suit, and he was there to assist in the repair but could not take over my role. He had his own responsibilities, and I was the one trained to do the now broken part of the repair. It was my job to fix this thing. I turned and looked into the cabin where my five crewmates were, and I realized nobody in there had a space suit on. They couldn't come out here and help me. And then I actually looked at the Earth; I looked at our planet, and I thought, *There are billions of people down there, but there's no way I'm gonna get a house call on this one. No one can help me.*

I felt this deep loneliness. And it wasn't just a "Saturday afternoon with a book" alone. I felt . . . detached from the Earth. I felt that I was by myself, and everything that I knew and loved and that made me feel comfortable was far away. And then it started getting dark and cold.

Because we travel 17,500 miles an hour, ninety minutes is one lap around the Earth. So it's forty-five minutes of sunlight and forty-five minutes of darkness. And when you enter the darkness, it is not just darkness. It's the darkest black I have ever experienced. It's the complete absence of light. It gets cold, and I could feel that coldness, and I could sense the darkness coming. And it just added to my loneliness.

For the next hour or so, we tried all kinds of things. I was going up and down the space shuttle, trying to figure out where I needed to go to get the next tool to try to fix this problem, and nothing was working. And then they called up, after about an hour and fifteen minutes of this, and said they wanted me to go to the front of the shuttle to a toolbox and get vise grips and tape. I thought to myself, *We are running out of ideas. I didn't even know we had tape on board. I'm gonna be the first astronaut to use tape in space during a spacewalk.*

But I followed directions. I got to the front of the space shuttle, and I opened up the toolbox and there was the tape. At that point I was very close to the front of the orbiter, right by the cabin window, and I knew that my best pal was in there, trying to help me out. And I could not even stand to think of looking at him, because I felt so bad about the way this day was going, with all the work he and I had put in.

But through the corner of my eye, through my helmet, you know, just the side there, I can kinda see that he's trying to get my attention. And I look up at him, and he's just cracking up, smiling and giving me the okay sign. And I'm like, *Is there another spacewalk going on out here?* I really can't talk to him, because if I say anything, the ground will hear. You know, Houston. The control center. So I'm kinda like playing charades with him. I'm like, *What are you, nuts?* And I didn't wanna look before, because I thought he was gonna give me the finger because he's gonna go down in the history books with me. But he's saying, *No, we're okay. You just hang in there a little bit longer. We're gonna make it through this. We're in this together. You're doing great. Just hang in there.*

And if there was ever a time in my life that I needed a friend, it was at that moment. And there was my buddy, just like I saw in that movie, the camaraderie of those guys sticking together. I didn't believe him at all. I figured that we were outta luck. But I thought, *At least if I'm going down, I'm going down with my best pal.*

And as I turned to make my way back over the treacherous path one more time, Houston called up and told us what they had in mind. They wanted me to use that tape to tape the bottom of the handrail and then see if I could yank it off the telescope. They said it was gonna take about sixty pounds of force for me to do that.

And Drew answers the call, and he goes, "Sixty pounds of force?"

He goes, "Mass, I think you got that in you. What do you think?"

And I'm like, "You bet, Drew. Let's go get this thing."

I get back to the telescope, and I put my hand on that handrail, and the ground calls again, and they go, "Well, Drew, you know, you guys are okay to do this, but right now we don't have any downlink from Mike's helmet camera." I've got these cameras mounted on my helmet, so they can see everything I'm doing. It's kinda like your mom looking over your shoulder when you're doing your homework, you know?

And they go, "We don't have any downlink for another three minutes, but we know we're running late on time here, so if you have to . . ." And I'm thinking, *Let's do it now while they can't watch!* Because the reason I'm taping this thing is if any debris gets loose, they're gonna get all worried, and it's gonna be another hour, and we'll never fix this thing. We've been through enough already.

So I'm like, *Let's do it now, while Mom and Dad aren't home. Let's have the party.*

So I say, "Drew, I think we should do it now."

And Drew's like, "Go!" And *bam!* That thing comes right off. I pull out my power tool, and now I've got that access panel with those 117 little bitty screws with their washers and glue, and I'm ready to get each one of them. And I pull the trigger on my power tool and nothing happens, and I look, and I see that the battery is dead. And I turn my head to look at Bueno, who's in his space suit, again looking at me like, *What else can happen today?*

And I said, "Drew, the battery's dead in this thing. I'm gonna go back to the air lock, and we're gonna swap out the battery, and I'm gonna recharge my oxygen tank." Because I was getting low on oxygen; I needed to get a refill.

And he said, "Go." And I was going back over that shuttle,

and I noticed two things. One was that that treacherous path that I was so scaredy-cat-sissy-pants about going over—it wasn't scary anymore. That in the course of those couple hours of fighting this problem, I had gone up and down that thing about twenty times, and my fear had gone away, because there was no time to be a scaredy-cat, it was time to get the job done. And what we were doing was more important than me being worried, and it was actually kinda fun going across that little jungle gym, back and forth over the shuttle.

The other thing I noticed was that I could feel the warmth of the sun. We were about to come into a day pass. And the light in space, when you're in the sunlight, is the brightest, whitest, purest light I have ever experienced, and it brings with it warmth. I could feel that coming, and I actually started feeling optimistic.

Sure enough, the rest of the spacewalk went well. We got all those screws out, a new power supply in, buttoned it up. They tried it; turned it on from the ground. The power supply was working. The instrument had come back to life. And at the end of that spacewalk, after about eight hours, I'm inside the air lock getting things ready for Bueno and me to come back inside, but my commander says, "Hey, Mass, you know, you've got about fifteen minutes before Bueno's gonna be ready to come in. Why don't you go outside of the air lock and enjoy the view?"

So I go outside, and I take my tether, and I clip it on a handrail, and I let go, and I just look. And the Earth—from our altitude at Hubble, we're 350 miles up. We can see the curvature. We can see the roundness of our home, our home planet. And it's the most magnificent thing I've ever seen. It's like looking into heaven. It's paradise.

And I thought to myself, *This is the view that I imagined in that movie theater all those years ago.* And as I looked at the Earth, I also noticed that I could turn my head, and I could see the moon and the stars and the Milky Way galaxy. I could see our universe. And I could turn back, and I could see our beautiful planet.

And that moment changed my relationship with the Earth. Because for me the Earth had always been a kind of a safe haven, you know, where I could go to work or be in my home or take my kids to school. But I realized it really wasn't that. It really *is* its own spaceship. And I had always been a space traveler. All of us here today, even tonight, we're on this spaceship Earth, amongst all the chaos of the universe, whipping around the sun and around the Milky Way galaxy.

A few days later, we get back. Our families come to meet us at the airfield. And I'm driving home to my house with my wife, my kids in the backseat. And she starts telling me about what she was going through that Sunday that I was spacewalking, and how she could tell, listening, watching the NASA television channel, how sad I was. That she detected a sadness in my voice that she had never heard from me before, and it worried her.

I wish I would've known that when I was up there, 'cause this loneliness that I felt—really, Carol was thinking about me the whole time. And we turned the corner to come down our block, and I could see my neighbors were outside. They had decorated my house, and there were American flags everywhere. And my neighbor across the street was holding a pepperoni pizza and a six-pack of beer, two things that unfortunately we still cannot get in space.

And I got out of the car, and they were all hugging me. I was still in my blue flight suit, and they were saying how happy they were to have me back and how great everything turned out. I realized my friends, man, they were thinking about me the whole time. They were with me too.

The next day we had our return ceremony; we made speeches. The engineers who had worked all these years with us, our trainers, the people that worked in the control center, they started telling me how they were running around like crazy while I was up there in my little nightmare, all alone. How they got the solution from the Goddard Space Flight Center in Maryland, and how the team that was working on that Sunday figured out what to do, and they checked it out, and they radioed it up to us.

I realized that at the time when I felt so lonely, when I felt detached from everyone else—literally, like I was away from the planet—that really I never was alone, that my family and my friends and the people I worked with, the people that I loved and the people that cared about me, they were with me every step of the way.

Michael Massimino, Ph.D., is a veteran of two NASA space flights (STS-109 in March 2002 and STS-125 in May 2009) and has logged a total of 571 hours, 47 minutes in space, and a cumulative total of 30 hours, 4 minutes during four spacewalks. A graduate of Columbia University and MIT, Michael is currently serving as executive director of the Rice Space Institute at Rice University in addition to his responsibilities in the Astronaut Office at NASA.

Life Flight

I get a phone call from my mom, and she tells me that my father is about to get on an emergency life flight from our home in Montana to go to Denver to get a liver transplant.

My mom is perennially optimistic, and she's telling me, "Don't worry. We're going to pull through this. It's going to be all right." But I know something is really wrong. I'm living in New York, so I get the next flight I can, hoping that I can get there before my father dies. And I'm really glad I got that flight as fast as I did, because I was able to spend a couple hours with my father before he passed away. And before I know it, I'm at the side of his hospital bed with my mom, and we're sobbing, because he's gone.

My dad was a strong, silent type. He grew up on a farm, and he was one of two eye doctors in town. So he could fix anything, you know? He could fix tractors or eyes. And he was always doing it behind the scenes. He never wanted to take credit for it.

It was apparent that my mom and I were going to have to be fixing things ourselves this time around.

And the first thing my mom did was to call my two brothers.

One's a year older; one is a year younger. And it was going to be really comforting to see my younger brother. We were really close. He was really going to support me.

It was going to be much more complicated seeing my older brother, Mark. We'd always had a really complicated relationship. And there was something really big about me that he did not know. The last time he saw me, years and years before, I was male. He was not aware that I had transitioned from being male to being female. And you know, I always wanted to tell him. I was trying to find the right time, the right place—trying to, you know, get up the nerve. I was worried about his reaction. He was a bit conservative. He had a temper, and I just kept putting it off—never found the right time. And now here we were, at the time where I had to deal with all this other stuff.

Mark wasn't the only one who didn't know my story. My hometown didn't know about me either. I was trying to find a way to tell Mark, but I kind of figured that with my hometown, I would just never go back there again.

So my mom calls my brother, and in one phone call tells him that he lost his father. And that he now has a sister.

I have to say, Mark, he was really great. He got off the plane. We met him at the airport. He gave me a hug. But it was awkward, as you can imagine.

And I think we did what a lot of families do at times like that—you just kind of fall back on tradition. And we wanted to do something that my mom and dad had always done, because, you see, it was my father's birthday. He had passed away twenty minutes before his sixty-fifth birthday. So we all went to Applebee's, and we got a slice of sizzling apple pie and put a candle in it. And my brother Mark, who really worshipped my father, got the honor of blowing out the candle.

And I still remember the expression on his face when he was blowing out the candle. He was trying to process my father's passing. He was figuring out why it had been so long since the two of us had talked, something that really frustrated him. And it was all coming together.

I took a business card out of my purse. It was for this job that Mark didn't even know I had. It had my new name on it. I wrote my cell phone number on it, and I gave it to Mark.

I said, "Look, you know, we haven't talked for so long, but here—anytime, anyplace, no barriers. We can talk anytime you want."

And my mom started crying because her children were re-uniting. And also because for years she had been running inter-ference between the two of us, and using every excuse in the book to explain why I wasn't getting back to him, or why pack-ages to me were being returned because they had the wrong name on them. And her job running interference was over.

So Mark was in shock. We were all in shock. And I was thinking about the fact that nobody in my hometown knew. And I was wondering if I could go back for the funeral—if I *should* go back, if my mom and my brothers really wanted me to, really deep down. I never even thought I was going to go back to my hometown, and now I was being pulled right back into it.

As contradictory as it may seem, as soon as there was a rea-son, I had this really deep yearning to go back. I had gone to school in New York and San Francisco, and traveled all over the world, and this was a place that I thought of as home. I think I had really repressed it, knowing that I couldn't go back there.

But as soon as there was a reason for me to go back there, a very strong reason, I really, really wanted to go. I wanted to see our house, the only house I had ever known growing up. I wanted to go back to my hometown and these people that comprised this community that I thought of as home.

And my mom reassured me that she wanted me to be there, that she in fact *needed* me there for support. My brothers too. And my mom had a plan to get us there. Our family had been separated for a long time, so she had the idea of all of us renting a car and driving the twenty hours from Denver back to Montana.

So before you know it, there we were in the car. My brother hadn't seen me for years, and never as female, and here we were. And we had so much to do. We were planning my father's funeral service. We were writing his obituary.

But also, my mom wanted to figure out—and I did too—how we could introduce the information about me while still keeping the focus on my father. So driving across Wyoming, seventy miles an hour, she had me take dictation. She wanted to invite her friends over for tea. She had this really strategic list. It was like, "You invite Judy," and she's going to tell all the people in the arts community that my mom was involved in, and "You're going to tell June, and June is going to tell all the people at Dad's office. And we'll find somebody else who's going to tell everybody at the church."

And the next night, there they are, eighteen of my mom's best friends and the minister from the church where the service was going to be performed. They're drinking tea.

And my mom says, "You all know very well by now that I've lost my husband. And I know a lot of you have wondered what happened to my middle son, who seemed to disappear. I want you to know tonight that I have a daughter, and her name is Kim. And this is my child, and I love my child, and I hope you do too, and we can focus on this tonight. We can talk about this tonight. You all are my ambassadors. If someone has questions at the funeral, and I'm caught up in things, I'm going to point them to you and let you tell this story, because you can talk about it in a sensitive way."

She takes a couple of questions from the people there. And the whole tea party ends slightly differently than the Tea Party we hear about in the news. The whole thing ends with everybody raising a teacup and saying, "Hip hip hooray for Kim! Hip hip hooray for Kim!"

There were a couple of "Amens" and some applause. And then everybody went home, and I swear there was a brownout from all the simultaneous phone calls that were being made, dispensing the information.

The next night there was a viewing of my father's body at the funeral home, and I had elected not to go, because I didn't want the focus to be on me. I was going to keep it on my father. But my best friend, Tim, from high school, was at the viewing, and he called me up. He had only known the new me for a couple of days. I hadn't even told *him* before.

But he knew me really well, and he knew I was chickening out. He called me from the funeral parlor, and he said, "Hey, got a lot of people here that really want to see you."

I should probably tell you that the people he was talking about were the football team. Because I used to be on the football team.

And so Tim says, "Where are you? I've got a lot of people

who want to see you." And I'm like, "Yeah, I don't want to go. You know, I want to keep the focus on my dad. I don't want to be the—"

And he's like, "Yeah, yeah, whatever. Either you come down here, or we're going to come up there. What's it going to be?"

And I say, "Come up here, I guess."

So before I know it, the football team is at my front door. And a couple of them have cases of beer under their arms. One case gets tossed in the snowbank to keep it cold. It's just like high school. And all of a sudden, they're in my living room. And it's this wake instantly. This show of support for me and for the memory of my father. And they're in my living room, this living room I never even thought I would see again.

And people are either laughing or crying, mostly laughing. And I remember looking around the room, and there's Kevin. He was one of the co-captains of the football team with me. And I look over there, and there are my brothers, Mark and Todd, and we were all very close in age, so we had friends in common, and they're telling stories about my dad.

And I look over on the couch, and there's Frank. He was an offensive lineman. It's the job of an offensive lineman to protect the quarterback.

I probably should have also told you before that, um, not only was I on the football team, but I was the quarterback.

And Frank is protecting me once again, twenty years later, under very different circumstances. He's got his arm around my girlfriend. They're laughing and knocking back cans of cheap beer, and that was the moment that I knew things were going to be okay somehow.

And there was one more person there that night, and that was my mom. And she told me something that we ended up repeating quite a bit that weekend, through the services. She came up, and she said, "You know, Dad was always fixing things, and it looks like he fixed this too."

And she said, "You know, even though your father has died, you've been reborn."

Kimberly Reed is a filmmaker living in New York City. She was named one of 25 New Faces of Independent Film by *Filmmaker Magazine*, one of Five to Watch by *The Advocate*, and the Best LGBT Character of the Film Year by Towleroad. Reed has been awarded Fellowships at the Yaddo Artists' Community and the Squaw Valley Community of Writers. She directed/produced *Prodigal Sons*, which *SF Weekly* calls a "whiplash doc that heralds an exciting talent." *Prodigal Sons* was a co-production with BBC Storyville and Sundance Channel; it premiered at the prestigious Telluride Film Festival with a record seven screenings. The film has gone on to be shown around the world in theaters, festivals, and on television, garnering more than a dozen jury and audience awards, including the Fipresci Prize. She has been featured on *Oprah* and CNN, among other media outlets. Reed is a summa cum laude graduate of the University of California, Berkeley, and a Montana native.

Angel

Everything happens for a reason. I'm here in front of y'all today to tell you what happened several years ago when I asked myself: *Why am I here?*

I was on tour with my band, Run-DMC. We were over in Europe, out there doing shows, getting $50,000 a night. But for some reason, something in me wasn't right, and I had no idea what it was.

On this particular evening after the show, I got back to my room, and I lay there, and I thought about everything that had happened to me.

OK, I'm Darryl McDaniels. I grew up in Hollis, Queens, New York. Byford and Banna are my mother and father. My brother is Alfred. I went to a Catholic school that my mother and father worked every day to pay for. I treated them right by coming home with straight A's. I was athletic. As a kid every day was Christmas. Life couldn't be better. After growing up in Hollis, I met Joe and Jay, and we did the things that young guys do, and then we started a rap group, and we put a record out, and then the record went number one, and we damn near created hip-hop.

We were the first to go gold, first to go platinum. All this good stuff—*Rolling Stone*, MTV—and now here I am in Europe getting $50,000 a night. But why am I so unhappy?

I was depressed to the point that I had suicidal thoughts. I don't think I really would have killed myself, but I did once go to the ledge and look over.

But I said, "I ain't jumping. It's gonna hurt."

I put poison in a glass, but I looked at it, and I said, "I ain't drinking that." I thought about a gun.

I knew something was wrong with me, even though life was good, because I had these suicidal thoughts.

But then I came to the conclusion, "I can't kill myself on the road while we're touring because Run and Jay's gonna be mad at me. So I'm going to just wait until I get home."

So we finished, and I came home very depressed. Didn't know what this void was that was in me, because when I summed up everything, I was supposed to be happy.

I got in the car, and the limo driver goes, "Do you want to hear some music?"

I was like, "Yeah, just turn the radio on."

"You have a preference?"

"No, just turn it on."

So he turned the radio on, and this was 1997, and on the radio was a record called "Angel" by Sarah McLachlan.

Now look, fame, friends, fortune, and even my family didn't mean nothing to me because I was suicidal, I was depressed, I was an emotional wreck. But for some reason, when I heard that record "Angel" by Sarah McLachlan, something in me said, "Life is beautiful. It's good to be alive."

So, for *one whole year*, all I did was listen to Sarah McLachlan's record "Angel." I went out and bought every record she ever made.

The only thing I was living for was listening to Sarah McLachlan. Over and over and over, everywhere I went.

I was driving my management crazy because they would be like, "Come on, Dee, we got to go on the road."

"Okay, but you got to put this in."

They would go, "No!"

And I'd say, "Then I ain't going!"

And they'd be like, "OK, we'll put it in for you. But there's something the matter with you. What's up with you?"

And at the end of the year, my manager goes, "Yo, Dee. I got tickets to Clive Davis's Grammy party."

Y'all know who Clive Davis is, right? If you win *American Idol*, you get a deal with Clive Davis. He discovered Janis Joplin and all these people.

But I'm like, "I have no time for Clive Davis and Hollywood because I have my Sarah McLachlan! That's all I care about."

He's like, "Yo, Dee, man, I went through a hard time to get these tickets," and blah, blah, blah.

I say, "OK. I'll go to the party, but I'm only staying one hour."

So I go to the party, Clive Davis's Grammy party in L.A. I'm counting the seconds: 59, 58, 57 . . .

I'm looking around, and there's Stevie Wonder, so fucking what; Alicia Keys, who cares about Alicia Keys; and paparazzi, and all this stuff, right? And I'm there hating on everything.

But guess who walks in? That lady! (She was "that lady" to me then.) *That lady* that made the record that changed my life.

I'm losing it, because nobody knows I'm an in-the-closet Sarah McLachlan fan.

So I get myself together, and I say, *OK, I got to go over there. If I do die, kill myself, whatever, I got to go over there first, and let her know what her record did for me.*

So I walk over to Sarah McLachlan. I'm in the whole Run-DMC garb—the hat, the black all the way down.

She sees me coming, and she goes, "DMC!" [*singing*]

It's tricky to rock a rhyme,
To rock a rhyme that's right on time. It's Tricky!

I'm like, "Wow." But in my head, I'm like: *That's a good reason to stay alive, because Sarah McLachlan likes my music.*

That's where I was at, y'all.

I go over to her, and I say, [*speaking very quickly*] "Hey Miss McLachlan, I just want to tell you your record 'Angel' saved my life. I was depressed. I was suicidal. But every day I listen to that record. I don't leave the house without listening to that record. Everything I do revolves around that record. And, listen, the record is called 'Angel,' you sing like an angel, people say you *are* an angel. But you're not an angel to me, you're *God*."

And on, and on, and on, and on. And she's looking at me like: *OK . . . where is this coming from? I just wanted to say hi to his ass.*

So I finish my little rant, she looks at me, and she goes, "Thank you for telling me that, Darryl, because that's what music is supposed to do."

So three years go by. I'm still trying to figure out what this void is in me. Then, I realize something. People know my musical legacy, what Run-DMC did—first on MTV, first with a record deal, all the firsts—but nobody knows about the little boy, Darryl, who *became* DMC.

So I say, "I'm going to write a book, and it's going to be, 'Yo, what's up? My name is DMC. Yeah, I'm the kid from Run-DMC. I was born May 31, 1964.'"

When I get to that point, I realize that's all I know about the day I was born. I've got to figure out the details of my birth.

So I call my mother up. "Hey Mom!"

"Hi, Darryl. How you doing? Love you."

"Love you too."

"Did you eat yet?"

"Mom, I—"

"You're losing too much weight."

"No, Mom, I'm working out. But whatever, I just need to know three things, because I'm writing this book. How much did I weigh? What time was I born? And what hospital?"

She told me those three things.

"Love you."

"Love you too."

Hung up the phone. About an hour later the phone rings. It's my mother and my father.

"Hey, son! How you doing?"

"Dad, yo. What's up?"

"We have something else to tell you—blahsy blah this, blahsy blah that—you were a month old, we think you're Dominican, and you're adopted, you're adopted, *you're adopted*, *you're adopted*, YOU'RE ADOPTED!"

Right then and there, the whole world stopped [*makes sound of screeching brakes*]. I thought about when I was lying in the bed three years earlier, summing up everything about me. *That* was the void, the missing link that had me going out of my mind. That was the one thing I didn't know about myself. So the void was now filled.

Now, if you think there's really a time to commit suicide, find out you're adopted at age thirty-five.

And people say, "Dee, they told you over the *phone*?"

I really wanted to kill myself, but then I remembered something Sarah McLachlan had said: *That's what music is supposed to do.*

So I said, "OK, before I get suicidally depressed again and do something really crazy, I need to write a record that's going to help that little orphan, or that little kid in foster care, who thinks: *They threw me away, I'm worthless, I mean nothing, no mother and father love me.* Because I may be DMC, but what I really represent is purpose and destiny, so I need to make a record that's going to inspire somebody the way Sarah McLachlan inspired me!

Then I got a bigger idea. I thought, *I'm going to call that lady back up and have that lady make the record with me.*

So I get Sarah McLachlan on the phone, and I'm thinking: *If she thought I was crazy three years ago, she's going to really think I'm crazy now!*

"Hey, Miss McLachlan! It's Darryl. Remember me?"

"How could I forget you, Darryl? You called me God."

"OK, here we go. Remember when I met you three years ago, and I told you what your record did for me?"

"Yes."

"And then you looked at me, and you told me that's what music's supposed to do?"

"Yes."

"Well, I just found out why I was depressed and suicidal. My father told me I was adopted. I need to make a record that's going to inspire others the way your record inspired me. Will you help me do this record?"

She says, "Yes!" real quick.

I was like, "Wow, that was easy." But I'm losing it now; I'm like: *She said yes!*

"I'll fly you to New York, put you in the Four Seasons."

She says, "No, Darryl, you can come to my house and make the record."

After three years of listening to this lady, I'm a fan, right? To make a long story short, when she said, "Come to my house," I fainted. I woke up. I was in Vancouver, Canada, at Sarah McLachlan's house, the lady whose record saved my life. It's beautiful there.

I said, "Miss McLachlan, I want to make a remake of Harry Chapin's 'Cat's in the Cradle,' and I'm going to put my adoption story there, and I'm going to give it a happy ending."

"OK, cool."

Took us two days to make the record.

I was on my way out the door, and she says, "Darryl, before you go, I've got to tell you something."

Now, I love her to death, her music, everything, what she did for me, I'm in heaven, I'm walking on cloud nine.

And I said, "What?"

And she says, "I was adopted too."

And I did not know that. Everything happens for a reason.

Darryl "DMC" McDaniels, one-third of the group Run-DMC, is a music icon. He is one of the most influential rap artists of all time and a pioneer in fueling the popularity of hip-hop into the best-selling musical genre that it is today. From being the first rap group to grace the cover of *Rolling Stone* to the first to appear on MTV, Run-DMC changed music, culture, fashion, and language, and made American history. Thirty million in record sales later, and more than ten years after the untimely death of his bandmate Jam Master Jay, DMC still continues to create, inspire, and motivate. He is the co-author of the critically acclaimed autobiography *King of Rock: Respect, Responsibility, and My Life with Run-DMC* (St. Martin's, 2001), and in 2006 released an award-winning solo album, *Checks, Thugs & Rock and Roll*. His story was the subject of the Emmy-winning VH1 documentary *DMC: My Adoption Journey*. In between his work as a musician, published author, and speaker, DMC co-founded the Felix Organization, a nonprofit that works with adoptees and foster children. In 2009, as a member of Run-DMC, he was inducted into the Rock and Roll Hall of Fame. More information can be found at www.me-dmc.com.

GEORGE DAWES GREEN

The House
That Sherman
Didn't Burn

So how many of y'all here are from the South? Well, you will know that in the South we sometimes have too many stories. And there was a story that my mother used to drill into me about when my great-grandmother was a little girl during the Civil War.

One day Sherman's troops came to visit our family plantation. And outside in the front yard, they found an area where the earth had been disturbed, so they decided that this was where the family was hiding the silver.

So they commenced to dig, and a woman came out on the veranda. She was very beautiful, but very frail.

She said, "Y'all won't find it. We sold it all long ago, and all that lies there are the remains of my boys—my twins—who died stillborn. And if you dig them up, you'll be seeing their faces for all eternity."

But they didn't believe her, so they dug. And when they

found the bodies of the two infant children, they were so shamed and remorseful and fearful that they just rode away.

That's why our family plantation house was left unburned when Sherman marched to the sea. However, I once talked to a cousin of mine who told me that he'd heard a rumor that the family silver had never been sold. That it had been, in fact, hidden *underneath the bodies of the two stillborn boys*. When he told me this, the expression on his face was a mixture of delight and a horrible loathing for everything that was our family. And this conflict of emotion is, I think, the mark of a true Southerner. We love what we hate, and we hate what we love.

The house that my great-grandmother presided over was called Treutlen Hall, and it was in Waynesboro, Georgia. And as you entered the foyer, you looked up and there was this horrifying mosaic of Medusa looking down at you. Then you walked in, and there were these two enormous dining rooms, the ornate library, and the staircase that was so grand and went up to the seven bedrooms and the five bathrooms. On the third floor was the grand ballroom where my mother danced when she was a little girl.

There was a nook in the house that contained what they called the Turkish Room, which was for intimate conversation. And when my mother had her sixth birthday, her grandmother led her into the Turkish Room. They were both named Inez. And on that day Big Inez gave Little Inez a plantation all her own.

Two thousand acres.

Then her little sister came running in and said, "Grandmother, can I have a plantation too?"

And Big Inez looked down and said, "Child, your name is Alice. You were named for your Yankee grandmother. Go ask your Yankee grandmother for a plantation."

But after the stock market crash there weren't any plantations for anybody. Everything was lost, and my mother married a poor writer and knocked around the North for many years and then wound up living on a little island off the coast of Georgia called St. Simon's Island, and she worked as a receptionist for an optometrist.

But she still had all her memories of Treutlen Hall, and she had all of these beautiful pictures, which I would not look at, because I hated all that stuff. I hated all that Confederate vamping. Mom wanted me to go to either Duke or Emory. And I dropped outta high school. I went to live on my own. Because I could not stand to be there.

I would go back for meals, and I was eighteen years old, and my mom would remind me to point my spoon away from me when I ate with it, because Big Inez had always said, "A little ship sails out to sea; I point my spoon away from me."

I would say, "Mom, let me eat, and leave me the hell alone."

I had a chip on my shoulder the size of the moon. And there was a guy who came down from Waynesboro, from my mom's hometown. His name was Lewis Ross. His father had worked as the gardener at Treutlen Hall. Lewis Ross had grown up and become very wealthy, and he was coming down to St. Simon's to build this huge resort for the middle classes. My mother reviled Lewis Ross. She said he was poor white trash. She said he was an odious little rodent.

So I went to work for him. Just to spite her. I worked on one of the construction crews building condos. One day we were out there digging footings, and Lewis Ross comes waddling up with his big bulgy eyes. And he's with the on-site architect, and he points to me and says, "Jones."

Now, my name's not Jones. Jones was my great-grand-mother's name. And when he spoke he had a little bit of bitterness.

So I was a little afraid, but I came up and he said, "Son, go and put your shovel down, and go over there to that shed, and bring me back some J-bolts."

I said, "I don't know what a J-bolt looks like."

He said, "Well, a J-bolt's kinda crooked, and it's about as long as your dick when it gets hard."

He was laughing, and all of my colleagues were laughing. And you know, I loved these guys, and all I wanted to do was to impress them.

So as I walked toward that shed, I knew that if it turned out that a J-bolt was any less than six inches long that I was destroyed—that for the rest of my life, my name would be J-bolt. So I got to the shed, and I looked in, and it was dark and hot. And there were all these wasps batting around in that shed. And I looked down and saw the J-bolts, and thank God, they were seven inches long. Even better, there were these anchor bolts, and they were about sixteen inches long, and they were iron and as big around as my wrist. And I got a bunch of 'em and carried 'em back to Lewis Ross and said, "I'm sorry, Boss, they're too small, but they're as big as I could find."

And my colleagues loved this. They were easy to please. And even Lewis Ross had to laugh. And later that afternoon I got summoned to Lewis Ross's office, and I went there, and he said, "Jones, let's go get a drink."

And we got into his bright red Cadillac, and we drove up to Macintosh County, to a brothel. Or kind of a brothel. It was a double-wide-trailer-in-the-woods kinda brothel. And I had lots of Southern Comfort, which is vile. But I liked it. And I liked the girls.

And Lewis Ross at one point said to me, 'cause he knew that I had lived up North, "Did you ever have a Yankee girlfriend?"

And I said, "Uh, well, yeah."

And he said, "Was she a hippie?"

And I said, "Sort of."

And he said, "Did you ever eat that thang?"

And I kinda had to nod, and he gave me this look of complete disgust, but he turned to the girl next to him, and he said, "Well, whyn't you do it to her while I watch."

And I looked at him and I realized that this man's skull was full of boiling shit, and that he hated what he loved, and therefore was a true Southerner. And I guess that I am also a true Southerner because I confess that I actually considered performing for him. Now, it's hard to say why. But I was eighteen years old. I wanted more than anything to impress him. He had a kind of bizarre grandeur. And he wasn't anything like anybody in my family.

But the girl saved me: She said, "Oh, no way!" And so we just had another drink.

Then Lewis Ross's eyes got very bulgy, and he told me that he had just purchased my family's ancestral mansion, Treutlen Hall, and his engineers were going to break it into four huge pieces and roll the pieces down to the Savannah River and put them on barges and float them down past the city of Savannah, down the intercoastal waterway to St. Simon's Island, where he would rebuild them as Treutlen Hall, his golf clubhouse and the crowning jewel of his resort. It would be like a beacon to tourists all over the world. And he wanted me to tell my mother that Lewis Ross would pay her twice what the optometrist was paying her if she would come and be the hostess at the house that she had grown up in.

He said, "I want to hire all you Joneses to work for me."

That night I didn't go right home. I went to Mom's first to

tell her about this, and she seemed somewhat distressed. And she said to me she didn't really want to put on a hoop skirt and a bonnet and go guiding grubby tourists all around her ancestral home.

And I said, "Oh, what's the matter, Mom? You don't like common people?"

She said, "I don't mind common people. This was my home."

I said, "Common people built Treutlen Hall."

And she said, "Are you drunk?"

I said, "You should like this, Mom. You can tell your story of the stillborn twins a thousand times. You can sell coffee mugs engraved with the story of the stillborn twins. Then that story will be worth something."

And she threw me out of her house.

I woke up the next day with the worst hangover that I'd ever had. I had this terrible remorse, and I called her to say I was sorry. But she said it was all right. She was gonna take the job, because Dad was sick, and they needed the money. But she wanted to go to Waynesboro one more time to look at Treutlen Hall in its real home.

So on Friday she drove on up. And on Saturday night around 3 A.M., I got awoken by a telephone call, and it was my mother, and she said, "It's all right. Treutlen Hall is safe."

And that was the night of the great conflagration. You can Google it. It's a famous night in Waynesboro, Georgia. The flames were seven stories high. And the gates were chained up so that nobody could get in there, and by the time they did, Treutlen Hall was gone. Treutlen Hall was chimneys.

And they determined it was arson, and that an accelerant, namely gasoline, had been used. Somebody had poured gasoline in every room—in the Medusa Room and the great dining rooms, and the Turkish Room, and the grand ballroom upstairs.

And I sat up all night, and I felt a kind of grief that I have never felt before. It was shattering. It was like a piece had been torn out of my side.

And then I felt a kind of pride, and I thought, *My mother did this.*

George Dawes Green, founder of The Moth and Unchained, is an internationally celebrated author. His first novel, *The Caveman's Valentine*, won the Edgar Award and became a motion picture starring Samuel L. Jackson. *The Juror* was an international best seller in more than twenty languages and was the basis for the movie starring Demi Moore and Alec Baldwin. *Ravens* was chosen as one of the best books of 2009 by the *Los Angeles Times*, the *Wall Street Journal*, the *Daily Mail* of London, and many other publications. He lives in Savannah, Georgia.

Cocktails in Attica

In 1975, I was twenty-eight years old, and I weighed in at 120 pounds. I found myself on a bus, chained to a West Indian brother, headed upstate to prison.

I had been busted for the sale of narcotics in the first, second, and third degree. I had been given "four-to-life" under the Rockefeller Plan.

During that time, whether you sold a bag of dope, a bag of coke, or even your own medication, you were going to get a sentence, but then it was going to have "to life" tagged onto the back of it. So you might get "one-to-life," "five-to-life," "twenty-to-life," etc. I knew that I was going to get some time one day because of the way I lived, but never in my wildest dreams did I think "life" was going to be at the end of my sentence.

I had done a couple of stints at Rikers Island and various county jails, but I had made the big time now—Attica Penitentiary. I was walking around the prison yard, seeing bullet holes still in the walls where the National Guard had shot inmates during the 1971 riot.

I was scared to death. I had heard about guys getting raped and stabbed, and I was just petrified. But as fate would have it, three of my old customers from the street that I used to sell dope to happened to be there, and they must have seen the fear in my face.

They said, "Sherman! Don't worry about a thing! We're going to look out for you, man, because you looked out for us when we was in the street."

I said, "Thank you, Lord!"

And so one of the guys said, "Sherman, when you go to the assignment board, tell them that you want to get your GED, and that you want to get into some kind of vocational program. You don't want no work assignment, you want to go to school, because that's the only thing they understand. That's what they call rehabilitation."

Sure enough, when I went to the board, I told them that I wanted to go to school. So they put me in typing.

My friend was getting ready to leave—he was going home on parole—and he told the guards up front to make me the waterman. Being the waterman, I'd get up early in the morning and pass out the water to everybody, because you had to have hot water to start your day.

So I'm thinking to myself, *I got a pack-a-day cigarette habit, I got a candy jar with little Snickers in them, but I'm only getting $20 a goddamn month from the state. So I got to come up with some type of fucking hustle to get me some cigarettes and candy.* Right?

When I was in Rikers, I worked at the bakery. And I remembered this guy showed me how to make hooch. We would get a big bucket and put a black plastic bag in the bucket, and we'd put yeast in there and several cans of concentrated grapefruit juice or orange juice. We would even put potatoes in there or grapes. I liked the grapefruit myself—it was much stronger. I liked to put the grapefruits and the grapefruit juice in there, put a little sugar with it, tie that baby up, and let it sit for about six or seven days, and voilà! You'll be in heaven.

So I said, "Well this is what I got to do!"

I had to make some connections, so I found friends of mine who knew a friend who knew a friend, who got in touch with the guy in the kitchen so I could get the yeast. Now, they sold the juice and sugar in the commissary, and every third day we had grapefruits for morning breakfast, and I'd get all the guys' grapefruit.

I started wheeling and dealing, putting stuff together. At first I was trying to figure out how I was going to distribute the wine. Then I figured out that everybody in the joint smokes or drinks coffee, so they have an old ten-ounce Folgers jar in their cell. I could put the wine in the coffee jars.

But once I made it, it started bubbling and stuff, and it started stinking. So I had to figure out a way to stop the smell.

In the commissary they had what they called Magic Shave. Now, Magic Shave was a paste you whipped up and put on your face (not only would it take the hair off your face, it would take the skin off too if you left it on too long). But it smelled like rotten fucking eggs—just stunk like hell.

So whenever the guards would come past my cell, they would say, "Shorty, I don't know how you put that stuff on your goddamn face! That shit *stinks*!"

But they didn't know I was whipping this shit up to keep

them from smelling the goddamn wine. I got the wine wrapped up in a blanket under my bed. I'm nursing this wine like I'm a nurse in the infirmary. I'm taking care of this wine, right? Because this is my livelihood.

The first batch was finally ready. Because I was the waterman, my cell was always open, so I collected everybody's coffee jars, filled them up with hooch, and passed them back out. For every ten-ounce coffee jar, I got five packs of cigarettes. So my cigarette packs and candy were stacking up. I was eating Snickers like a motherfucker, eating M&M'S like a motherfucker. I was doing good, right?

Mr. Ronny Worth and Mr. Frank Yonkerman, who were the guards, they had taken to liking me because I was the smallest guy in the joint, but I was always in the face of someone who was many times taller than me, talking shit, you know?

So they'd say, "Shorty, you got a set of balls on you! We're glad we chose you to be the waterman."

Mr. Frank Yonkerman had this scar on his face, which reminded me of Al Capone.

So I'd always go to him and say, "Mr. Capone—I mean, Mr. Frank!"

He'd go, "Ha ha, Shorty, you're a little shit! Where do you want to go?"

I'd say, "I just want to go next door, mister, a friend of mine's next door."

"You go on, Shorty!"

Now, if anyone else asked, he'd tell them, "Fuck you, I'll lock you in!"

"But you let Shorty go!"

"Stop snitching! And lock the fuck in!"

But I was all right with him. And so I'd take my wine and put some in my coat pocket and some in my back pocket, and go across the hall and sell it.

One guy told me, "I don't got no five packs. But I'll give you a joint."

I said, "That's cool." So I gave him the wine, I got the joint. Now I'm really kicking! I got reefer, candy, cigarettes, I'm eating cookies, I'm really wheeling and dealing.

But then Big Frank Yonkerman and Ronny Worth took a vacation. And some new guards came on, but they ain't cool with me like Frank and Mr. Ronny were.

So I was lying there one night, and my wine was cooking. I had a couple of guys in the back and a couple of guys in the front, and whenever the guards would come, they would say, "Pass the pen! Anybody got paper?" That was our signal that the guards were coming, and I would hook up the Magic Shave.

But this particular night the guards scared the shit out of them, and they didn't say nothing. And the next thing I knew my cell door was being cracked, and the captain was there with about four guards.

He said, "Shorty, you want to step out?"

I said, "Man, it's eleven-thirty at night. What is this all about?"

He said, "Shorty, you want to step out or would you like for us to help you out?"

And he comes in the cell and goes under the bed and gets the bucket and pulls it from under the bed.

In the prison rule book it says you can't mess with a guy's

religious artifacts, so I had a big Bible and several Christian pamphlets on top of my wine.

I said, "Man, you can't be touching my religious artifacts!"

He said, "Don't worry, Shorty, we ain't going to mess up your Bible and stuff." He picked it all up and put it on the bed.

Then he pulled the wine out and opened up the bag, and the fumes jumped up, and he said, "Oh my God! How do you drink this shit? This will take the wax off the floor!"

I said, "What shit? It ain't nothing but punch. I just put some grapefruit in there with some juice and some sugar. You know, the Fourth of July's a couple of days away. I was going to give the fellas a little celebration with some punch."

The captain said, "Do I look like a goddamn fool to you? You forgot one ingredient, the yeast! Motherfucker, get your ass back in the cell! Write him up!"

So they took my wine away and wrote me up. The next day I went to the adjustment committee.

The deputy said, "You Sherman Powell?"

I said, "Yes, sir."

He said, "You stupid or something?"

"No, I'm not stupid."

"What'd you say?"

"Yes, sir, I'm stupid."

He said, "Your name is Powell, not Gallo. What the fuck you doing selling wine in my prison? You in here for selling dope, and you're going to come to my prison and sell wine? What do you think you're doing? Are you OUT OF YOUR GODDAMN MIND?!? Take his ass back downstairs and lock him up! Thirty days no rec, thirty days no commissary, thirty days no visits."

So I told my friend, "Look, go to my people and tell them to send me a block of yeast. I'm going to whip up another batch."

He said, "You're crazy, man! You're on key-lock!"

I said, "That's the best time to make it! They don't think you got it, right?"

But he said, "Look, man, if they bust you again, your ass is going to be shipped to Dannemora."

Now, Dannemora Clinton Penitentiary was the worst penitentiary in the state of New York. So I had no intention of going to no goddamn Dannemora.

But still my greed overtook my common sense, and I wanted to make another batch because my supply of M&M'S and Snickers was down. And so my man went and got the yeast, and I made me another batch.

By this time Ronny Worth had come back from vacation. And so I was sitting there, reading my book. I had gotten all the jars from the guys before they went to rec, and I had filled all the jars up with the wine, so as they came in, I was passing out the jars, and everybody was getting their wine, right? And I was collecting my cigarettes.

So I'm sitting there, and all of a sudden my friend said, "Mr. Worth said he wants you to come to the front."

So I came out front, and Mr. Worth said, "Shorty, you done made some more of that goddamn wine, didn't you?"

And I looked at him, and I thought: *Who the fuck done snitched on me that quick? I didn't see nobody.*

But he said, "Don't lie! You want to know how I know? Open the fucking door."

So I pulled the door open that led to the cells, and all you could hear was the black guys playing their boom boxes loud, singing Motown at the top of their lungs.

And all the Spanish guys are beating on their lockers and desks:

Boom boom bop bop! Boom boom! Bop bop bop!

And all the white boys got their guitars, singing country songs in their Southern drawls.

So everybody was in their own world, right?

And he said, "Shorty, I know that you done passed out that shit because it's total chaos back there. It's normally quiet as a church mouse. People be reading their Bible, studying, writing letters. Only when you pass out that bullshit is it like that in there! So you want to know who snitched on you? Your customers snitched on you!"

And then he said, "Look, Shorty, you going to board in a couple of months. I don't want to see you get in no trouble. Go right back in there, empty that shit out, get some pine cleaner, clean your cell out, and retire from being a bootlegger. You get my drift?"

I said, "Yes, sir, I get your drift." So sure enough, two months later I went to the board, and they gave me a parole date and let me go.

And if it wasn't for Ronny Worth and Frank Yonkerman being all right with me, had they decided to bust me, I had a life sentence, I could have been there until the next eclipse.

It dawned on me how stupid and childish I had been, doing that shit. And I made up my mind that there's a time to be defiant, and there's a time to be compliant. And when you're in the penitentiary, be compliant!

Sherman "O.T." Powell was born and raised in St. Louis, Missouri, and has traveled extensively from coast to coast. He is a graduate at the advanced level of The MothSHOP Community Education Program, and his stories have appeared on *The Moth Radio Hour* and *The Best of The Moth* CD series. He was featured in a brief write-up in *New York Magazine* after a 2004 Moth appearance, and he is currently studying to become a substance abuse counselor and writing his autobiography.

Whatever Doesn't Kill Me

You wake up in the morning, get dressed, put on your shoes, and you head out into the world. And you assume you're going to come back home at night, go to sleep, and get up to do it again. That rhythm creates a framework that you use to form a life, and you make plans, and you count on continuity.

John Lennon said, "Life is what happens to you while you're busy making other plans."

I woke up one morning, and I wasn't wearing any of my own clothes. I had two chest tubes, a hose going up my nose to drain my stomach, a catheter, and a morphine drip. And I woke into this fog of pain that felt like I had broken through the ice into a lake of frozen hurt.

At the end of my bed I could see the surgeon who had spent all night saving my life, and he was holding my foot. He had given me about a two percent chance of living. Next to him were two homicide detectives. The *homicide* detectives had gotten the case because they didn't think I was going to make it, and they didn't want to have to do the paperwork swap when I died.

And let me tell you, when you start your day with two homicide detectives explaining what happened the night before, it's downhill from there. They told me they had five young men in custody, and they wanted me to identify them from the mug shots before I died. They just wanted me to make an "X" next to the pictures.

What had happened is that these young men had come in from Brooklyn, and they were part of a gang. The initiation for them to move up into the upper echelons of their gang was to come into Manhattan and kill somebody. And they had set up this little ambush where they had one lookout at either end of the block, and then three guys would sit on a stoop in between with their hidden knives. And they would wait.

It was late at night, the night before Thanksgiving, so the city was really empty. The kids had told the detectives that some *other* guy walked around the corner and headed down the block. The two lookouts gave the go-ahead, and the three guys stood up and started walking towards him. But he had his key out, and he put his key in the door and went in the lobby, and the door closed behind the guy, and the gang initiates were locked out. The guy pushed the elevator button, and he went upstairs, got undressed, and went to bed. And he never knew what just *didn't* hit him.

And I was the next guy to turn down the street.

I came down the block, and one of the very lucky things from that night was that when I was in college at Notre Dame I was on the boxing team. So I got one good punch and knocked the middle guy out. They caught him, and he gave up everybody else, which is how they had these five guys in custody.

So nobody expects me to make it, but I do. I live. They take me off life support, move me into ICU, and the nurse comes in with the clipboard, and she wants to talk to me about my insurance. I was self-employed at the time, so I like to say I was insurance-free.

And when they found that out, the nurse who came in the next morning said, "It's amazing how well you're doing, and we think you ought to go home." And they gave me a bottle of Percocet and a cane, and a bag to put my stuff in, and sent me on my way.

The flowers hadn't even wilted yet.

So I ended up in my apartment, at home, in very bad shape. The nightmares were unbelievable. I couldn't eat. They had removed about a third of my intestines, I had two collapsed lungs, I was missing organs that I hadn't known I had. Things were very difficult.

In New York, if you can't go to work, make money, and pay your rent, you don't get to stay in your apartment. So I would try to do my job—I had a little business building custom furniture. But whenever I saw a young man that had any hint of menace, this feeling would hit me, and the feeling was like this:

You know when you're driving late at night in the winter on a snowy road, and you're going a little fast, and you come into a turn, and you feel all four wheels slip, and you see the guardrail, and you know there's nothing you can do? And then all of a sudden, you hit the dry pavement, and the wheels grip, and you're back in control and nothing happened.

And then you get hit with this adrenaline. It's a feeling in the back of your knees and in your palms, and you taste it in your mouth. But you're driving, and you're like, *Nothing happened.* I would have that feeling seeing teenage kids on the street six, seven, eight times a day, and it wore me out.

I was having post-traumatic stress symptoms.

I ended up losing my apartment, and essentially then becoming homeless, and losing my business. I went to the district attorney's office for an appointment, where I had five attempted murder trials that I had to handle. And I broke down crying.

I was like, "I'm so lucky to be alive, but now I'm homeless." And he gave me a number—a little late I thought—for the Victim Assistance people.

And so I go, and this girl comes out, and she's like Reese Witherspoon in *Legally Blonde*. She's got the turtleneck, and the ponytail, and she leads me back to her cubicle. And I'm in a really dark place, and I have this feeling that we're not going to connect. I get to her cubicle and pinned up on the wall next to her monitor is that poster—I know you know it—of the kitten with the branch saying, "Hang in there, baby." And I just don't feel like she's going to be able to help me.

She gives me this paperwork to fill out for Medicaid, and she gives me some more paperwork on how to get on a list for subsidized housing. ("It's an eighteen-month wait but, you know, at least you're on the list.") And another sheet with some addresses in the Bronx where I can go for free group counseling.

I feel like a drowning man who's just been thrown a kit to build a boat.

I walk out of there, and I go to my favorite bartender, who's this cute Lebanese-Canadian girl. She's a poet. And she lets me move in and stay on her couch. She's rocking this Simone de Beauvoir look, and she's smart and funny.

But the biggest thing is she *listened*, which was amazing. Because most people—and they were all very well-meaning—had one of three responses.

The first response was, when I tried to talk about my feelings, and my fear, and this turmoil in my head, they would say, "Well, everything happens for a reason." And that made me want to punch them in the face, and ask them if they knew what the reason for that was.

The second thing that people tended to say was "You've just got to get over it, man. You're alive. You're lucky. You've just got to put this in the past, and move on." And that made me want to stab them six times and come back and talk to them in six months and go, "So how's it working out, you got any advice for me now? Because I could really use some help from somebody who knows what I'm going through."

And the third thing that people would say, and again, very well-meaning, but it just was absolutely no help, was that "whatever doesn't kill you makes you stronger."

And I mean, I had read Nietzsche too. I had gone to college, and I was up all night in the student union drinking coffee going, "Yeah, if it doesn't kill you, it makes you stronger, *man*."

The problem with that was I had come to New York, started this little business, built a life, and I had lost *everything*.

I felt like I was actually broken. That things could happen in life that would just break a man. And that not only wouldn't you be stronger, but you would never ever again have what you had before. And I felt like things had slipped in a way that I would never be able to recover.

And this girl that let me move in with her was getting a little worried because I was just so sad all the time.

To try and make money, I would gather my little set of chisels and tools and go up to the Upper East Side of Manhattan, where there's always some billionaire working on his mansion. I would see a construction site, and I'd go up and knock on the door and ask if they needed anybody to work, just a day laborer. And the foreman, you know, he'd see a guy with his own tools, who knows his way around a job site, English is his first language, and he'd be like, "All right, put him down there and see what he can do."

And I'd go, and I'd start working. I'd be in this incredible mansion that was being renovated, and I'd look around at the unbelievable materials, and I'd think of how lucky these people were to be living there. When we were done with this work, they'd be surrounded by amazing craftsmanship.

So I'd be there working, and I'd be making a mortise for an offset pivot hinge in a rosewood door, and the beauty of everything that I was working on contrasted with my life, and I would just start to cry. And so I'd be on my hands and knees, sobbing.

And one of the laborers would go tell the foreman, "The dude you hired, man, he's sobbing in the library."

And the foreman, usually, you know, an Irish guy, would come and say, [*in an Irish accent*] "Eddie, I can go ahead and pay you for the day. Go and have a drink, man. We don't need you anymore." And then that would be it, I'd get fired.

I was getting fired again and again. And these people didn't know what had happened to me, they just knew they couldn't have some guy weeping in the basement. I couldn't hold a job, and I was getting angry.

The Canadian poet-bartender—she's my girlfriend now—and she's worried because my attitude is becoming not so good.

One day I leave a site after being fired once again. I walk out onto Park Avenue, and I see this guy walking by. His hair is perfectly coiffed, and his tie is knotted, and his shoes are shined, and he's in this impeccable suit with his shiny briefcase.

And I see that guy, and I just want to tackle him and kneel on his chest and punch him in his face and go, "You know, you're not good! You're just *lucky*, man. You think that every-thing you know and all you're doing is keeping you where you are; but you're just lucky, because it can all be gone, you can just lose it!" And I have this rage towards him.

I don't do anything—I let him keep walking—but I've just wanted to hurt an innocent stranger, a passerby, to make a point about what is wrong with my life.

And in that moment I realize I've lost who I was before. I've become more like the kids who stabbed me.

It's incredible to feel like you're not who you used to be. I was going down a road where I was going to meet the guys who were my attackers. And I was going to be in hell, because I would go there alone, because that path was just bitterness.

And for the first time I realized I could *never* get back to where I was before: that guy, that business, that whole life was just *gone*. I had lost it. But up until that moment I had never believed that I had lost it. I had always thought I was going to get back to being that guy again.

As I sat there, I thought, *I've got to do something* new.

It felt liberating. It was like, *All right, I can't go back, because that's gone. And I don't want to be evil and bad. I'm going to do this new thing. I can do it!*

And then I remembered, *I have this girl.*

And I run home, and I'm like, "OK, I'm not going to be the sad guy, and I'm not going to be the mad guy. I'm going to change, and we're going to work this out—will you marry me?"

And she's like, "No! You need a little more work here," but she's enthused by my enthusiasm.

And she knows I'm never going to ask her again. So after about another year and a half, she feels like we have something, and *she* asks *me* to marry *her*. And so we do. And we end up building this routine again, and setting up a life.

And now we have a two-year-old daughter. And I put her shoes on in the morning, and I head out to work.

In his day job, **Ed Gavagan** is the owner of PraxisNYC, a design/build firm practicing across a broad spectrum but specializing in boutique residences. Ed creates homes and furniture for fancy people and humble folk the world over. He is a founder of Design Starts Here, an architects' collaborative that offers free design services to the public from a pop-up storefront in Manhattan. Two weeks after the 2010 earthquake in Haiti, Design Starts Here mobilized a fund-raising effort, and Ed traveled with a three-man team into Haiti on a relief mission, delivering tons of food, medicine, and clothing to refugees, clinics, and hospitals. In 2009, Ed began telling stories with The Moth at a StorySLAM in Manhattan. From there, he has won a Moth GrandSLAM and contributed to The Moth Mainstage events, The Moth iTunes podcast, *The Moth Radio Hour* on public radio, and various Moth outreach events. He designed and built The Moth offices in 2011. Ed gave a TED talk at TEDMed2012 based on one of his Moth stories. He was one of forty innovators invited by Todd Park, the chief technology officer of the United States, to participate in the Safety Data Initiative organized by President Obama's Office of Science and Technology Policy. Ed lives in Manhattan with his wife and daughter.

Generations

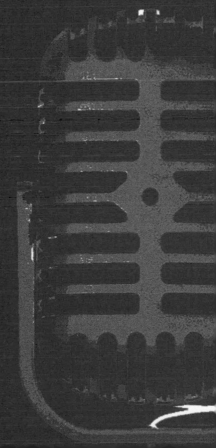

LOL

The story I want to tell you tonight is a simple story about myself and my son Luke. Some of you may have read about him over the years. I write about him often enough. And the truth is we've always been pretty good friends. Father and son, of course, but we've always shared a lot in common. We lived through Paris together, and we love football. I've taught him to love hockey; we even love the same hockey team, the Montreal Canadiens.

But recently he turned twelve, and in New York City, because everything is a little accelerated, twelve is really thirteen. And when thirteen happens to kids, as you all know, something profound changes. They begin to become adolescents; they approach being teenagers. And the bond, no matter how strong it is, between a father and son, or a mother and son or daughter, begins to change. It begins to alter. And suddenly they become more distant from you.

And it's like—if I can even use the word in this context—it's sort of like the mortality of parenting. That is to say, you know it's going to happen, but you can't believe it's going to happen to you. You think, *It happens to other people, but it won't happen to me*.

And so about a year ago Luke started coming home from school at three o'clock. I work at home, and I write. Three-fifteen I would open the door, and I would do the thing that no parent should ever do, but that no parent can resist, even though you hear the chorus of parents past behind you saying, "Don't do that!" The doorbell rings, and you open it, and there's your twelve-year-old, and you can't help yourself, you say, "How was your day at school?" And the twelve-year-old hunches his shoulders and droops his head and walks into his room without saying a word, and the door shuts.

Now you know what's going on on the other side of that door; he's on his computer. You sort of wish you could smell the healthy whiff of marijuana or hear the sounds of adolescent groping because that at least you can connect to from your own adolescence. But there's not a chance of that. They're on their computers; they're instant messaging each other, six or seven at a time, talking about just what big schmucks their parents are. And that's appropriate.

And you never learn! The doorbell rings the next day at three-fifteen, you open it, and the great chorus of parents past chants, "Do not ask the question!" And like Oedipus you do the thing you're never supposed to do, you say, "How was your day at school?" And you get a shrug, and he walks into his room and shuts the door. Well, I understood it. And I knew that he was back there in the silence instant messaging his friends, as I say.

Now, instant messaging is something that I could not understand. I couldn't understand the appeal of it, and I couldn't understand the prevalence of it. Because the truth is when I was twelve years old, we used the telephone all the time. We had a series of phone conversations with everyone we knew. And it always seemed to me that had the telephone come second and the instant message been the thing that Alexander Graham Bell invented a hundred years ago, there'd be no question that the telephone call would be the huge technological break-through. If Steve Jobs had invented the phone call, it would have been on the front page of the *Times* the next day, and there'd have been giant back-page ads everywhere you looked talking about "Finally, real voices! Real communication!"

"Liberate yourself from the pressure of the keyboard. Hear your sweetheart talk!" It would have been the great break-through of the twentieth century. But because that was the nineteenth century, kids only instant message. That's the only way I can understand it.

Well, Luke is always insisting that I download software—Skype, or Limewire—and he insisted that I download AOL Instant Messenger, and I did. And I had it on my desktop. One day he comes in, I ask the question, he walks into his room, the door shuts, I go back to my little study, and I'm writing, and suddenly I hear a *ping* on my screen. And I look down, and it's an instant message from Luke.

"Hey, Dad! Wuz up?"

And I write, "Nothing much. Wuz up with you?"

And he says, "Oh, I had a terrible day at school."

And right away—he's fifteen feet away from me—we have the conversation that he denied me at the door five minutes be-fore. And I realized, of course, what it was really all about. The appeal of instant messaging is that you control—the child controls—the means of communication. You're not accepting the three-fifteen third degree. You're claiming the right to con-trol your own conversations.

And so every day from then on it became a sort of ritual. It was practically Japanese. Doorbell would ring, I would open the door, Luke would come in, we would bow at each other, he would say nothing. He would walk into his room, shut the door, I would go back to my office and shut the door, and about thirty seconds later a *ping* would go on, and it would be Luke.

"Hey, Dad! Wuz up with you today?"

And we would instant message each other and have a conversation about our days. And sometimes we'd actually be sitting on the same bed watching a hockey game together, instant messaging each other in total silence.

Now I loved instant messaging, once I'd gotten the hang of it. I loved the simplicity of it, I loved the autonomy of it, and I loved the language of abbreviations that instant messaging has. And Luke taught me all of the abbreviations: "brb" means "be right back," "U2" means "you too," "g2g" means "got to go."

And then there was one that he didn't even have to teach me because it was so self-evident and that was "LOL." And I knew right away that it meant "lots of love" because he put it at the end of every message that he sent me. And even when I sent him a really sententious message (you know, one of those "Just do the things you've got to do, and then you'll be able to do the things you want to do. I had homework too."), he would always write back, "OK, Dad. LOL—Luke." And I was really moved by this because even when I was lecturing him, he was able to absorb it in a mature way and send "lots of love" back to me as he thought about it. And I thought, *This is such a beautiful telegraphic abbreviation for the twentieth century because it's like a little arrow of love you can send out to anybody you know.*

And for the next six months I was infatuated with instant messaging and its power of emotional transmission, and I sent "LOL" to everybody I knew. My sister was getting divorced out in California, and I wrote to her, "We're all behind you and beside you, LOL—your brother." My father got ill, and I sent him "LOL" in Canada. Everybody I knew at work, at home—*everyone*—I sent them "LOL." I was an instant messaging demon.

Well, one evening I'm in the lounge at LaGuardia waiting for a plane. I have to travel a lot to speak. And I was IM'ing with Luke, and he and I were discussing this. And I was really full of emotion. I hate traveling, I don't like being away from the children. And I wrote to him, "Luke, I just want you to understand that every weekend I'm away is a weekend I hate, but I have to do it to live the life we want to live and to make money for us. LOL—your dad."

And suddenly on my screen, there at midnight in the lounge in LaGuardia, I see coming across my screen giant letters, like an incoming message from NORAD—*Bombers are on the way!*—and it says, "DAD! WHAT EXACTLY DO YOU THINK 'LOL' MEANS?—LUKE"

And I write back, "Lots of love, obviously."

And he writes back, "No, Dad. It means 'laughing out loud'!"

"No it doesn't."

"Yes it does, Dad."

And, of course, it does. It's all it means.

Well, I was miserable. Not only had I been totally misunderstanding the degree of ridicule that Luke had been shooting at me for six months, but I was going to have to repeal six months' worth of "LOL." I was going to have to go through every single person I'd sent an instant message to and apologize for having made fun of them in the midst of their suffering. And I thought to myself, *This is the real nature of every communication between parent and child. We send them lots of love, they laugh out loud at us, and we don't even know they're doing it.* We stopped instant messaging each other.

And then a couple of months later, Luke and I went off on a trip together. And my computer broke, and I had to send something in to work, so I said to Luke, "Luke, can I use your computer?" And he said OK.

"Well, just give me your password so I can get on."

He said, "Eh! I don't want to give you my password."

I said, "Luke, why don't you want to?"

He said, "Well, *you* give me *your* password."

"Well, my password is you—Luke94. Your name and the year you were born."

He said, "Really?"

I said, "Yeah. So tell me, what's your password?"

And he said, "It's, uh, Montreal Puck." It wasn't exactly "Dad," but it was pretty close; it was something that we had shared, and that secretly he had encoded as his way out into the world. It was as though he were packing his suitcase, but he was packing it with something that I had given him.

And from that night on, when we got back to New York, we started IM'ing each other again. And every time we would, we would include it—LOL. Because here's the thing that I think is true, what I've learned, and that is that through all of those months when Luke was laughing out loud at me, and I didn't even know it, he never thought there was something strange about our miscommunication. He never stopped to think that there was something wrong about the way that I was using LOL. Because, if you think about it, there are very few times in life when saying "I'm laughing out loud in your presence" and saying "I love you a lot" aren't really close enough to count.

They're not exactly the same—if they were we would never grieve when someone we loved died. But in most of the exchanges that we have, between ourselves and our children, saying "I'm laughing" and saying "I love you" are a reasonable hit, a near miss, good enough to carry on with.

And so now every night, the last thing we do, me from my bedroom and Luke from his, is to send each other an instant message, and we always end it "LOL."

"LOL, Dad!"

"LOL, Luke!"

And it doesn't matter what it means. It means laughter or love, or whatever it might mean at that moment to us.

Adam Gopnik has been a writer for *The New Yorker* since 1986. He is the author of the essay collections *Paris to the Moon* and *Through the Children's Gate*, both of which include many of his pieces from the magazine, and also two children's novels, *The King in the Window* and *The Steps Across the Water*. His other works include *Angels and Ages: A Short Book About Darwin, Lincoln, and Modern Life* and *The Table Comes First: On Family, France, and the Meaning of Food*.

Liberty Card

My story goes back sixty-two years, to the autumn of 1940. I won't fill in the blitz and Wendell Willkie running against FDR for the third term. The story, such as it is, took place in a sprawling borough by the sea, Brooklyn, in a neighborhood tucked into the northwest corner on the East River, known as Williams*boig*, to distinguish it from Williamsburg, the colonial restoration.

My parents were very late immigrants to the United States. My mother came with nine siblings in 1930. My father had come in the 1920s, it seemed—that side of the family never disclosed much. I have a feeling he did something infamous, because World War I was involved, and the borders changed, and then there was the Russian Civil War and Lenin attacked the Poles, and you know, God it was terrible. Who knows what people did to survive?

But he never told stories like Herbie Kleinman's father, who was a baker with a baker's great belly. You know, "I sewed jewels into my underwear and snuck out of Odessa!"

So they married and settled in Williamsburg, where my

mother's family lived, where the Satmar live now, the very pious Jews. My family was not pious in that energetic way.

We lived in the part of Brooklyn that had row houses, not *A Tree Grows in Brooklyn* Williamsburg—Betty Smith's Irish tenement Williamsburg—but a row house that had been lived in by the Brooklyn bourgeoisie. It had been broken up into not floor-through apartments, but half floor-through, and we lived in a succession of them.

I was overprotected. I was treated as if my parents had had a child before I came along . . . and that child had died.

My parents had come here as much out of fear of what had happened as what *was* happening, and what was *likely* to happen in Europe. They escaped the worst of it, but there was a mixture of hope to be sure. America was called *the Golden Medina*, and there were so many great success stories: David Sarnoff, Eddie Cantor, you know, I could run the list now.

But their fears were great. My father worked terribly hard— left early, came home late, I hardly ever saw him. He went along with my mother, who said, "No bicycle for him." We could afford it. We had boarders who helped pay the rent, like Mr. Lichtenstein, who was a retired watchmaker. So it wasn't the money.

But a bicycle? "You could fall!"

Roller skates? Well the hills in Williamsburg weren't great, but there was an incline, and "You'd lose control and you'd be on Bedford Avenue and those buses . . ."

And playing marbles in the gutter, that wasn't dangerous, but I'd be amongst the common ruffians. My parents were not educated, they were not rabbis, but they had a sense of themselves. I can't think of the proper Yiddish word—doesn't matter. You lived a fine and dignified life. And most of the people around us were noisy and sat outside on the stoops in their undershirts. So I couldn't do those things.

As it turned out, I loved school. And though I was not the master of the streets, the second day I went to PS 122, I came home and said, "I will walk to school by myself." Four blocks, two avenues, past the big armory to PS 122.

Going to school and coming back, the streets teemed with activity. Laundry delivered, big electric-driven trucks with chain drives, the bakeries, Dugan's delivering rolls, the milk from Sheffield Farms on Heyward Street. I even remember horse-drawn carts. The Italian vegetable and fruit man came with an old nag, who was just two steps this side of the glue factory.

And then there were so many other people. There were street singers, and I remember the cutler, who ground knives. He would come peddling with a big stone wheel in front of him and a bell. He'd get to the middle of the block and hit the bell. All the mammas knew what the bell meant, and they came scurrying out of the houses with their aprons wrapped around scissors, knives, and the funny little chopping things that they used for "soul food"—chopped liver. You could hear the whirring, the screeching noise, and see the sparks as the stone whetted the metal.

So the streets were safe and full. Still, no bicycle. No roller skates. No scooter made of a stolen box, attached to old roller skates.

But the thing I craved most, because I loved books and reading, was a library card. The boarder taught me Hebrew when I was about two. I puzzled out the Yiddish paper once I figured out you read it from back to front. And we didn't have much English in the house, but there were ketchup bottles.

I knew that the books were in this big, very elegant building with red brick, limestone, and marble, just a few blocks away, near Eastern District High School and the YMCA, the civic center of that part of Williamsburg.

But I couldn't get my mother to walk me over and get the library card, 'cause anything involving public institutions reminded her of Brest-Litovsk in Poland, where every uniform meant danger, including the police, and every public office meant procrastination and insult and bribery and curses and humiliation. And of course walking that way also took you to the elevated train on Broadway—just a couple of blocks more—that took the men like my father across the Williamsburg Bridge into Manhattan to work, as many of them did, in the garment center. My father was a furrier.

So two things frightened her: the men's world and the public world. And she wouldn't do it.

But I came home from school one day, and I had the ultimate weapon:

"Teacher says."

I listened to the teacher.

I said, "Mom, teacher says to get a library card."

For some reason you had to show a gas bill. I guess they thought maybe you could forge rental receipts, and maybe electricity was not as widespread as I thought. Or maybe it was democratic—somebody who owned a house paid a gas bill as well as someone who rented. I don't know.

But we took the gas bill over and found the appropriate desk. You had to be able to write your name or print it, and I was frightened because I never had the Spencerian copperplate hand that of course all the girls picked up. But with my tongue sticking out in concentration, I wrote my name, showed the gas bill, and got a temporary library card. Thirty days later, the permanent card came.

I don't think I took out picture books. Because words were what I was interested in, and I would list them, and go over to the big dictionary and schlep the pages over, you know, looking for words.

My parents, in silent partnership with this great republic in which they had the most tenacious toehold, insecure in language and so much of American ways, had gotten me, in that unlaminated card, my ticket out of ghetto-mindedness. Unknowingly, somewhat unwillingly, they had given me a chance to satisfy my curiosity, such a powerful instinct for a lonely, lost, and rather sullen child.

And with it, in time, after Doctor Dolittle and the boys' editions of Kipling and Stevenson and Victor Hugo, Alexandre Dumas, and, of course, Mark Twain—I haunted libraries—it was Dickens and Orwell and de Tocqueville. So that in time, and I'm proud of this, I'd achieved an *independence of mind*. And thanks to my humble self-extinguishing parents, enough of the *independence of spirit* that has to sustain independence of mind.

A line of poetry, which I'm not much given to, came to me. It's a line of Shelley's, and I think my parents would have loved it:

To hope and hope and hope till hope creates from its own wreck the thing it contemplates.

They did. We must.

Marvin Gelfand was a longtime New Yorker, born in Brooklyn. A product of the public schools of the city and the state of New York, he taught economics at the university level, was a literary editor at *The Washington Post*, freelanced as a book reviewer, and wrote speeches and orated for many, many worthy losing candidates. For years he lectured, consulted, and led walking tours about the history of the city of New York. He died in 2011, and we miss him.

Discussing Family Trees in School Can Be Dangerous

I'm a geneticist. I study how chromosomes are inherited in dividing cells. But my story tonight will have more to do with my own genetics.

I'm English. I was brought up in the 1950s and 1960s in London. My family wasn't very rich. I had two brothers and a sister. My dad was a blue-collar worker. My mum was a cleaner. My siblings all left school at fifteen.

I was different. I did quite well at school, and I passed exams, and I somehow got into university, got a scholarship, and then did a Ph.D.

I wondered, *Why am I different to the rest of my family? Why did they all leave school at fifteen?* And I didn't really have much of an answer, but I felt a bit unsettled about that. I wondered about it occasionally. But I carried on with my life. I got a job in a university. I got married. I had two children, Emily and Sarah. And, you know, just got on with things.

Then my parents, who were living in London, retired to the country, and we used to visit them regularly; but the truth was it was a bit boring, you know? They lived in the middle of nowhere. Nothing much happened there, and my kids got a bit bored. One day when we were visiting, Sarah, my eleven-year-old, had a project at school. And the project was family trees.

I said, "I've got a great idea. Why don't you talk to Grandma about her family tree?"

So we got there, we had dinner, and then off Sarah trotted with her grandma to talk about her family tree. Five minutes later, in came my mum, absolutely white.

And she came over to me, and she said, "Sarah's been asking me about my family tree, and I have to tell you something that I've never told you."

I was in my thirties by this time. She said, "I never told you . . . I'm illegitimate." She'd been born in 1910. Her mum wasn't married. She'd been born in the poorhouse. She wasn't from a wealthy family. She was brought up by her grandmother, and her mother had married somebody else, who I'd thought was my grandfather, but that wasn't the case. My grandfather was unknown. So I'd lost a grandfather.

Then she said, "And actually it's the same for your father too."

So in two sentences, I'd lost two grandfathers. Well, this was a bit of a shock.

And then I began to think about it, and I thought, *Well, maybe this is where I got some exotic genes, and they sort of recombined, and that's why I'm a bit different.* And then I remembered that my middle name was Maxime, and I got it from my dad, who was called Maxime William John. And, you know, he was a sort of farmworker in the country. That's where he came from, in Norfolk, and I tell you in Norfolk, farmworkers are not called Maxime usually. This is a French-Russian aristocratic sort of name. So I began to imagine that perhaps I had an exotic grandfather, a French-Russian aristocrat, and, you know, blah, blah, blah. And that was why I ended up how I was.

And so that seemed okay. That seemed a reasonable explanation, and I got on with my career, and I became an Oxford professor, then a departmental chair. Then they knighted me, and then I got a Nobel Prize a few years ago. So that's all hunky-dory.

Then in 2003, I decided to come to New York City. Both my parents had died. They lived into their eighties and nineties. And I came with my family to New York City to be president of Rockefeller University, on the Upper East Side.

And a couple of years ago, I thought I should try and get a green card. Have you ever seen those poor bastards queuing up at the airport when you come through immigration? They're all people like me, who have to wait there for an hour and a half and have their fingerprints done. But if you have a green card, you avoid that.

So I applied for a green card. Huge amount of paperwork. You have no idea how complicated it is. Sent the thing off, waited a number of months.

Came back. And I was rejected.

I thought, *How come I'm rejected? I'm a knight. I've got a Nobel Prize, and I'm president of Rockefeller University, and they reject me for a green card? I know Homeland Security has high standards, but I mean, this does seem more than a little ridiculous.*

So I looked through all the paperwork, and I eventually found out they did not like the documentation I'd sent with my application. They particularly didn't like my birth certificate.

So I got my birth certificate out, and it was a so-called "short birth certificate," which we have in Britain, which names who you are, where you were born, the time you were born, your citizenship, and so on. It doesn't name your parents, but it's a perfectly official document.

And so I thought, *Well, I can go and get the long certificate.* I knew the registry office would have it. So I phoned up London and said, "Please send that in the post."

I told my secretary in my office, "When it arrives, bundle it all off again. Send it off to those silly jerks in Homeland Security."

I went on holiday for a couple of weeks. Went to New Zealand. Came back. Was undoing all the mail, looking at my e-mails, and so on. Several people in my room—my secretary, her assistant, my wife, my lab manager. So quite a few people around.

And then I remembered that I had told my secretary to get this package sent off. So I asked her, "Did you manage to do that?"

And she turned to me, and she said, "Well, I didn't do it because the certificate arrived. I looked at it, and I thought, um, maybe you got the name of your mother wrong."

I said, "Of course I didn't get the name of my mother wrong. Don't be absolutely ridiculous."

So she hands me the certificate, and everybody starts to look at me, you know? It's a bit of a strange conversation to have. So I open it, I look at it, and there is the name Nurse, my mother. And I think, *Well, you know, not a problem there.* And then I look at it again, and the name is *Miriam* Nurse.

And that was not the name of my mother at all. It was the name of my *sister*.

So I'm looking at this, thinking, *Oh my god, the people at the registry office have cocked up again*, you know? And then I look a bit further, and where it says "Father," there's just a line. Just a dash. No father.

And then my wife comes up and says, "You know what this might mean, Paul?" And I was a bit slow, actually. I really didn't quite realize what it might have meant. And then slowly the clouds rolled away.

My sister was eighteen years and one month older than me. Both my parents, who were actually now my *grandparents*, had died, but so had my sister, who was really my mother. She had died early of multiple sclerosis. So I had nobody to confirm if this story was true.

However, on the birth certificate was the place where I was born, and it was my great-aunt's house, about a hundred miles from London, in a city called Norwich. And my great-aunt had a daughter who was eleven years of age when I was born.

So I phoned her up, and said, "Do you know anything about this?"

And she said, "Yes, I do."

She said, "Your sister became pregnant at seventeen, and she was sent to her aunt's in Norwich." This is like a Dickensian novel, as you can see. "And she gave birth to you. Her mother, your grandmother, came up and pretended that the baby was hers. And she sent your real mother back home, and several months later she took you back, pretending that she was your mother."

And we all lived together in this two-bedroom apartment for two-and-a-half years, and then my real mother got married and left home. And there's a photograph of me in this wedding. And my mother, my *real* mother, is holding the hand of her husband in one hand and my hand in the other. Because you realize, this was her leaving me with her parents. She never told her husband, so the whole thing was kept secret for over half a century.

Now, at the same wedding, I crawled under the table, a gate-leg table, which had the wedding cake. And I managed to move the leg, and the wedding cake fell off the table and smashed into pieces. I wonder whether I was revolting at the thought of my mother being taken away.

But I was brought up happily. A little dully, maybe, by my grandparents, but this was only a tragedy for my mother. She had three other children, and she kept four photographs of babies by her bed. I only learned this after her death. Three were her legitimate children, and I was her fourth, illegitimate child.

Well, the final irony here really is I'm not a bad geneticist. And yet my rather simple family kept my own genetic secret for over half a century.

Paul Nurse is a Nobel laureate and is president of the Royal Society of London and director of the Francis Crick Institute, where he also continues to do research in cell biology. He is the former president of Rockefeller University and chief executive of Cancer Research, UK. In 1999 he was knighted in Great Britain for his contributions to cancer research.

The Mug Shot

How you doin'? My name's Steve Osborne. I was a New York City cop for twenty years. Now, a few years back, I was a sergeant in the Fugitive Division. Our job was to go out and hunt and catch the most wanted fugitives. This was the greatest job in the world. I loved this stuff. I used to love hunting these guys down, tracking 'em to wherever they would try and hide.

We'd find 'em, catch 'em, jump 'em, handcuff 'em, and drag 'em in. It was loads of fun.

I once tracked a guy down to the maternity ward while his wife was giving birth. Now, before you go "Ooh" and "Ahh" and all of that—he shot five people. When you start shooting that many people, I'll get you wherever I can get you, you know? All's fair. We would start work at four-thirty in the morning. We did that because we wanted to catch them in bed, sleeping. They were tired, they were groggy, and they were less likely to go for a gun or a knife or something else stupid.

Now, when we would come into work, I'd grab my coffee and sit at my desk, and there'd be a stack of warrants—five, six, seven of them, the guys that we were going after that day.

They'd usually be in priority order—the worst guy would be on top.

Now, the guy on top this day was this kid by the name of Hector. At the age of twenty-six, Hector was already a hard-core bad guy. He had been locked up a whole load of times, for everything from smoking weed to assault, robbery, criminal possession of a weapon, and his latest collar, an attempted murder. That was the one that I was concerned with.

Turns out he got into a beef with a guy, pulled out a gun, and shot him. The guy didn't die, so *attempted* murder. Hector gets arrested and goes through the system. He goes to his arraignment, and the Bronx being the Bronx, the judge lets him out on bail with a return date of thirty days later.

Well, surprise, surprise, thirty days comes and goes, and Hector's nowhere to be found. Judge gets pissed off and issues a warrant for his arrest. Now he's my problem. I gotta go find him and bring him in.

Every warrant comes in a package. There's the warrant itself, signed off by the judge. There's the arrest report. And stapled on top is a mug shot.

Now, you've all seen police mug shots. You know, a guy standing there with the numbers across his chest? It's the worst possible photo that anybody could ever take. I don't think Pamela Anderson topless could take a good mug shot. Well, you know, maybe her, but, really, I don't think anybody else.

So I'm looking at this kid's photo. He's sitting there, and he's looking out at me, you know? He's got the numbers across his chest. I've been doing this for a long time. I've made hundreds and hundreds of arrests. And I can just tell by looking at this kid's face that he is going to be a pain in the ass. He has these black beady eyes, high bony cheekbones, a pointy chin, a scraggly goatee, and a pockmarked face. And he has a scar under his eye, like he got cut in a fight.

Believe me, it was a face that only a mother could love.

Now it's time to get to work, so I go through my checklist. I got my vest, gun, backup gun, handcuffs, flashlight—all the tools of the trade, everything you need for hunting down bad guys. I get my team of six detectives together, and we head out the door.

And I got that spring in my step. I love this stuff.

We head over to his building—real bad building. I've been there a couple times before. Every time we go there, there's a problem. Either they're throwing bricks and bottles off the roof at us, or perps are fighting with us.

But it was early in the morning, and everything was quiet, so I was hoping to slip in, get this guy, and get the hell out before anybody even knew we were there. We go through the front door and into the lobby, and it's a dump. There are bullet holes in the wall and graffiti everywhere. There are crack vials on the floor, empty beer bottles, urine in the corner. The place is a mess.

He lives in apartment 4B. We figure out the "B" apartments face front.

So I tell two of my guys, "Cover the front window."

Now, you might think, like, *Who would jump out a fourth-floor window and try to escape?* But I'm telling you, desperate men do desperate things. And I guarantee you if he jumps out that window and kills himself, his family's gonna be on the six o'clock news that night, swearing to God that I threw him out the window, trying to sue the city for $50 million. So two guys covering the window might save me a little bit of aggravation.

We go up to the apartment, and it's like it's choreographed.

We do this every day. I take one side of the door, one of my guys takes the other side of the door, and we listen. We're listening for anything—voices, a TV, a radio playing, kids, a dog barking. Anything that might give us a clue about what we're walking into.

We listen for a minute. Nothing. Everything's quiet. So it's time to hit this thing.

Now, the last thing I do before we hit a warrant is I always take the mug shot out, and I study it. I look at that face and commit it to memory. 'Cause a lotta times you go into these apartments; it's dark, and there's a lotta confusion. The family may be fighting with us. Somebody could be going for a gun or a knife. And there may be a brother, a cousin, an uncle, a nephew—somebody that looks just like him. So you want to know exactly what your bad guy looks like.

I take out the photo, and I'm studying it. And I see the little black beady eyes staring at me and that pockmarked face and that goatee and the bony cheekbones and that bony chin and the scar under his eye. I take the photo, and I hand it off to the next guy. He does the same thing. Everybody passes it around, and then I stick it back in my pocket.

And it's time.

Now you might think that we knock the door down, but we really don't. We knock. If I have to, I got a battering ram and sledgehammers and stuff in the car, and I'll go down and get them, and I'll knock your door down. But usually knocking works. So I knock on the door. We're listening. Nothing. I knock a little louder.

Finally I hear a woman's voice on the other side of the door. "Who is it? What do you want?"

We tell her, "POLICE! We got a warrant. Open the door."

I hear on the other side of the door, *click, click, click, click, click*. You know, she's got like, twenty locks on this door. As she's doing that, we're turning on our flashlights, unholstering our guns, and getting ready.

The door opens up, and there's this little Hispanic woman standing there, with this pink fluffy robe and these little pink fluffy slippers. She's in her late forties or early fifties.

And I say, "Police. We got a warrant. We're coming in," and we push our way past her.

So we go into the apartment, and we do our thing. We're going from room to room flipping up beds, pulling clothes out of the closets. The reason that we do this is because these guys will hide in the tiniest, most unbelievable places. So you gotta be thorough.

So we're tearing the place apart looking for him. No sign of him. I go back out to the living room, and I grab Mom.

I say, "Ma. Where's Hector? I gotta talk to him."

She has this confused look on her face, and she says to me, "My son is dead."

My first reaction is: *Bullshit. Don't lie to me.*

You might think that I'm being a hard-ass, but I'm not. Believe me when I tell you, I've had little old ladies with rosary beads and Bibles in their hands swearing to God that they haven't seen their little Johnny in months. Meanwhile, the prick's behind the bedroom door with a butcher knife, waiting for us to come in.

It's dangerous work, and I trust nobody.

So I tell her, "Look, you're not helping him. Tell me where he is. Don't make me hunt him down out in the street. That's how bad things happen. Tell me where he is, or get him to turn himself in."

With that, the daughter comes out of the bedroom. She grabs her mother, and they interlock their arms and hug each other. They're scared. And it's understandable; the cops are busting in their house early in the morning, tearing the place apart.

So I say to the girl, "Where's your brother? I gotta talk to him."

And she looks right at me and goes, "My brother's dead. He was shot and killed last week down the block." And with that, she goes over to the refrigerator, and she gets a business card, and she hands it to me, and she says, "Here. Talk to this detective. He's got the case. He knows everything."

So I take the card, and I hand it to one of my guys, and I say, "Make a call."

We make a couple of phone calls. Sure enough, everything checks out. Hector was a homicide victim about a week earlier. He got shot and killed down the block, but the paperwork for that case hadn't caught up with the paperwork for my case. So I tell his mom, "Look. I'm very sorry for your loss. I'm very sorry for the way we had to bust in the way we did, but we had a warrant, and this is the way we do things." And I explain to her, "Look, I'll go down to court. I'll get the warrant vacated. I'll make sure that nobody comes and bothers you again. I'm very sorry."

With that, it's time for us to go. In reality, I got five or six more Hectors we're going after that morning. But before we leave, I take the mug shot outta my pocket. I just want to make sure there's no mistaken identity, you know, that we're talking about the same kid.

So I take the mug shot, and I show it to her, and I say, "Is this your son?"

She takes one look at the photo, and tears start rolling down her face. And she starts sobbing—that really deep, mournful sobbing, that only a mother crying over her child would have in her. So, I believe her. Obviously this is her son.

So I take the photo and stick it back in my pocket, and I tell her again, "Look, I'm very sorry for your loss," and we turn to leave.

But as I turn to leave, she says to me, "Can I see the picture again?"

I'm like, "This, this picture?"

I'm confused. Didn't she get a good look at it before? Is she not sure? I'm not sure where this thing is going now. So I take the photo out, and I show it to her. And she reaches out, and she takes it from my hand, and she clutches it to her chest. It's like she's hugging him.

And she says to me, "Can I keep this picture?"

I'm thinking: *That picture?* You want to keep *that picture?*

So I tell her, "Look, it's police department property. We don't normally give them out to the public."

But she goes on to tell me that she has no photos of him because he was never around. His whole adult life, he was either out tearing up the streets, or he was in jail. He never really came around for Mother's Day or Christmas or anything like that, and she has no photos of him. She has nothing to remember him by.

When she told me this story, I felt terrible for her. You know, I'm a hard-core guy, but my heart was breaking for her a little bit. She seemed like a nice lady. I mean, this building was a dump, but the apartment, she kept it clean. She put that thick plastic on the sofa so that it wouldn't get dirty. And she wasn't cursing me out, like a lotta other mothers do, blaming me 'cause their son's got a warrant, and he's gotta go back to jail. She just seemed like a nice lady who lost her son to the streets, which in that neighborhood happened a lot.

So I told her, "Okay. If you got nothing else to remember this kid by, go ahead, be my guest. It's yours."

And she reaches out, and she shakes my hand, and she thanks me. She's clutching her robe shut, and she still has those little pink fluffy slippers. She shuffles across the room and goes over to this bookcase against the wall that has all these family photos in nice silver and gold frames. You know, there was Grandpa in his World War II uniform, and wedding photos and graduation pictures with the cap and the gown.

And very lovingly and tenderly, like only a mother would do, she took that mug shot and she placed it right in the middle of those family photos.

Steve Osborne was a New York City police officer for twenty years and retired as a lieutenant assigned to the Detective Bureau.

Good News Versus Bad

When I was about twelve years old, my mom said she wanted to talk to me about something. My mom and I didn't have a lot of talks. I loved her very much, but she was kind of an intimidating figure. She was one of those corporate working moms with the beeper and the pants suit and the rolly suitcase. She yelled important things into phones, and she was away a lot on business.

But she sat me down in the living room, and she told me that she was pregnant. And it was kind of strange the way she said it, almost like she wasn't that happy about it. It had been eight years since my brother was born, but even I could remember how excited everybody had been—how everyone had ideas for names, how all the grandparents had flown in from out of town, how barely a day went by that we didn't get some kind of massive delivery of balloons or a giant stuffed animal. But this time there were no balloons. There weren't even any cards.

But I was still very excited. I had never expected to have another sibling after my little brother, and I was optimistic that this time I'd get one who could throw a baseball. So I told everyone the big news. I told everyone at school, everyone at church, my Girl Scout troop, the next-door neighbors, the kid who mowed our lawn—everybody. And they were all just as excited as I was. Except after a while, I started to notice that when these people would inevitably congratulate my dad on the big news, there would be this sort of whispered exchange, and then that person would say, "Oh my God, I'm so sorry." And I didn't know what that meant until one day when my dad took me out for ice cream.

My dad was my best friend when I was a kid. He was the dad who would read to us every night before bed and would listen very seriously to my thoughts on the Roald Dahl masterpiece *James and the Giant Peach* and the film version's inherent inferiority. He taught me how to throw a baseball, and at one point really believed he could teach my brother the same. He taught us that Darth Vader had to wear that suit because he had been injured in a car accident, and so my brother and I better always wear our seat belts unless we wanted to end up like him. Imagine my disillusionment when I saw the *Star Wars* prequels. (Disillusionment on so very many levels, but anyway.)

Because my dad and I were so close I knew what ice cream meant. Every time my dad has bad news he takes us out for ice cream. It's kind of his M.O.

Don't ever go to the Cold Stone Creamery with my dad—just don't do it. Unless you want to find out that Grandpa has cancer, or your dog's been put to sleep, or your nanny's been fired for stealing your mother's jewelry, just don't go.

So we get our ice cream of doom, and my dad takes a deep breath, and he says, "The baby your mother is pregnant with is not mine." And I can see him looking at me trying to see if I understand at twelve years old what he means.

As it just so happened, I had conveniently just learned what sex was in school, when my science teacher forced poor Craig Berken to read it out loud from our biology textbook. I can still remember the exact words, as read in Craig's shaky, giggly voice: *The man jiggles his penis inside the woman's vagina.*

Yes, jiggles. Even at that age I was like, *I really feel like that is not the right word for this context.* "Jiggles" is a word that's neither sexy nor scientific, and probably only belongs in a Jell-O commercial. But you know, it did the trick. I learned what sex was, and I understood exactly what was going on here. I understood what my dad was telling me, and I could tell how hard it was for him to tell me. And I knew that as much as he didn't want to tell all of those other people, I was the very last person that he wanted to tell.

And then he says, "Do you know who the father is?" And I realize with sudden clarity that I do know, that I have perhaps always known but have not realized it until this exact moment.

"Andy?" I said, and my dad nodded.

Andy was my mom's coworker, this British guy about ten years younger than her, who would take me and my mom and my brother on little trips and buy us expensive presents. He'd even, oddly enough, gone to church with us. I thought he was our friend.

I realized now that I'd been wrong, and that I'd been stupid not to realize it. And as a result, not only had I failed to prevent this disaster (and like every child I truly believed in my heart that I could have, with a well-timed tantrum or the right number of slammed doors), but I'd also made it infinitely worse for the person who deserved it the least, my father. I'd been coming home for months saying things like, "Dad, look at the awesome Lego castle Andy brought us." I'd been calling him to say, "Dad, guess what, we taught Andy how to play baseball today," never noticing the tense silence on the other end of the line. Not to mention I'd publicly humiliated him by telling everyone about my mother's pregnancy.

I was devastated, and I was no longer excited about the new baby. Shortly after this my parents got divorced, and my mom bought a house down the street from my dad's because the neighborhood didn't already have enough to talk about. We were supposed to go down there every now and then when my mom was home, and one day I went down and there was cake on the table and my mom said, "Andy and I got married today. Do you want a piece of the wedding cake?"

No, I did not want a piece of the cake of lies.

The next time I went down, I was met with an even bigger surprise, this time in the form of a strange pink baby who I was told was my new sister.

"Do you want to hold her?" my mom asked.

No, I did not want to hold her. I didn't want to look at her, at this baby who had broken my father's heart. I loathed this horrible creature, and I decided then that I always would. I made a commitment in that moment to hate this baby for the rest of my life, possibly longer.

There was just one problem . . . I don't know if you've ever tried to hate a baby, but it is fucking difficult. Because everything they do is magical as shit. And this was especially true in the case of my sister, Emma, who had a little Pebbles Flintstone ponytail on top of her head. Every night that I was at my mom's house, she would refuse to go to sleep until I came and sang to her. It was the same song every time, "Shoe Box" by the Barenaked Ladies, which is kind of an inappropriate song to sing to a little girl since it's about statutory rape. But she'd heard me playing it in my room, and that was what she wanted, so who was I to argue?

Soon I found myself bonding with my mom for the first time in a long time over our mutual love for Emma and our mutual hatred of the Teletubbies. Slowly all my anger fell down like dominoes. When I forgave my sister, it was easier to forgive my mom, and when I forgave my mom, it was easier to forgive myself. I'll admit I never quite forgave Andy, but that was okay because it turned out that his stay with us was only temporary anyway. He met another married woman with children and started going to church with them, and presumably started this story all over with someone else.

As for my dad, I never had to ask for his forgiveness. It was always there.

Emma is fourteen years old now, and she's gone from Teletubbies to *Twilight*. Clearly she has questionable taste—in a few years it'll probably be Dan Brown novels. But despite that, we're great friends, and I love her very much, and I can't regret anything that happened because without it we wouldn't have her. Although she never did learn how to throw a baseball.

Erin Barker is a writer, a Moth GrandSLAM champion, and the senior producer of science storytelling project the Story Collider (storycollider.org). She would like to thank Justin D'Ambrosio, Ben Lillie, and Jenifer Hixson for their support and advice with this story and others, and her family for being awesome.

EDGAR OLIVER

The Apron Strings of Savannah

Mother used to always say to us, "Savannah is a trap. It'll try to imprison you. Even if you manage to find a way to get away, it'll drag you back."

Mother also used to say, "Beware of other people. They won't understand you. We're different. We're artists." So all throughout my childhood it was just the three of us—Mother, Helen, and me. And then there was the world as though we were lost in it. Never were three more lost children than Mother, Helen, and me.

No one ever made it into our house, especially relatives. Mother was deeply suspicious of relatives. And if some old friend from Mother's past did dare to pay a visit, they wouldn't have been there very long when Mother would begin sobbing and screaming, "You've been listening to the vicious gossip about me! I can tell! You've been listening to the vicious gossip about me!" And she would advance on them, and they would back out the front door and flee, never to return. At which point we would all three jump in the car and zoom off with Mother driving like a maniac.

All throughout my childhood we drove obsessively, at least two hundred miles a day, sometimes three hundred. They were aimless drives. It didn't matter where we went just so long as we were on the go. Helen and I did our homework in the car, which to this day I believe deeply affected both Helen's and my handwriting, which no one can decipher.

At night we would return to the house on 36th Street and lock ourselves in. Then we would plunge the downstairs into darkness and all three make the terrifying journey upstairs together, where we would lock ourselves in for the night. We were all three so terrified of the dark that it never would have occurred to any of us to have a room of our own. So we all three slept together in the upstairs front bedroom. The rest of the rooms upstairs were stacked to the rafters with chests of drawers and trunks and armoires and boxes that were all locked and filled with Mother's secrets.

We'd all three lie on our narrow beds in the front bedroom beneath dim-shaded lamps, and Mother would shuffle her gypsy-witch cards, and Helen and I would read, which we did madly. And Mother would ask the gypsy-witch cards things like what she should have to eat the next day. Eventually the gypsy-witch cards convinced Mother to go on a banana-split diet.

Invariably at some point Mother would beg Helen and me to rub her feet, so Helen and I would take turns sitting at the foot of Mother's bed for hours kneading and twisting and tickling and pulling at her feet. We played "This Little Piggy Goes to Market" with Mother's toes deep into the night.

Often in the middle of the night, Mother would decide that

we had to talk to the Ouija board. So we'd all sit around the board with our fingers poised lightly on the planchette. When Mother was at the board, the planchette would fly around wildly, and the board would say things like "Tonight is the night of the killer. Don't go to sleep or you'll wake up dead!" So we'd sit in our beds waiting for the killer to strike.

But sometimes the Ouija would say, "He's coming tonight! Get out now!" So we would all dash downstairs and jump in the car and go check into the Travel Motor Lodge on Bay Street, which Helen and I always loved because we loved staying in motels. But the man at the reception desk always found it rather odd because he knew that we lived in Savannah.

Helen and I had almost never spoken to a grown-up. In fact grown-ups used to wonder out loud what our voices sounded like. The only time we would speak to grown-ups was when we went to drive-ins, which we did a lot since we were always driving. And Mother was so paranoid that she would refuse to place an order. She didn't want to speak to the people at the counter. So Helen and I would have to go up and make the order.

And invariably the girl at the take-out counter would peer over the counter at us and say, "Y'all talk funny. You're not from here, are you? Where are you from? Are you from Transylvania?" And then she would say, "Come look at the two little Transylvanian children! Are you two twins?"

If ever any of our friends from school did walk home with us, as soon as they saw what house we lived in this look of terror would come over them, and they'd say, "You live in *that* house? How do you dare go inside? I wouldn't dare set foot on the front porch! That house is haunted!"

And then their look of terror would transfer itself from the house to us, and they would back away from us and say, "Your mother is a witch!" And then they would run off without even saying good-bye to us over their shoulder.

Helen and I always wondered why other children reacted that way. And we decided that maybe it was because sometimes, when Mother's sorrowful rages took hold of her, she would go into the backyard and climb a ladder onto the roof of the shed, and she would stand on the roof and claw the air and curse the sky in her rage.

When I was thirteen and Helen was fourteen, we began to study French obsessively. It became our secret language that Mother couldn't understand. And we would speak French together madly while rubbing Mother's feet. Those conversations with Helen in French were some of the most passionate conversations of my whole life. We dreamt of being poets and painters and wild Bohemians rolling drunk in the gutters of Paris.

Even when I was in high school it never occurred to me that I would ever learn to drive. Helen never learned to drive either. I think that we somehow thought that Mother would always be there to do the driving.

We did, however, both get bicycles, which we kept in the downstairs hall. At this point Mother had begun to practice self-hypnosis. Helen and I would sit beside Mother as she lay on the upstairs couch and put herself through a series of hypnotic autosuggestions. Mother would tell herself that she would feel full of self-esteem and wildly good about herself, and that she would no longer be driven to eat banana splits.

And when Mother had placed herself in a deep, sound sleep, Helen and I would rise quietly and sneak downstairs. Mother kept a folding chair wedged under the front doorknob with two long strands of camel bells dangling from it. Mother said that the ringing of the bells would warn us in case a burglar tried to get in. But Helen and I had become convinced that Mother kept the camel bells there so she would hear us if we tried to leave in secret.

Very slowly and carefully we would move the chair out from under the doorknob without making a single one of the camel bells ring. Then we would grab our bikes and run outside and quietly shut the door and zoom off—alone, without Mother, together—the most wild, adventuresome feeling!

But invariably, no matter how far we'd gotten into whatever godforsaken part of town, we would look back over our shoulders and there would be Mother's blue Chevy II bearing down on us at top speed, with Mother at the wheel biting her lip and driving like a maniac, trying to drive us off the road. It seemed like Mother didn't care whether she killed us, so long as she stopped us from going off without her.

Our longing to get away from Mother began to grow very deep.

When I graduated from high school, we all three took the train up north to Washington. Helen and I were going to attend George Washington University, and we were all going to live together in that room on the top floor of Mr. Schwoyer's rooming house in Georgetown and it would be the three of us, like it always was, like it always would be.

But Helen and I knew that that summer would end differently. We were going to run away together to Paris.

We had made our plane reservations in secret. We had some money in trust from our father, who had died before I was born of a morphine overdose. We wrote to the bank in secret, asking that the monthly checks be sent in our names, and no longer in our mother's name. By running away, we were pulling the financial rug out from under Mother's feet.

At the end of the summer I began to pretend to go to my classes at George Washington, but instead I would go every day to the Greyhound bus station to put quarters in a locker where we had our luggage kept.

The day came for us to fly away. Neither of us had ever flown before, but what concerned us was getting Mother to go to the National Gallery alone, without us. I think I said that I had to go to my classes at GW, and Helen said that she was feeling sick.

I kissed Mother good-bye and walked downstairs and waited in the alley that ran along the side of the house. Helen was going to pull one of the blinds down in the top-floor bay window as a signal to me that Mother had left.

I was waiting in the alley—waiting to betray Mother. I peered around the side of the house. Mother had just walked out the front door. She was walking away. Her back was to me. She was walking downhill to catch the bus at the foot of 30th Street. She was wearing her big Harris tweed men's overcoat like she always did, and her crocheted hat that she had made herself that was shaped like a ziggurat, and her loony boots that she'd ordered from the Marcia Hill shoe catalogue that had fur tongues and that looked like boots a bear would wear. Her wild hair was poking out all around from under her crocheted hat. She was swinging her arms as she walked. She looked happy and innocent. She looked like a clown walking away.

Edgar Oliver is a playwright, poet, and performer. After Edgar and his sister Helen ran off to Paris, his mother became a security guard at the National Gallery, guarding the paintings she so loved. Edgar is a member of the Axis Theatre Company, which is under the direction of Randy Sharp and which is located at 1 Sheridan Square in Manhattan. His one-man show, *East 10th Street: Self Portrait with Empty House*—produced by Axis and directed by Randy Sharp—was the recipient of a Fringe First award at the 2009 Edinburgh Fringe Festival. Three collections of his poems are available from Oilcan Press: *A Portrait of New York by a Wanderer There*, *Summer*, and *The Brooklyn Public Library* (oilcanpress.com). His novel, *The Man Who Loved Plants*, is available from Panther Books (www .goodie.org). Mr. Oliver's latest one-man show, *Helen & Edgar*, opened in New York City in October of 2012 and was called "a revelation" by Ben Brantley of *The New York Times*.

A Kind of Wisdom

There's a kind of wisdom that fathers have, and then there's the kind of wisdom that *my* father has. He thinks he's totally brilliant, but I just think he's crazy.

For example, when we first immigrated from Hong Kong, he thought it would be a good idea for all of us to have American names, which would make sense because it would make transition a lot easier. And so my dad chose as his American name "Ming" even though it's not American or even his real Chinese name, it's just another Chinese name—it's a dynasty.

When we first came to America, we came to Boston. Being from Hong Kong, we had never experienced New England winters. We were penniless; we had very little money. My dad had the brilliant idea of making me my first winter coat, which he designed himself. He got this pink quilt material, which was totally inappropriate for a coat. The actual bodice of it floated away from my three-year-old body, so all the cold air could draft up. He didn't have construction skills to make sleeves, so there were just these two slits in the front that I could use to grab things. It was this big pink bell. The design made no sense. But to this day he thinks it's *the best* design.

Another example: one day he came home and there had been a sale on belts, and he'd bought a monogram belt, and he was so excited.

He was like, "Look at this!" and it had this big, shiny letter "A" on it, even though our family name is Lee.

And I was like, "Dad, why did you get a letter 'A' belt? That doesn't make any sense."

And he was like, "Oh, I got 'A' because 'A' is for 'Ace.'"

You have to understand something about Chinese people. Chinese people are obsessed about being number one. Like, *I have a belt now that says so. I'm number one! Ace!* If you've never noticed, in Chinatowns across the country Chinese business-people always have to find the best "number one" name for their business in order to bring in money and good fortune, which is why everything is an "Imperial Dynasty," "Lucky Dragon," or "Number One Kitchen."

That is my dad, that's his mentality.

So in the first few years of being in this country, he had no time off and worked like crazy, and managed to save a little money to start up his own business. It was a very modest grocery store in Boston's Chinatown. And of course he called it "Ming's Market," but in Chinese the name of it was 平價超級市場, which literally means "bargain price market."

And even as a little kid, I didn't understand. He told me one day he would mark up something by just 5 cents, mark up another thing by 10 cents. I was like, "How are you ever gonna make money? This business model is insane."

But you know, strangely enough, almost immediately he developed a really loyal following in Boston's Chinatown, because for the first time working poor families actually had a place where they could buy affordable, healthy groceries, and eat well, which is no small thing when you're poor.

So after about ten years he built it up to be a very successful business, and by 1989 he had moved into an enormous space—it became New England's largest Asian market.

I was a snotty teenager. I still thought, "Well you're still crazy. You're a successful businessman, but you're nuts. You have crazy ideas."

So he'd been running his business on the first floor of this vacant building. It had been vacant for thirty years. And the landlord was trying to renovate the other floors to rent them out as retail space. But he was doing everything on the cheap, so instead of hiring a contractor, he was welding and renovating on his own without getting permits. And one day something got out of hand and this big fire broke out as he was welding. But it was OK, they evacuated the building—about 150 people—and the fire trucks arrived immediately and everything was fine.

Until the fire department hooked up their hoses to the hydrants and there was no water to fight the fire. And they were like, *Huh, that's weird.* So they went down a couple of blocks and tried the next hydrant, and it was also totally dry.

What had happened was, a few months prior, the city of Boston had done road construction, and generally if they drill deep, they turn off the water pressure in case they hit a water main. And when they sealed up the road, they forgot to turn the pressure back up, so the firefighters had no tools to fight the fire.

It was a disaster. An hour later, the building was still on fire, and there was still no water. They were trying to jerry-rig something from a nearby hydrant, ten blocks away.

And as if things couldn't get worse, the fire jumped an alley and the building next door caught on fire, and on the top floor were ten thousand square feet of illegally stashed fireworks.

Now firefighters couldn't safely scale the ladders, and it was a surreal moment because things were exploding in celebration as my dad stood there, completely helpless, watching his life's work being destroyed in a moment through no fault of his own.

So I got a call. I was a sophomore in college at the time, and I went out to his store the next day, when it was just smoldering; it wasn't on fire anymore. And as I made my approach to the store, I remember seeing three elderly women, and they were crying.

I went up to them and said, "Is everything OK? Why are you crying?"

And one of the ladies looked at me, and then she looked at my dad's burned-down store and pointed, and teary-eyed she said, "Where are we gonna go now that we don't have a home?"

And that was a turning point for me. I hadn't really thought about my dad's store in that way. I just thought it was something he was doing to provide for the family, but in fact he was providing for a greater community. These elderly women, they didn't have a community center to go to. They didn't have a public park in Chinatown. This was the only place where they would actually run into their friends. And they spent a lot of time there. In a way it *was* like a second home.

I guess it is true. It sounds corny, but you do only realize what you have when you lose it.

So in the months that followed, I kept begging my dad for more stories. I asked him what he did with shoplifters, 'cause I was really curious.

And he said, "Well you know, one day I caught a kid

shoplifting. He was only ten, and he didn't know who I was. I was kinda following him around, and he was just taking stuff, stuffing it in his bag, putting it in his pockets. And at one moment he actually took a break from stealing and sat down and actually started eating the food he had stolen, right in the middle of an aisle."

My dad told me that he came up to him, and he said, "Hey little boy, have you had enough to eat?"

And the little boy rubbed his belly, like *almost*, you know?

And my dad's like, "Hey, so where are your parents?"

And the little boy said, "Well, um, they're at work."

My dad said, "Oh, well why aren't you at home?"

The little boy's like, "Because there's no food at home."

And my dad said, "Well you know, when you take stuff, especially if it's at a store, and you don't pay for it, it's actually stealing."

And the little boy got really nervous, like, *This guy is gonna get me in trouble.* And he was kind of angling for a way to get out.

But my dad said, "So in the future if you don't have anything to eat at home, would you just come and find me and ask me for whatever you need? If you ask, I'll give you whatever you want; just don't steal, because stealing is wrong." And in the months that followed I think my dad really looked forward to seeing the little boy.

It was these stories that I was craving, because in some way I think I was trying to re-create something that I had lost, taken for granted.

Whenever we went to Chinatown, lots of people would come up to us and say, "Please, we need a store like this again. When are you going to open up your store?"

And it was hard because my dad was basically penniless.

The fire had caused about $20 million worth of damage, and he barely had enough insurance to cover it. So he really had no money. But he had this idea that maybe he could pool together what little money he did have with a lot of the original employees, people who were immigrants and had gotten their first jobs through my dad at the store. Some of them had been working there since the 1970s.

So they pooled together, and it was a big risk. The only location they could find was just on the outskirts of Chinatown, which in the early nineties, during the last recession, was like a no-man's-land. It was so unsafe, and the only reason you would ever go there was to get a prostitute or drugs. And at the time I remember thinking, *What's the wisdom in that? Why are you going there? It's so unsafe, no one's gonna go, you're gonna lose your life savings.*

But he did it anyway because he's crazy, and almost overnight the place was revitalized. There were really loyal people, families from the suburbs, who came and gave patronage to my dad. And people walked from Chinatown. Soon thereafter many businesses started popping up, and then there was more and more foot traffic, and then families started moving back into this neighborhood. And it was an amazing thing. He kind of helped revitalize this neighborhood, to the point that, fifteen years later, it became one of the most valuable pieces of real estate in Boston.

Which is why my dad got an eviction notice from the owner. He wanted to kick my dad out and knock down the whole block and build luxury condos.

At the time, my dad was seventy, and I said, "You know, Dad, what do you want to do? You have ninety employees, and they're all in their forties and fifties. They don't speak English. They're very hard to employ. What's gonna happen to them?"

And I remember my dad said, "You know, I'm seventy years old. I'm too old for this. I'm too old to fight."

And I understood. But I decided that *I* wasn't too old to fight.

So I organized the community and led this grassroots movement to fight city hall and fight one of the largest developers in all of Boston. And at our first public hearing, there was a really amazing turnout, and we got enough press that even the mayor changed his tune and started supporting us.

And after the first initial hearing I went to the store, and when I walked in, there were these two older women who were my dad's employees.

They rushed right up to me, and they said, "Thank you so much for what you did last night. You know, we normally don't think that we have a voice, and we normally don't think we can advocate for ourselves in that kind of way, so thank you for doing what you did." And when I looked into their eyes, I saw so much compassion and humility and grace.

And it was at that moment that I understood the wisdom that my father had given me.

Ellie Lee is an award-winning director, writer, and producer of animated, fiction, and documentary films, which have screened at the Berlin Film Festival and over a hundred festivals worldwide. She is a five-time National Emmy Award nominee and won the 2009 Alfred I. duPont–Columbia University Award for excellence in broadcast journalism. She is a 2013 Sundance Institute Screenwriters Intensive Fellow and serves on the board of the nonprofit Karen Schmeer Film Editing Fellowship. Currently, she's producing a new animated comedy Web series, *Chinafornia* (www.china fornia.com).

A Perfect Circle

In August of 1998 I was trying to give birth, and it was well attended. I had a nurse, two midwives, my boyfriend at the time (who was not the father), my foster brother, and two women who were also awaiting the birth of *their* first child, who also happened to be *my* child.

Seven months prior to this, after many glasses of water, visits to the bathroom, and sticks peed upon, I had come to accept the fact that I was pregnant. This was not the best of news for a bunch of reasons. One of them was that I was sixteen. More so than that, my life had been a lesson in negatives. It had been a lesson in what not to do.

My mantra had been "How not to be my mother." My mother was a prostitute, and I had grown up with her, and many other prostitutes, and the men that handled them. When she died in the 1980s, like so many from AIDS, I went into foster care. I did a year and a half there before my mother's parents, my grandparents, took me in under duress. As you might note, people who don't want children probably shouldn't have them. I went from being touched much too much in really painful and monstrous ways, to never being touched at all. Sometimes, I wasn't sure which was worse. They lasted about five years with me before they threw in the towel, retired to Florida, and put me in a Southern Baptist children's home.

I lasted about a year and a half there before I thought, *I could do better than this. I could raise myself.* I mean, the bar was pretty low. I studied a lot, and I took a lot of tests, and I graduated high school two and a half years early. I got on a Greyhound and went back to New Jersey, because that's where I grew up and that's where I felt safe. And I started college at a local community college. I got my first full-time job with full health benefits, and I got my first place. I was sixteen. And by the end of my sixteenth year, we get to the point with the bathroom and the pee sticks, and a wrench was thrown in the works.

I knew a few things right off the bat: I wasn't going to abort. A lot of people asked me why I wasn't going to abort (a surprising amount of people were willing to ask, "Why don't you abort?"). And it wasn't because of some misbegotten belief in God or because I'm pro-life, because I'm not. It was because I really, really wanted this baby. I desperately wanted this baby; the want was a pain. I had always wanted a baby. I always wanted to be a mother. I always wanted a family. I always wanted something that was mine and pure and good and whole.

I wanted it, but I couldn't keep the promises I had made to myself about having a family. That whole mantra about not being my mom; I couldn't give this kid a home. I couldn't give a life without fear or want. I couldn't promise that I would be there all the time. I couldn't give unfailing support or provide a net. And so I had to find another solution. I looked at traditional adoption, but I couldn't have a kid grow up the way I did, with so many questions about who I was and where I came from.

And I looked at fostering, but again, you know, I had traveled that road. It hadn't really gone so well.

Finally, someone explained open adoption. It means that the adoptive parents want an ongoing relationship with the mother; and the mother—she gets to choose the parents. And I thought, *I can do this. If he never has questions, if he always knows where he comes from, I can do this.*

So I attacked this like I attack everything else in my life, like a research paper. I made a lot of calls and took a lot of notes, and I finally found an agency that could meet my criteria.

I had three. My first was that it had to be a same-sex couple, because, at this time, it was a little harder for them to adopt. Additionally, despite my own sexual ambiguity, I realized that if I ever found anyone to settle down with, it would be another woman. I never wanted *that* to be an issue.

Number two: they had to not have any extreme religious affiliation. I had had religion shoved down my throat, and I thought faith should be a choice and something questioned. Number three: they had to want an interracial child as their first choice. The father of this baby was black, and I was half very white and half something very brown and short. I wanted this kid to be a first choice. I didn't want it to be something they settled upon because they couldn't find a perfect blond-haired, blue-eyed baby, or because they were trying to better their karma. Even with those narrow parameters, I had over two hundred couples that were viable choices, and each of them had a brochure. Each brochure was full of pictures of their family and friends and their homes, and information about how well educated they were, how much support they had, and how financially stable they were. (If you're ever thinking of adopting, I recommend a background in marketing.)

After going through those, I found about forty or fifty couples that I really liked, and I made a long list of questions. Some of them were what you might expect, like "Why are you adopting?" But a lot of them were a little different, like "How are you going to do this kid's hair?" and "Why don't you believe in God?" and "What do you do when you're mad?"

Eventually I found a couple that I really liked. Their names were Gwen and Gretchen. I did not pick their names, but it's really fucking cute. They lived up in Portland, Maine, which was far enough for me. I didn't want them to be too close, because I totally knew I might be a stalker mom, and I didn't want to find myself on a playground. So they were close enough that I could get there if I needed to, but also far enough away that I couldn't run there in ten minutes.

They came down from Maine to meet me. Gretchen is tall and strong and unflappable, and Gweny is tiny and sweet and nurturing. And I liked them, and they liked me, which was really important because they had to deal with me for a really long time, and a lot of people had not really hung in there.

I knew they were the right ones. I knew that they would work. I chose them, and they gave me an 800 number so I could always reach them. And we waited the wait of expectant parents, and I got bigger.

Eventually we found ourselves in this delivery room, and after twenty-three hours of back labor, I gave birth to an eight-pound, six-ounce baby boy.

And he was perfect. And he was whole. And he was so beautiful, and he had all of his fingers and toes.

I had forty-eight hours with him, and I sang him every song I knew. I tried to say hello to him, and I tried to say good-bye to him. And at the end of that forty-eight hours, I brought him downstairs, and I helped them strap him into a car seat, and I watched these strangers drive away with my baby.

I hoped I had made the right choice. I hoped they were the right people. I hoped he would forgive me.

Up until this point I had never cried, but when I went home, I finally did. I shattered. I broke into a million pieces. I looked at my body, this seventeen-year-old body that should be healthy and strong and young, and it was broken too. I had stretch marks that looked like purple claws from my belly button to my pubis. My stomach that had so recently been filled with life was flaccid and dead. My breasts were heavy and hard and swollen and leaking, trying to feed a child that wasn't there, a baby that was gone.

And I didn't know what to do. I had had such a good start, but I stopped living the mantra of how not to be my mother. I did my best to prove I was just as bad as her. I was someone that could give away a baby. I was the person that could throw away a child. And after never drinking and never smoking and never doing anything bad, that's all I did for the next three or four years. I tried to destroy myself as quickly as possible.

After four years, I made my way to Maine. I finally got up the courage to visit this family that had my child. I went to their home, and it was beautiful, and everyone in it was the kind of person that did what they said they were going to do as a child—they're actors and inventors and dancers. The kitchen was the kind of place where everyone goes to tell their story and friends meet. And all I saw was everything I wasn't; all I saw was a bar I would never meet. And I watched these people raise a child that I was incapable of holding or touching or saying "I love you" to, because I didn't know how to do that. I didn't know how to do it for myself; I didn't know how to do it for him. I just hadn't been given those tools in my life.

I did realize on that trip that I had to get my shit together. I had to be someone who—when this kid was old enough to ask questions—was worthy of being asked.

I went home, and I stopped doing all of those horrible things to myself. I made better friends and started building my own family of supporters. Eventually I got better, and every year in August I would visit them, and every year it was a little easier to talk, and it was a little easier to share, and it wasn't so terrible when people stared at me and said, "You look just like him."

When he was turning nine, I realized I really needed to change. I was invited to a meditation seminar about an hour north of Portland, and I went with two of my best friends. We were given homework. We were asked to bring something we needed to get rid of, and I had a lot to get rid of. But the one thing that I had to really get rid of was this concept, this idea that I was Henry's mother (that's his name, Henry), because I wasn't.

There's a big difference between the person that gives birth to you and the people that raise you. I knew that from my own life; it just took me a long time to learn that lesson for myself.

After the shedding and meditation, we went to Portland. It was the first time I brought friends with me. It was the first time I didn't second-guess myself every time I spoke to them. It was the first time I didn't stop myself from touching him. I realized this meditation hadn't changed me as a human being, it had just changed my perception. It had changed how I saw them, because I realized these people—these wonderful people who did such an amazing job raising this brilliant kid—had given me the only blueprint I had. They had given me the foundation for what a family should be, what love was and loyalty, and what a mother could be. What two moms could be. I left there, and it was the first time I did not cry all the way till Boston and scream until New Jersey.

The year he was turning ten, I found I was pregnant again, but this time it was so different because I had spent these years trying to build a real family. The people in my life were so excited because this baby was the first in our family of friends. I was still poor, and I still hadn't completed my formal education, but I wasn't alone. I had this wonderful family of friends; and they called, and they wrote, and they put ads on craigslist, drove all over the tri-state area, and filled a storage space with so many baby things that I had to give away two of many things.

When my daughter was born, this birth was also well attended. So many people were there that they had to turn people away at the maternity ward. Everything was so different.

Henry carries a picture of Asha in his wallet. (I named her Asha; it means "hope" in Sanskrit.) My son will be fourteen this year, and in April, when Asha turned four, he came with his mother, Gretchen, to our house and shared our home and stayed with our family and all the people that chose to be there, and I watched him hold her and play with her. I saw them as part of my family for the first time, really understanding that they were part of me too. I watched this beautiful, brilliant, strong boy carry his beautiful, brilliant little sister and realized that he had become a part of the net that would hold her up.

Carly Johnstone is a work in progress, please excuse the mess.

Shot Through the Heart

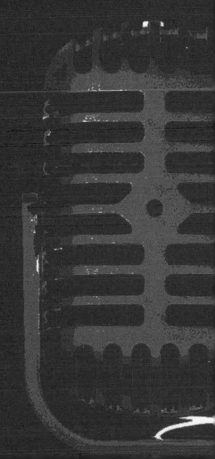

War

I first went to war when I was thirty-one. I grew up in a wealthy suburb. I spent my twenties writing short stories and trying to wait tables. And I got to thirty, and I guess the best way to say it is I didn't feel like I was a man. And I thought war would be exciting and intense, and that it would transform me in some way.

So I got a backpack, and I put a sleeping bag in it and some notebooks and pens and a few thousand dollars, and I went to Bosnia during the civil war, to Sarajevo, to try to learn to be a war reporter.

And war was all those things that I thought it would be. The thing about war is it does not disappoint, but it's also way more than you bargained for.

For example, this: the first time I saw a dead body, it wasn't a fighter. Most of the people who die in wars are civilians. It was in Kosovo during the civil war. It was a girl, sixteen, seventeen years old. And I always imagined that she was probably really beautiful. She'd been taken by Serb paramilitary forces, and they took her up to a field above a town called Suhareka. And they did whatever they did to her, and then they cut her throat.

And when I saw her, it was a couple weeks later. It was summer. It was hot. And the only way you could tell she was a girl, or really even human, was that you could still see the red fingernail polish on her nails. That girl stayed with me for a while. She was more than I'd bargained for.

I remember the first time I prepared myself to die. I was in Sierra Leone during the civil war. And I'd been out at the front lines, and it was getting pretty bad out there, and I was trying to get back to Freetown. I got in a jeep with a few Sierra Leonean soldiers who really weren't good for much, and with a couple of journalists, and we were driving down this empty road, back towards Freetown, and these rebels stepped out of the jungle in front of us, with their guns leveled at us.

We came to a stop, and we just stared straight ahead while they argued about whether to kill us.

And I tried to get ready. I was hollow. I was numb. And I didn't have any grand thoughts. I just kept thinking, *I hope this doesn't hurt.* That's all I thought. And the guns were pointed at us. I saw the little black hole that the bullet comes out of. At one point a guy racked his gun and started to shoot, and another guy grabbed the barrel and jerked it up. It was like that for fifteen minutes, while all these little black holes were staring at us. And I thought, *There's eternity inside those holes. They're so small— the thickness of a pencil—and eternity's in there.* And I couldn't bring myself to look at the rebels.

For some reason, they didn't kill us, and we drove back to Freetown.

And I kept going back for more. I kept going to more wars. I felt like there was something I needed to understand about war that I didn't understand yet, and I kept looking for it. I kept going back.

I remember the first time I froze in combat. You know, you go to war, you think you're gonna be brave. If you don't think that, you probably don't go to war. And sometimes you are brave, but then other times you're not. And so this time I was out at a small American outpost in Afghanistan, an outpost called Restrepo, a twenty-man position up on this ridge. They were getting attacked all the time.

But this day it was really quiet. Hot. Nothing was going on. I was leaning against some sandbags and some dirt flew into the side of my face. And what you have to understand about bullets is that they go much faster than the speed of sound, so if someone shoots at you from four hundred meters, five hundred meters, the first thing that happens is you ask yourself, *Am I getting shot at?* Because the sound the bullets make when they go past you is pretty subtle. And then the gunfire arrives a moment later. *Yes, I am getting shot at.* And then everything goes crazy.

The bullet hit two inches from the side of my head and kicked dirt into my face. That's what I had felt. What's the angle of deviation at five hundred meters that gives you two inches to the right? You know, what's the math on that angle? You don't even wanna think about it, and then it's all you can think about.

I was paralyzed. Bullets were coming in, hitting the ground, hitting the sandbags, smacking into everything. I was behind some sandbags.

And our gear was right over there, just a few feet away—cameras, bulletproof vests. We're getting attacked from three sides. They're coming up into the wire. It's really bad, and we can't get to our gear. There's too much gunfire. And I'm paralyzed.

THE MOTH

The guy I was working with, Tim Hetherington, a photographer—we were on assignment out there—he finally jumps across that gap. He throws my camera to me, and he throws my bulletproof vest. He grabs his stuff. He's throwing ammo to soldiers because the soldiers are pinned down too. And he gets back, and I have my camera in my hand, and I start shooting; I start working. And then I'm fine. I'm not scared anymore.

Tim was an amazing photographer and obviously very, very brave—a lot braver than me—but he was also really thoughtful about war. I remember at one point he said to me, "You know, war might be the only situation where young men are free to love each other unreservedly, without it being mistaken for something else."

That was Tim. And that's why we were working together. We decided to make a documentary about this little outpost. We were going to call it *Restrepo*, and we were going to spend as much of the deployment as possible at this little spot on this ridge in eastern Afghanistan.

We were going to alternate trips, and I had torn my Achilles on this trip, so I had to go home to kind of heal up, and Tim took the next trip. He was on a weeklong combat operation up in the mountains on foot, a very bad scene; a lot of American soldiers got killed and wounded. At one point the American positions got overrun, and the Taliban dragged off a wounded American soldier at night, in the middle of a firefight. The US forces got him back, but it was bad out there—way worse than anyone back home really knew, you know?

And in the middle of all that, Tim broke his leg. He was at ten thousand feet, up on the Abas Ghar, with a broken leg, and the platoon was moving down the mountain all night long.

And the medic examines his leg and says, "Well, it's broken, and we can't get a medevac, and we have to be off this mountain by dawn, or we're gonna get hammered. Here's two Advil."

And Tim knew that if you're not prepared to walk all night on a broken leg for the sake of thirty men, you shouldn't be out there. And he did it. I don't know how, but he did it. He got down off that mountain.

So we finished up our deployment—that's how we started to think of it, our deployment. And the rest of it was okay. The worst was in the beginning, actually, and then we started making our film, *Restrepo*. And the film did really well.

It started with this scene, and it took me a long time to be able to watch it, actually. I would always close my eyes when it came. It was a scene where I'm riding in a Humvee ('cause I took the next trip after Tim broke his leg). And I'm riding in a Humvee, and all of a sudden everything goes orange and black, and the Humvee gets blown up.

The explosive went off under the engine block, though, instead of under us, so we lived. And that whole rest of the day, I was just on this crazy, jagged high. I mean, there's nothing like not getting killed to crank you up. It's incredible. And that night I just sank. I spiraled down into this black hole.

War is a lot of things. It's incredibly exciting. I hate to put it that way, but I'm not up here to lie to you. It's really exciting. And it's really scary. And it's really intense. And it's really meaningful. But it's also incredibly sad. And sadness is a kind of delicate emotion that's easily trampled by other feelings, and that night I got in touch with the sadness of the whole thing.

Politics aside, just the fact that people are doing this to each other, it crushed me. And that sadness lasted exactly until the next time we got shot at. Then I was back in the game.

But I had the camera rolling when we got blown up in the

Humvee. And that bit of footage, I could not bring myself to watch, because when I tried to watch it, my heart rate went to 180. I just couldn't do it.

But we put that in the beginning of the movie, and the movie came out, and it did really well. And Tim and I were just on this amazing ride, you know? It was incredible.

But the Arab world was in flames now, right? The Arab Spring was just this incredibly important upheaval in the world. And Tim and I were dying to get back to work, to get back out there, you know? We're journalists. We decided to go to Libya to cover the civil war.

At the last minute, I couldn't go, and Tim went on his own. And on April 20 last year, I got the news—through the Internet, on Twitter actually, which is a way I hope I never get bad news again—that my good friend Tim had been killed in the city of Misrata. An 81 mm mortar had come in and hit a group of fighters and journalists and killed and wounded a bunch of 'em. Tim was hit in the groin, and he bled out in the back of a rebel pickup truck, racing for the Misrata hospital.

And I felt nothing. I was hollow again, just like in that jeep in Sierra Leone when I was waiting to see if I was gonna die—completely hollow. I felt bad that I didn't feel bad. I mean, I realized later I was in shock. And you know, the shock spares you for a little while the things you're gonna have to feel later.

In the middle of that awful day I got an e-mail from a Vietnam vet that I'd met in Texas. Tim had met him too. He'd really liked *Restrepo*. He'd been through a lot of bad stuff, and he read my book and Tim's book, and he liked our work. And he sent me an e-mail and said, "Sebastian, I'm so sorry about Tim, but I have to tell you something. It might sound callous, but I've gotta tell you. You guys, with your books and your movie, you came very close to understanding the truth about war, but you didn't get all the way. The core reality of war isn't that you might get killed out there. It's that you're guaranteed to lose your brothers. And in some ways you guys didn't understand the first thing about war. And now, Sebastian, you've lost a brother, and you understand everything there is to know about it." And he was right. It wasn't callous. It's the truth. The truth can't be callous. And now I know the truth about war, and I'm never going back again.

Sebastian Junger is the bestselling author of *War*, *The Perfect Storm*, *A Death in Belmont*, and *Fire*. As a contributing editor to *Vanity Fair* and contributor to ABC News, he has covered major news stories in Liberia, Sierra Leone, and many places around the globe. He won a National Magazine Award and an SAIS Novartis Prize for journalism. His reporting on Afghanistan in 2000 became the subject of the National Geographic documentary *Into the Forbidden Zone*. Junger's time in the Korengal is the subject of the documentary feature film *Restrepo*, which Junger shot and directed with award-winning photographer Tim Hetherington. *Restrepo* won the 2010 Grand Jury Prize at the Sundance Film Festival. After Hetherington's death in Libya in 2011, Junger made a documentary about him called *Which Way Is the Front Line From Here?*

We'll Have to Stop Now

So my therapist, Phyllis, is in her chair on the other side of the coffee table, and she's got her shoes off in front of the Saul Steinberg lithograph. Her legs are tucked up underneath her in these kind of billowy, white summery pants, and she's looking at me funny. And I'm on the couch looking back at her funny, because in the middle of the coffee table between a box of tissues and the African primitive carving is a bottle of Maker's Mark bourbon. She's my therapist; she knows what I drink. And next to that is a bottle of Glenfiddich scotch. She's my therapist; I have no idea what she drinks, but I assume this is for her. And she's wearing a little more makeup than usual, you know, enough so that I can notice. And three days ago, the last time I saw her, her hair was brown, and now it's red. She's been messing with it for a while. First kind of light brown combed back and then dark brown with bangs, and every time she shows up with a new do she asks me how the change in her makes me feel, like maybe she's doing it for me. So I spend about twenty dollars' worth of therapy telling her how great she looks, because just in case she is flirting I want her to know that I know.

So now she's a redhead, and there are these bottles and glasses with ice there. And she wants to have a drink with me, right now, in the middle of a session, right here in her office, which is also her living room, which means there is also a bedroom here someplace. I am on the verge of a massive therapeutic breakthrough. After three years sitting here listening to her say "And how do you feel about that?" while I'm trying for one guilt-free second to forget my girlfriend back at home and imagine Phyllis getting up and tiptoeing across the room to squeeze in next to me and ask me, "And how do you feel about this?"—now with the whiskey bottles I feel like it's my move, although I'm not much of a mover. I'm more the shaker type. That's why I'm here. And I have a girlfriend, that's also why I'm here. At the time I was a fifty-three-year-old man who after sixteen years was still calling his girlfriend his girlfriend.

One day my girlfriend and I were home when we had only been living together for about thirteen years. And we're watching TV, and we're talking about our future, when she stops and laughs and says, "Forget it. You'll get married when hell freezes over."

And I stop for a second and think, and say, "I never agreed to that."

And she laughs again because, you know, it's a funny line, and she has a great sense of humor. But after that the conversation kind of fades away and stops. Because it's time to talk, which for me means it's time to talk to a mental health professional, which is when I find Phyllis.

Phyllis is probably about fifty, like I am, because she remembers and forgets a lot of the same things that I do. But she looks a lot younger, and she's tiny and kind of pretty. So she's cute enough to inspire my fantasies and old enough so I don't have to feel like a midlife-crisis cliché. It's the best of both worlds, really. But the attraction isn't really a physical thing. I just think we make kind of a nice couple. Unlike every other therapist whose spirit I've broken, Phyllis always looks happy to see me, and also unlike those others, she has human reactions. She's appalled when I say something appalling, like the time I was in the men's room and a moth flew out of my pants, right out through the fly like it was an empty old purse. And when I say something funny, like the time the moth flew out of my pants, she laughs just like my girlfriend. And because we haven't been living together for sixteen years, she always at least pretends to be listening, and you can't expect that from anyone. So I'm kind of in love with her, which is okay because you're supposed to fall in love with your therapist. And I swore to myself and to my girlfriend that I was gonna do this right this time.

So she started changing her hair, that was the first thing I noticed, and shortly after the hair thing I noticed that she started losing the little midriff belly bulge that she had that you could only see when she wore certain pants. It was like she was working out maybe. Then a little while after that I stopped bumping into her other patients as I was walking in and out of the office. I wasn't avoiding eye contact with Mr. Handsome with a Chiclet-sized cell phone anymore, and that was okay with me. I didn't think he belonged in therapy anyway. After a while it was just Phyllis and the Saul Steinberg lithograph and the African carvings and the shark's teeth and the rain-forest white noise machine. And me. And her place was like my place, like our place, and now she wants to pour cocktails like we're a couple and we just got home from work and have to unwind before dinner.

And she asks if I want a drink, and I say sure, you know, if you're having one. And she says, "I know the whole drink thing is totally unprofessional, but I've been struggling with a way to bring this up." And I know what's coming. I know it's gonna be big, and suddenly I am terrified.

It's like when I took a few flying lessons. I was really into the whole idea of it—the green headphones and the logbook and the flight bag and the shrink-wrapped set of instruction manuals. But I always kind of hoped the lesson would be canceled because of bad weather. You know, give me a license, but keep that plane away from me. So now I am kind of nervous about how she's going to crack open this whole thing that is going on between us.

So I sit back and let her start. She pours the drinks, she looks at me for a while, and she says, "I've been sick. I am in the middle of a course of chemotherapy right now. You must have noticed me losing weight."

And I can't say anything. I am frozen. I am shocked. I am scared, and I'm whatever a bigger word for sad is. And I'm ashamed about what I was expecting to happen, and I can't help it, but I'm disappointed and that makes me ashamed again. And she says she's not saying that we have to stop our work right now, she doesn't want to. Maybe it's selfish, but some work is good for her because it helps her forget and stay centered. But even though the treatment's pretty successful now, things could change anytime without much warning, and I'm the one who has to decide what to do, to stay or go.

I look at her, trying to figure out what to say, still tongue-tied. She says it's up to me, and she hands me a list of other therapists in case I decide that she can't help me anymore.

I say, "When have you ever helped me before?" And she

laughs, and it's great because she gets one of those human looks again. I can't believe how much I would miss her if I left. And she looks happy about it when I say, "I'm not going anywhere."

She looks at me again for a second and says, "You're the only client I'm seeing right now." And my heart explodes.

She says, "Well, you and one other person, on and off."

I ask if it's the handsome guy with the cell phone. She says that's none of my business, but no. And then she looks at the clock, and she says, "We'll have to stop now," like it's any other session. But I'm not ready to stop; I'm just beginning to think of things to say. I ask her if she has anybody to talk to. And she looks at me funny and says, "Like do you mean a therapist?" and I feel it's the stupidest question in the world. She says, "I'm fine, you know I have plenty of friends and family." And I get this quick flash of her real life.

When she gets up to show me to the door, for the first time I see how really thin she's gotten. Her pants are hanging from thin hips in these loose folds so that her legs barely touch the material when she walks. When I get to the door I hug her. I've never done that before, but she doesn't act surprised, and she doesn't let go before I do. And it feels the way I imagine it would feel hugging a duckling—small fragile bones under a soft coat. But her hair doesn't feel soft, it feels coarse and artificial, because it is. It's a wig—they all were.

Then she kisses me on the cheek, and she says, "I'm sorry this has all been so weird."

And I tell her, "I'd sit through anything for a kiss." And I wonder if she kissed the other guy.

So we go on, every Monday and Thursday. Every once in a while her hair changes, but I stop telling her how nice it looks, because I don't want her to notice that I'm even looking at her at all, because she'll think I'm looking for changes, because I am. And after a while I stop asking her how she feels because I just want her to feel like nothing has changed. So she sits there, being dissolved from the inside by chemicals, and I talk about how my girlfriend left the dishes for me to do again. Sometimes we quit early because she's tired.

Then she leaves a message to cancel an appointment. And I call back, but I get her voicemail. I keep calling back for a couple of days, until I get a phone call from this man with a European accent, and he says his name is Morton. He's Phyllis's husband. I find out she is married, and without any kind of preamble, he says she died the night before.

And I knew it was coming, but it feels exactly like it felt when I was five and Dad said that he was leaving. And I tell him how unbelievably sorry I am for his loss and how much I'll miss her, and he just grunts. I can tell that he is sick of hearing how much strangers are gonna miss his wife.

But I don't feel like a stranger. I knew her, she knew me, every Monday and Thursday. And I'm sorry now that I stopped asking how she felt. I wonder if she thought I just didn't care, or maybe she enjoyed the escape from reality twice a week the way I did. And I'm sorry I stopped telling her she looked nice. Morton tells me that she left a list of people that she wanted notified about the service, and I'm on it, and that's why he called. The next day my girlfriend is ready to go to Riverside Memorial with me, but I tell her, "Go to work instead, I'm fine." Because I just want to go and be alone with Phyllis one last time.

And I get there, and for about forty-five minutes—like the length of a therapy session—people get up one after another and talk about her. I finally find out little bits about her life now that she's gone. She married Morton three years ago, when she was fifty-two, right around the time I started seeing her. He was the love of her life. It was her first marriage. Almost every Friday they went to the theater together. Everybody who goes up there and talks about him calls him Morty, not Morton, because they're all friends and family. He's sitting in the first row sobbing through the whole thing, devastated. And there's an empty seat next to him. And I think that if this were a theater and last week even, that's where she'd be sitting.

Then this guy walks up to the front with a guitar, and he's about thirty-five, nervous-looking. And he says he's grateful for the opportunity to be here. That he's not a friend or family, he just knew Phyllis as one of her patients, and he just saw her a few days ago. It's the guy. It's the other patient. And I wonder which one of us saw her last. He says he's gonna play a song that he wrote himself, and I'm jealous. I play guitar, I write songs. And he kind of apologizes and says he's not very good, and he starts. And he's not very good. And I'm less jealous, and I'm kind of embarrassed for him. And a couple of lines into it I realize, along with everyone else, the song isn't even about Phyllis, it's about this guy's wife, who's apparently sitting in the back of the room because he's kind of singing over everyone's head. My song would have been about Phyllis. He keeps playing and singing as people are shuffling and whispering all around them, *What's going on? What's up with this guy?* But he keeps going, and gradually the whispering subsides, everyone gets quiet. And by the time the guy is done, everyone is either crying or smiling to themselves, and I'm jealous again. And he says he had to come to say thank you to Phyllis, that she was the reason he and his wife were here together.

I told my girlfriend to go to work, because I didn't want my real life and my imaginary life mixing up in the same room. I mean this kind of nervous, earnest guy saw her to work out his life, whatever problems he had. I saw her to escape from my life, skip out on it. I saw her for almost three years to work on a fantasy with someone that I loved because she was so real.

I squandered her.

The list of therapists that Phyllis gave me on the day she told me she was sick had six names on it. They were all men. And I thought back then, with my last shred of fantasy, maybe she couldn't imagine me seeing another woman. But now I know that she knew, especially with her life getting realer and shorter—enough make-believe. And I want to tell her that I can see that, and we can work on that now.

But I can't because it's too late, because our time is up, and we have to stop now.

Andy Christie is creative director of Slim Films, a NYC-based animation and illustration studio. His writing has appeared in *The New York Times* and in the Thomas Beller anthology *Lost and Found: Stories from New York*. His autobiographical stories have been heard on *The Moth Radio Hour* and WFUV's *Cityscape*. He is also creator and host of a live storytelling series, *The Liar Show* (www.TheLiarShow.com).

Her Way

Many years ago, I ruined a beautiful friendship, and it was over a song, which sounds like a strange thing to ruin a friendship over. And what makes it even stranger is that the song was sung with the utmost love and affection.

My friend's name was Craig, and I met him at college. We both went to a place called Trinity at the University of Toronto, and it's this weird little place. We would wear long black academic gowns, and jackets and ties to all meals, and we would say Latin grace before we ate. We didn't really have jocks because we weren't large enough, and we didn't really have a party culture because we were too nerdy for that.

All we really ever did was sit around and make fun of each other. Which I realize all students do, but we did this to an extraordinary extent, and the person who was best at that game of making fun of everyone was my friend Craig.

Craig was this tall, incredibly handsome guy, and he had this extraordinary charisma. Women flocked to him. He was just this sort of legend with the ladies. He had this sense of humor that was something that I had never encountered before in my life. And he really kind of led us like the Pied Piper.

At one point he decreed that everyone should have a nickname, and not just a casual nickname, but a serious nickname that had been considered and thought about. So, for example, there was a woman named Felicity Smith who was this busybody. She ran everything, and she was always in people's business. And we thought long and hard about what her nickname should be, until Craig finally said, "Falickity Split."

And there was a guy named Kai Carmody who was this incredibly serious, studious guy, and we wanted to have a nickname for him, but it was very difficult because he was so boring. We thought about it and thought about it, and finally Craig said, "High Comedy."

Now, that makes it sound like Craig was all sort of sweetness and light, but he actually wasn't. There was a kind of a mean streak in him—he had an instinct for the jugular. He really could expose and identify someone's weakness, but it didn't matter because there was something about his sense of humor that made it possible for him to pull that off. For example, there was a guy who was this brilliant, incredibly good-looking person, who everyone loved—he was just a kind of winner. And he did all kinds of wonderful things on campus. And he had one very small weakness, which was that he wasn't nearly as successful with women as you would have thought. And Craig decreed that he should have a nickname, and we couldn't think of one. This guy was so perfect. And finally Craig came up with one. The guy's name was Saul Pinkston, and Craig said, "Small Dinkston."

But nicknames were just part of it. Craig's real gift was songs. He had this ability to, almost on the fly, make up songs about people, and he would sing them at the most inopportune moments—it was this gift that I'd never seen before in anyone.

I remember once there was a guy at college called Phil Walk. And Phil was this big, schlubby guy. He always dressed really bad, and his hair was always sticking out in every direction. He was always charging around. And one time we were sitting in the dining hall—we would sit around Craig in the dining hall for hours after every meal—and Phil Walk charges in, and Craig just starts singing the Phil Walk song. We'd never heard it before, and we think he made it up right in the moment, but it was to the tune of "Feelin' Groovy" by Simon and Garfunkel:

[*singing*]

> *Slow down, you hulking mass.*
> *Your jeans are ripped, we can see your ass!*

And there was a whole long verse after that and the chorus. I just remember the chorus:

[*singing*]

> *I'm Phil Walk, I'm big and goofy!*
> *Do do do do do do do do do, big and goofy.*

I realize, in retrospect, that I was in love with Craig in that way that you are when you're eighteen and you meet someone who's just more brilliant and whose light shines brighter than yours. And all I wanted to do was to be as funny as him, and to make him laugh, and to bring him jokes and songs and see if I could seize his interest. And, you know, I was never as good as

him, but it never seemed to matter because there was this quality of generosity about him; he really wanted everyone around
him to be as funny as he was.

It was even an honor to be made fun of by Craig, because he
did it with such panache and such joy. And I can remember the
time that I thought that for the rest of my life, whenever I had
some funny thought or came up with some funny song, I would
just call up Craig and sing it to him and make him laugh, and
that was going to be a part of who I was for as long as I lived.

But then something happened that changed everything,
and that is that Craig met a woman named Leigh, and they decided to get married. Craig met Leigh at graduate school. And
they were like night and day. Craig was from a small town called
Barrie in northern Ontario, from a very modest background.
And Leigh was from Phoenix, and she was really wealthy; her
father was some hotshot Republican defense contractor. And
Craig was kind of an indifferent student—he was still working
away on his Ph.D. because he spent so much time with people.
Whereas she had gotten her Ph.D. already—she had gotten it
in two years, and she was off. And more than that, she was incredibly dominating. I mean, we thought Craig had a powerful
personality, but she put him to shame. She would finish his sentences. She would pay for everything. She would boss him
around.

Worst of all, she didn't have a sense of humor at all. She had
none of Craig's wonderful, whimsical take on the world. She
was the anti-Craig in many ways.

I realize now, looking back with the perspective of history,
that I hated her. I really did. Not just for the fact that she had
taken Craig away, but because she had changed him—she had
changed who he was and what he meant to me.

But at the time I didn't realize that at all. None of us did. All we knew was that this beloved figure in our life was getting married, and what kind of gift do you give to someone like that, the ultimate songster? Well, you give him the gift of a song, right? Not just any song, but the best possible song you can come up with. And that was where the trouble started.

The wedding was in Phoenix, which is where her family was from, and her parents were called Dick and Celeste. They looked like they had fallen asleep under a heat lamp. They were uptight "Republican country club" kind of people. And the wedding was this extraordinarily elaborate affair. There must have been seven different events, and we drove up and down the interstate in these air-conditioned vans with chauffeur drivers.

And I remember the rehearsal dinner was at this Western-style steakhouse, and there were big plates of glistening steaks; it was just obscene. And we had planned our song for the wedding, and we had decided that at the rehearsal we would just do a little teaser. And so at the end of the evening, my friend John was elected to do the honors, and he reached into his pocket, and he took out a huge folded paper, and he said, "I just want to say a very simple thanks to the people in Craig's life who have made him who he is. I'd like to thank his parents for giving him that joy. I'd like to thank his science teacher in high school for giving him a love of chemistry, and I'd like to thank his Boy Scout leader who gave him such a love of the outdoors. And most of all, I'd like to thank the women in his life who paved the way for this relationship with Leigh."

And he just started to read, "Rachel, Mary, Julie, Lauren . . ."

And then he unfolded the paper, and it reached all the way to the floor. And he just started to read one name after another, and we of course were collapsed with laughter. We thought this was the funniest thing of all time. But I happened to look across the table at Leigh, and there was this mixture of loathing and contempt and pure rage on her face. And I had this feeling like, *Oh my God!*

And when we went back to the hotel, I said to my friends, "You know, maybe we can't do this song. I don't think Leigh's going to take it well."

And for a moment we were going to shelve everything, and I wished to God that we had, but we didn't because I think, in some ways, we could not wrap our minds around the fact that our friend Craig had grown up and moved on. In our minds, we were still sitting around the dining room table at college with him singing songs.

The wedding was the next day, and it was at some extravagant resort off in the desert outside of Phoenix, and every defense contractor in the state of Arizona was there, and they all had wives with the hair and the bosoms out to here. And there were big pitchers of martinis on every table, and all kinds of backslapping and admiring references to Ronald Reagan, and long speeches.

And finally it was our turn, and we were really nervous because we had been preparing this gift for so long, and it meant so much to us that this was what we would give Craig on the greatest day of his life.

And so the three of us walked to the front of the room, and we turned to the band, and we said, "Do you know Frank Sinatra's 'My Way'?"

And they said, "Of course."

We said, "Well, our song will be sung to that."

And we started to sing.

[*singing*]

And now, the time has come for us to toast the boy from
   Barrie.
He lived a life that's true and swore that he would never
   marry.
But then, he met a girl who set him straight he couldn't
   run away.
So Craig, he tied the knot.
He did it his way.

And after we finish the first verse, I look over at Leigh, and she has that same look on her face that she had before, and I can tell she knows what's coming. She knows enough about Craig, and, more importantly, about *us*, to know that this will not end well. And were I a savvier or a smarter person, I would have just cut it off then. But I couldn't. Because we were in mid-song. [*singing*]

Girlfriends he's had a few, in fact a lot, the list is endless.
But Leigh is a woman that's true. She set him straight and
   now he's friendless.
He met her mom and dad, who planned his wedding along
   the freeway.
So Craig, he tied the knot.
He did it their way.

And then I look across at Leigh, and I see that she's standing up, and then she grabs Craig by the hand, and she pulls him up, and I realize to my horror that they're leaving their own wedding reception.

And as they walk towards the door, he looks back at me.

And the look in his eyes is a mixture of pain and confusion

and betrayal. It's one of the most painful moments of my life. And it's also the last time I ever laid eyes on Craig.

But what are we going to do? We're only halfway through the song. We haven't even gotten to the bridge. All of our best material is still ahead of us. So we keep singing to this random group of defense contractors in the middle of Arizona.

[*singing*]

> *What is this man? What has he got? A shelf of bricks; a*
> *squeaky cot.*
> *She pays the bills. He sits and rots. She has her doctorate,*
> *and he has not.*
> *He's on a leash. He's made his peace.*
> *He'll do it herrrrrrrr wayyyyyyyy!*

Malcolm Gladwell has been a staff writer with *The New Yorker* magazine since 1996. His 1999 profile of Ron Popeil won a National Magazine Award, and in 2005 he was named one of *Time*'s 100 Most Influential People. He is the author of three books, *The Tipping Point: How Little Things Make a Big Difference* (2000), *Blink: The Power of Thinking Without Thinking* (2005), and *Outliers: The Story of Success* (2008), all of which were number one *New York Times* bestsellers. His latest book, *David and Goliath*, will be published in October 2013. From 1987 to 1996, he was a reporter with *The Washington Post*, where he covered business and science and then served as the newspaper's New York City bureau chief. He graduated from the University of Toronto, Trinity College, with a degree in history. He was born in England, grew up in rural Ontario, and now lives in New York City.

CYNTHIA RIGGS

The Case of the Curious Codes

I was born on Martha's Vineyard, and I come from a long line of Vineyarders.

I spent many years off-island, working as a boat captain, and then I returned to the Vineyard and came to live in West Tisbury with my mother—Dionis Coffin Riggs, a poet. She and I opened a bed-and-breakfast catering to poets and writers.

After her death when she was almost ninety-nine, I was kind of at loose ends, and a bed-and-breakfast guest suggested that I go back to school and get a degree in creative writing. So I filled out an application form, and they accepted me.

Somebody told me I ought to write murder mysteries. Two years later, when I was seventy, my first murder mystery was published by St. Martin's Press. I've now had ten published, and the eleventh is on Kindle, and I'm working on the twelfth right now.

Well, about six months ago, a mystery came into my life that was totally unexpected. I had thought about a guy that I'd met many years before. His name just sorta popped into my mind, and so I looked him up on Google, and I couldn't find him, so I sorta forgot about it. Well, two weeks later, I got a package from him.

Now, it included his name, and when I'd Googled it, I'd spelled it wrong. The return address was a latitude and a longitude. I opened the package, and inside was an archival envelope that had a whole bunch of old, dried-up, yellowed paper towels in it. The paper towels were all covered with scrawled-out cryptograms. Also in this package there was a little note, with a more modern cryptogram.

Well, I had no idea what this was all about, so I looked at some of the messages on these paper towels, and it all came back to me.

When I was eighteen years old, I was a marine geology major at a college in Ohio—of course. My college managed to find me a college job lasting for four months in San Diego, working for Scripps Institution of Oceanography sorting plankton at a research project. Now, I was just thrilled. I'd never been out West before. I was working in a real laboratory. I was eighteen. Most eighteen-year-olds are clueless; I was particularly clueless.

My coworkers were a bunch of guys who had been working sorting plankton for much too long. They were bored, and they were rather bright, so they came up with some wonderful practical jokes, like nailing my lab drawers shut. And I had no idea how to handle this, all these little practical jokes that were played, or talking in codes that I didn't understand. But there was one guy in the lab. He was an elderly man—he was twenty-eight. He started defending me against my tormenters. My dad had been in the army, and he'd introduced me to cryptograms. I just loved the idea of these secret messages, so I wrote secret messages, as cryptograms, to Howie, on these paper towels.

Now he'd kept them for sixty-two years.

Well, I have a group of young women in my Wednesday writers' group, and I said to them, "What do you think of all this?" They all said, "You've got to get in touch with this guy. You just have to. This is wonderful."

And so I thought about it, and I thought, *Well, how am I gonna get in touch with him?* This was latitude and longitude. So I Googled it. I found . . . there was sort of a circle right around Baja California. Now, I knew that Howie had a dental degree, so that was kind of a clue. I figured, okay, there was a golf resort somewhere within that latitude and longitude, so I called this golf resort on their toll-free number, and I said, "Is there a Dr. A. registered there?" No, there wasn't.

Then I figured, okay, that circle could include the coast of Baja California. So I thought, *Aha! He's on a cruise ship.* So I found a cruise ship tracking site on Google. This is all true. But there were no cruise ships in the area at that time. So then I was sure I had it—he had a private yacht. He was a retired dentist after all. I figured the captain had come up to Dr. A. and said, "Dr. A., sir, this is your latitude and longitude." But that was kind of a dead end.

By the way, I'm sort of diverting, but at the time I happened to be writing a book called *Blood Root*, which was based on a murder in a dentist's office.

The next thing I figured, okay, I'll go to the California Dental Association. And I found him! I found him, and I found an address. Now, he'd been a public health dentist for one of the counties in California, which sorta shot the idea of the yacht.

So I went back to my Wednesday writers, and I said, "Now what?"

And they said, "You've got to get in touch with this guy. You just have to." Well, I figured I could write him maybe sort of a noncommittal note. So I did that. I said, "Well, I just got that packet that you sent, and I've decoded the message." And that was it.

In the meantime the Wednesday writers, representatives of which are here tonight, had formed sort of a cheering section, and it was going something like this: "This is every woman's fantasy. This man has spent a lifetime loving you and searching for you."

Now, you need to know a little something about my background. I wasn't totally off on men, but I was a little uncomfortable because I'd been married for twenty-five years to a very brilliant but a very abusive husband. We'd been divorced for thirty-five years, and he'd stalked me for twenty of them. So I was not comfortable opening any doors to any kind of intimacy. And these paper towels were things that could lead to intimacy.

Well, I sent this letter off to what might or might not have been his current address, and, by golly, I got a postcard back, and it said, "Nicer than nice to hear from you." So I knew I had the address right.

The next thing I did was to send him a book of poetry. I had a daughter who had died about five years before, and this was a book of her poetry. And he wrote back, and he said, "I had a son who died at the same time your daughter died, about the same age."

As you can imagine, this broke down a lot of barriers in a hurry. If you think of the worst thing that can happen to parents, it is to have a child die. And to have two of us sharing this painful experience . . .

So we started corresponding. And we started finding out about more coincidences. It wasn't just me writing *Blood Root*.

And it wasn't just the kids' deaths. It was also the Manganese nodules.

Since I'm speaking to a group that is near the ocean, probably many of you know what Manganese nodules are, but most people don't. They're knobby little lumps of black/gray-looking mineral deposits that are found only in the deep sea. Few museums have these Manganese nodules, and very, very few individuals have them. Howie happened to have one that came from the Marianas Trench, which is the deepest part of the Pacific Ocean, and he sent it to me.

Well, I just happened to have been on an Antarctic research cruise. I had a small sack full of Manganese nodules. I sent him four. I made sure they were smaller than his.

The next thing he sent me was a CD, a piece of music that his son had composed called "Cactus on Mars." Well, my son-in-law, who's a geophysicist, was evaluating research proposals for Mars.

These coincidences went on and on and on.

Howie found out that I'm an avid gardener, so he sent me seven seed packages. One was hollyhocks—**H** for Howie. And one was catnip—**C** for Cynthia. And in between he had **L**eeks, **O**kra, **V**inca, **E**ggplant, and **S**pinach.

This was a real romance.

By the way, at this time, the young woman in the West Tisbury Post Office got involved. She would say, as she gave me a package, "Another letter from your boyfriend!"

And at this point, the Wednesday writers stepped in again and said, "You have to go see this guy."

I had no intention of going to see him, but you have no idea what these women are like.

So I have a ticket to California on my desk.

I'm going out to see him. But now, here comes a question: when I appear, is he going to have in his mind this eighteen-year-old that he fell in love with? I mean, I'm eighty-one now, and he's ninety.

I asked the Wednesday writers, "Well, what can you do?"

And they said, "Oh, *plenty*."

Howie has actually changed my life. I had been pretty much closed up. But what he did was he gave me some very gentle warmth. He also introduced me to a calm love that I'd never thought of before. And he introduced me to a sweet passion. You'd be surprised at what you can do in letters and codes.

But most of all, the thing that's really affected me, is he gave me back a sense of great self-worth. And with that, I hope you all can find a Howie, or his equivalent.

Cynthia Riggs is the author of eleven books in the Martha's Vineyard mystery series featuring ninety-two-year-old poet Victoria Trumbull. She was born on Martha's Vineyard and is the eighth generation to live in her family homestead, which she runs as a bed-and-breakfast catering to poets, writers, and other creative people. She has a degree in geology from Antioch College and an MFA in creative writing from Vermont College. For twenty years she held a U.S. Coast Guard Masters License for 100-ton vessels. She has five children and thirteen grandchildren. A few months after she told this story, Cynthia flew to California to meet Howie. He proposed within two hours of seeing her. They were married in the spring of 2013.

OPHIRA EISENBERG

The Accident

It was the summer after third grade, and my mom was looking for activities to keep the kids busy. She took me, my brother, my best friend Adrienne, and her brother to the Jewish Community Center to go for a swim and hopefully tire us out.

On the way back, we were driving home, and my mother took a left turn to drop Adrienne off. And at the same time, an eighteen-year-old ran a red light and hit our car.

My brother was in the front seat, and his knees went into the dashboard, and he was unconscious, but he was okay. My mother broke her wrist trying to crank the steering wheel in a last attempt to avoid an accident, and she was conscious. Adrienne and I were little crumpled messes in the backseat, but her younger brother, who was in the hatchback of the Honda Civic—back when you used to do that and think it was okay—actually walked away without a scratch.

I don't remember the accident at all. It's all put together from other people's accounts, and observations, and interpretations. But I do remember the hospital. I remember waking up in intensive care, and my mom and dad talking to some doctors. It seemed like there was quite a kerfuffle going on, because my mother kept going, "It's a step backwards. It's a step backwards."

They wanted to give me an operation, and she was afraid that it was going in the wrong direction, and that we were just putting off the inevitable.

But the next thing I knew, my dad was by my side, and I looked at him. He was always a pillar of strength, you know, a real authority figure. And he had this look in his eyes that I'd never seen before—he looked a little scared.

But then it evaporated into a warm smile, and he said, "Listen, you're gonna go to sleep for a little while, and then when you wake up, I will buy you anything you want. So I want you to think really hard about what you want, and when you wake up, I will buy it for you."

My dad had never said anything like this to me in my entire life. I was the youngest of six. We lived well, but very modestly. The idea that he would buy me anything—I mean, my brain almost exploded.

I went in for this operation, and I woke up. I had a tracheotomy with a metal plate in my neck.

My twenty-year-old sister came to visit me, and we were playing this game where she would pretend to see steak and scrambled eggs going through my feeding tube, and I would pretend to taste them. And I told her that I had this dilemma with the present that I wanted Dad to buy me. It was between a TV and a phone for my room, or the Barbie Dreamhouse.

And my sister said, "Listen, you're gonna have a lot of TVs and phones in your life. You should go for the Barbie Dreamhouse."

My mother was there every day, from the second I woke up,

all through the months when I was in the children's ward. Every second, she was by my side. And when I was well enough to start eating solid food, and I would complain about the hospital food, she brought home-cooked meals to me in Tupperware containers. When I didn't like the hospital gowns and the weird pajamas, she brought me clothes from home, and new clothes, and toys, and games. She was always there.

Everyone kept telling me how strong I was, what a strong, brave girl. And I relished this attention. I *loved* it. It was like I had accomplished something, but I didn't really know what exactly I was doing. I felt like I wasn't doing anything.

Adrienne's mother would visit me a lot too. And I would always ask her, "Why aren't you bringing Adrienne? I want to see Adrienne." But somehow, she would just change the subject, and I would go with it.

But one day I just wouldn't let it go. I kept pushing, "Why won't you bring her to play with me?"

And she and my mother looked at each other, and they said, "We think that you're healthy enough to hear this now, but remember when you described being unconscious? It felt like you were sleeping for a really, really long time? Well Adrienne never woke up."

I heard what they were saying, but I don't think I got it. I don't think my eight-year-old brain could comprehend that. I didn't cry, because I didn't know what that meant. I just knew that I should stop asking for Adrienne.

Time moved on, and soon I was well enough to finally leave the hospital. I couldn't wait to get home to my bedroom and my dog. And I walked in the house after all these months, and there, waiting for me, was the Barbie Dreamhouse. And it was more beautiful and bigger than I'd ever imagined. And my mom said I could set it up in the living room.

I wasn't even *allowed* in the living room.

I loved it so much. I really wished that Adrienne could play with it with me, because she would have loved it too. And, I mean, I played with it *a lot*. I would wake up in the morning before school and play with it at breakfast. I would come home at lunch and play with it. I would play with it after school. Then I would play with it after dinner. And I played with it for years—in some people's opinion, too many. But I loved that Barbie Dreamhouse.

And life, you know, continued to move on. I went back to school, and Adrienne wasn't there. They put me in a different class, with different classmates than I had been with in former years. It wasn't actually like continuing my old life; it was like someone gave me a new life.

And my parents pretended like everything was normal. They didn't treat me special. They didn't pander to me. They didn't tell me I couldn't do certain things. Everything was normal. They both survived World War II, my dad in Israel and my mother in Holland, so they were very versed in moving on.

And all that special attention just evaporated, and I kind of missed it, even resented not having it anymore.

When I was about sixteen years old, my favorite pastime was snooping around the house, because it had occurred to me that adults hide their secret lives from children, and now that I was sixteen, I wanted to know *everything*. We had this beautiful antique dining room buffet that had all these tiny cupboards and drawers with tiny old keys. I used to love playing with the keys when I was a kid, but now I realized I could use them to unlock all of the cupboards.

THE MOTH

So I unlocked one of the drawers and found all this cool stuff. There was an old pocket watch from my grandfather, and my mother's first passport photo, and all these letters.

One letter caught my eye. It was from Adrienne's dad to my mother. It was written about a week after the car accident, just after the funeral.

It had never even occurred to me that there was a funeral, because the whole time I was in operations, and there was all this attention on me. It was the first time I'd ever thought of that.

He wrote that he would never blame my mom for what happened, that day was when God wanted to take Adrienne, and that his family prayed for us and my recovery.

I'd never thought of what my mother went through, because she never showed me her pain or vulnerability for one second. I can't imagine the guilt she felt. The responsibility of taking care of someone else's child, and then it all going horribly wrong.

But she showed nothing but love, and things were going to be just fine while she was braiding my hair, and reading me stories, and driving me to ballet.

And my dad really was a pillar of strength. And him offering me that present was his own genius way of trying to give an eight-year-old a reason to live, something to look forward to.

I wasn't really the strong one; *they* were the strong ones, because they had carefully led me to this place where I could live like an absolutely normal sixteen-year-old kid.

And Adrienne was never gonna be sixteen. It hit me hard, staring at the handwriting of her mourning father. And I couldn't run off to my Barbie Dreamhouse.

And for the first time, I sat down at that dining room table, and I cried.

Ophira Eisenberg is a stand-up comic, writer, and host of NPR's new weekly trivia, puzzle, and game show, *Ask Me Another*. She has appeared on *The Late Late Show with Craig Ferguson*, Comedy Central, and VH-1. She is also a regular host with The Moth, and her debut comedic memoir is *Screw Everyone: Sleeping My Way to Monogamy*. She would like to dedicate this story to the memory of Adrienne, and her dad.

Sing Sing Tattoo

This time of year in Sing Sing prison it gets very hot in the cellblocks. Cellblocks are huge buildings where inmates live. They're like warehouses for human beings. It gets so hot that when inmates come out of their cells to exercise in the yard or the gym, they often aren't wearing shirts and you get to see some surprising things. You see a lot of scars, because a lot of inmates have been stabbed and shot, and you see a lot of tattoos. They're not tattoos as you'd see in the Village so much as jailhouse tattoos, which are cruder, homemade, and often self-inflicted. And they're often kind of, well, they're not artful.

On this one day in July of 1997, an inmate I knew a little bit named Delacruz came out of his cell, and I learned for the first time that he had emblazoned across his chest the word "AS-SASSIN" in three-inch letters, which didn't surprise me. That's not an unusual thing to see in Sing Sing prison. But as he walked away and I followed him, I saw that his entire back was covered in tattooed script. He had a big back—he was in excellent bodybuilding shape, like a lot of inmates in Sing Sing—and every single inch was covered in script, and from what I could see—I just caught a brief glimpse—it was in Spanish.

When he came back in, I said, "Hey, Delacruz, what is that on your back?"

He said, "Oh that? Conover, that's a poem, man."

I said, "A poem? What poem is it?"

He goes, "Nothing. You wouldn't know about it, Conover."

I said, "Try me."

He says, "It's nothing," and goes into his cell.

Delacruz was a guy who interested me a lot because within a week of arriving on the floor where I worked, he was put on disciplinary restriction. He had tried to extort money from another inmate in the commissary, which surprised me, because he seemed like an intelligent and calm and reasonable guy, and this was before we knew each other. I said, "Hey man, what's this about? Nobody gets a ticket so soon."

He said, "Conover"—no, he said "C.O." because he didn't know my name then—so he said, "C.O., you gotta do what you gotta do." C.O. means correction officer or prison guard in the most direct language.

Every day I traveled as a prison guard, about thirty miles north of here, to Ossining. Sing Sing Prison has been there for a hundred and seventy-five years. The passage of inmates from Manhattan to Sing Sing gave rise to the phrase "up the river," which describes the way they got there. They went in boats up the river to Sing Sing. This is also where the phrase "the big house" originated, because the first cellblock in Sing Sing was massive. It held over a thousand inmates. In the forties, two more cellblocks were built: A Block and B Block, which hold 650 and about 500 inmates each. These are two of the biggest cellblocks in the world. They're out of date. Prisons don't work when they're this big. They're chaotic, they're impersonal, and they're harmful in all kinds of ways, but Sing Sing still has them.

I worked in B Block, and that's where Delacruz was. I wanted to get to know this guy. Often the guys on restriction are the ones you get to know because they're stuck in their cells twenty-three hours a day. They're not let out. One day when I saw him sitting there sort of pensively, I said, "Hey, Delacruz, what's on your mind, what are you thinking?"

He said, "Conover," and he looked like he wasn't sure if he should tell me, he said, "I'm not going to lie to you. I'm thinking about my next job."

I thought, *Wow, this is good. He's thinking about the work he's going to get when he gets out.* He says, "No, no. I mean the job I'm gonna pull, man."

I said, "What do you mean?"

He said, "That's the reason I'm here. It's 'cause I didn't think out the last job. Next time it's gonna go right, man. It's all planned. I know it's not a positive thing, but I'm not going to lie to you. That's what I'm doing. I've got plenty of time to do it, and if I do it well enough, I won't be back in here again."

Delacruz was a man in his late twenties. This was his third felony sentence. His first one had been in Virginia, where he'd entered a prison known as "the Wall" at age sixteen, because he'd come from Puerto Rico on a birth certificate that belonged to his dead brother who was two years older. His mother had brought him over on that birth certificate, so the state thought he was eighteen when he was only sixteen. He told me how scared he was that day. It's hard to get inmates to tell you things like this, but he was unusual, and I think he knew that I would respect what he was telling me.

I asked him about a week later, "Delacruz, what's on your back?"

He said, "Oh that poem, C.O.? You never heard of it, man. It was by this Jewish girl during World War II, man. She got trapped by the Nazis in her house. She wrote this book."

I said, "You've got to be kidding me—Anne Frank?"

And he looked at me like, *You know Anne Frank?* Because this would be a very strange thing for an inmate. Most hadn't appreciated an officer who not only read but knew things you read in high school—poetry, important social documents, *The Diary of a Young Girl.*

I said, "Yeah, I know that. I know that diary. So what does the tattoo say?"

He says, "Oh no, never mind, C.O."

A couple of days later I got a day off, and I went home and read it cover to cover, looking for a poem. There's no poem in *Diary of a Young Girl.*

I came back and I said, "Hey Delacruz, there's no poem in there, man. You're confused."

He said, "I'm not confused! You think I'd put a poem on my back, and I don't know what book it comes out of? You think I'd translate it from English to Spanish and have some asshole tattoo it on my back, which took a month, and not know what it came from? It's from Anne Frank."

I went back and checked it again. It's not there.

I go to Delacruz, "Hey, you want to read that book again?"

He goes, "You got it?"

And I said, "Yeah."

It's against the rules for an officer to bring a book to an inmate. It's contraband. It has to go through channels, but I said

I'd bring it to him. He spent the next two days in his cell glued to that book.

On the third day I said, "Well, how was it?"

He goes, "Man, it's the best book I have ever read. I cried the whole way through. It is the best book I ever read."

I said, "So what does it say on your back?"

He said, "Get out of here, Conover. Get lost, man."

And that was that. Delacruz got transferred upstate, and I left the state service. But a couple months later, I wrote him a letter and asked if he remembered me. He said he did.

I wrote him again, and I said, "What did that poem say on your back?"

So he wrote it down in Spanish for me. He transcribed his tattoo. And with renewed vigor I went to the New York Public Library. I figured there was an edition of this book that had the poem. There are like, fifty editions of the book, and I checked out twenty-five of them. No poem. I called up a woman in Woodstock who'd written a one-woman play about Anne Frank; I said, "Do you know of any poems written by Anne Frank?"

She said, "She wrote a couple. They're not in the diary. Most people have never seen them."

I read her what the poem basically said and she said, "No, nothing like that."

I thought, *Shit*. I thought I'd done everything I could. I read the whole book one more time. I got to the last page, I got to the last sentence, and there it was. It was the last sentence of *Diary of a Young Girl*, and this is what it says:

> When everybody starts hovering over me, I get cross, then sad, then finally end up turning my heart inside out, the bad part on the outside and the good part on the inside, and I keep trying to

find a way to become what I'd like to be, and what I could be, if only there were no other people in the world.

And at that moment, I understood a little bit more about Dela-cruz, and I understood a lot more about officers—officers who don't want to talk to inmates, officers who don't want to find out about inmates, officers who, I think, at the end of the day, couldn't bear the sadness of what they'd find.

Ted Conover's *Newjack: Guarding Sing Sing* describes the ten months he spent working undercover as a guard at the famous prison. Finalist for the Pulitzer Prize and winner of the National Book Critics Circle Award, *Newjack* was initially banned by the state and now is censored before inmates are allowed to see it. Conover's writings are frequently based on firsthand participation: He is also the author of *Rolling Nowhere*, an account of riding the rails with modern-day hoboes; *Whiteout: Lost in Aspen; Coyotes*, a classic tale of life among Mexican migrants; and most recently *The Routes of Man: Travels in the Paved World*. He contributes to *The New York Times Magazine* and other publications and is a Distinguished Writer in Residence at New York University.

Carpe Diem

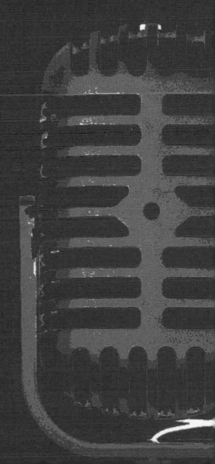

My First Day with the Yankees

I grew up a huge fan of the New York Yankees. When I was very small, I'd go to games maybe once a year with my father and watch Reggie Jackson. When I was a little bit older, we'd watch Dave Winfield. And then when I came into my teens, Don Mattingly, who was my absolute favorite player.

I went to high school in New York, and it was a big moment when I started going to Yankee games by myself. It was at one of these games, sitting in the bleachers in the fall of 1991, that I noticed for the first time this kid in right field wearing a Yankee uniform playing catch with the right fielder.

I'd been to Yankee Stadium so many times, but I had never noticed the batboy before.

And this kid could not play catch for his life. He was throwing the ball over Jesse Barfield's head, or he was one-hopping him. And I was like, *I'm not a great athlete, but I can play catch at least as well as this kid can. I don't understand why he has that job, and I'm sitting in the bleachers.*

So I went home that night, and I tore a page out of the program that listed all the different Yankee executives. I wrote a handwritten letter to everyone from Steinbrenner on down to Stump Merrill, who was the manager at that point, and basically said, "My name is Matt, and I'm 16 years old, and I'm a huge fan of the Yankees. I don't know if you can apply for this batboy position, but if you can, I really would like an application. And I'm so excited to hear from you that if I don't hear from you soon, I'm going to follow up with a phone call."

I sent these off. And after two weeks I hadn't heard anything, so I picked up the phone and called the Yankees switchboard number.

The secretary answered the phone, "Hello. New York Yankees."

I said, "Hi, this is Matt McGough. I sent a letter in a couple weeks ago about applying for a batboy position. Nobody got back to me."

So she's like, "Okay, well, I'll take your name and number down, and I'll have somebody get back to you."

Another week goes by, and I don't hear anything. So I pick up the phone again, and I call and this woman answers the phone, "Hello. New York Yankees."

I say, "Hi. This is Matt. I've sent some letters in about the batboy position, and I called last week and somebody was supposed to call me back."

I thought it was kind of rude that they hadn't.

And she laughed, and asked me, "How old are you?"

I said, "Sixteen." And she laughed some more. I didn't really understand what she was laughing at, but she took down my name and number.

She said, "I'll make sure that somebody gets back to you."

A few days later, sure enough, a letter arrived in the mail on official Yankee letterhead. It invited me to come up to the stadium for an interview with Nick Priore, who was the clubhouse manager.

So I put my jacket and tie on. I didn't even tell any of my friends about this, because it was way, way too weird to explain. I took the 4 train up to the stadium. This was October, and the Yankees weren't playing in the World Series back in '91, so it was very quiet. I walked into the Yankee lobby, and there was a security guard there.

I introduced myself, and I said, "I'm here for the batboy interview."

He picks up the telephone, and he's like, "Nick, some kid's here to see you," and he says to me, "Have a seat."

So I sit down in the pinstripe lobby, and I'm passing about ten minutes waiting for this guy, Nick, to come up for the first job interview of my life. I'm trying to think of the questions that he might ask me. I'm ready to tell him what my favorite subject is in school, why I think the Yankees need a big bat behind Mattingly to win the pennant next year, and what Mickey Mantle's batting average was in 1956.

I'm passing the time, when these double doors burst open, and this guy walks in—obviously Nick, but he doesn't introduce himself. He could be anywhere from forty to eighty years of age. He has this greased-back hair and a stogie between the two teeth left in his mouth and a chaw of tobacco. He's wearing a wife-beater T-shirt, blue Yankees shorts, and white athletic socks pulled up to his knees. He has these black sneakers that are obviously shoe polished.

He looks at me and says, "Are your parents gonna mind you taking the train home late at night?"

So I say, "I take the train to school every day. I think it'll be fine."

And he says, "Well, come back Opening Day."

I go home. I think I have the job. I'm not really sure. Six months later, Opening Day in 1992, I put on my jacket and tie, and I show up at the stadium at 9 A.M. I go back downstairs, through these tunnels, and come to this big steel door—the Yankee Clubhouse.

I walk inside, and it's complete pandemonium.

All these ballplayers that I'd only seen before on TV or across rows and rows of stadium seats are here in the flesh, right in front of me. I had a poster of Don Mattingly above my bed for my whole life, and he's standing on the right. Jimmy Key, the ace of the pitching staff, is over there.

Opening Day at Yankee Stadium is not just a sports event. It's a news event, and it's the beginning of spring in New York City. Mayor Dinkins was in the clubhouse with his entourage, and like, it's *Mayor Dinkins* and *Don Mattingly*, you know? I'm walking around, and I'm kinda lost, and I figure I better go find Nick.

So I walk up to Nick, and I say, "Nick, I'm Matt. We met a couple months ago. This is my first day of work. What do you want me to do?"

And he says, "Stay the f— outta my way."

I kind of shrink back and throw my backpack over on the side, and I'm wandering around in a daze, when I feel a tap on my shoulder. I turn around, and it's Don Mattingly.

He sticks his hand out, and he says, "How's it going? I'm Don Mattingly. Are you gonna be working with us this year?"

I'd never really thought about the experience in those terms. He could've said so many other things that wouldn't have been as cool.

He could've said, "Who are you? Are you the new batboy? Are you gonna be working *for* us this year?"

But he said, "I'm Don Mattingly. Are you gonna be working *with* us this year?"

So I said, "I know who you are, Mr. Mattingly. I'm Matt. I'm the new batboy."

He's like, "Great to meet you, Matt. I have a very big job to ask of you. I've just unpacked all my bats from spring training, and I don't know if it was the altitude of the flight up from Florida or the humidity down there or what, but the game starts in about two hours, and I need you to find me a bat stretcher."

I say, "Okay."

I go and find Nick, but Nick is busy. Probably half a dozen ballplayers are bothering him for batting gloves or AA batteries or this or that.

I walk up to him, and I'm like, "Nick, I need a bat stretcher for Don Mattingly."

Nick lets loose with a stream of expletives that fell on—I swear—completely virgin ears. I'd never heard that type of language in the movies before or anywhere, let alone directed at me.

So I rock back on my heels and go and find Nick's assistant, Rob.

And I say, "I need a bat stretcher for Don Mattingly, and Nick told me to go f— myself, and I don't know what to do."

So Rob goes, "Chill out. I saw Danny Tartabull using one in his locker." Danny Tartabull is the new power-hitting right fielder.

I go to Tartabull's locker, and he's getting dressed in his uniform. I stand off on the side, and he says, "How's it going?"

And I'm like, "Fine. I'm Matt. I'm the new batboy. I need a

bat stretcher for Don Mattingly, and I heard you were just using one."

Tartabull says, "Well, I was using one, but I left it in the manager's office. You should probably go check in there."

I say, "Thanks," and I go into the manager's office. I walk in, and Buck Showalter, the manager, is having a press conference with probably eight or ten reporters. I stand off on the side, and the conversation comes to a standstill basically because there's a sixteen-year-old kid there in his Easter blazer and jacket, standing in the manager's office at Yankee Stadium two hours before first pitch on Opening Day, looking very lost and anxious.

Showalter turns to me, and he's like, "Can I help you?"

And I say, "I'm Matt. I'm the new batboy. I'm really sorry to interrupt, but I need a bat stretcher for Don Mattingly, and Danny Tartabull says that he left it in here."

So Showalter looks down beneath his desk. Then he's like, "Well do you need a right-handed one or a left-handed one?"

This is the first question I heard that day that I could answer with complete confidence, because you couldn't have grown up in New York at that time without knowing that Mattingly was the best left-handed hitter in baseball.

I say, "I need a left-handed bat stretcher."

Showalter says, "Well, I think we maybe have a right-handed one around here, but probably not a left-handed one. You should try down at the Red Sox clubhouse. See if they have one."

So I said, "Okay, thanks. I'm sorry to interrupt." By this point, I'm sprinting down the hallways in the tunnels beneath the stands. I run into the Red Sox clubhouse and find their equipment manager and give him the whole story [*talking very quickly*]: "I'm Matt. I'm the new batboy for the Yankees, and

Danny Tartabull left his right-handed bat stretcher in Buck Showalter's office, but I need a left-handed one, and the game's about to start."

He's like, "Calm down. We don't have one, but we *need* one. Here's twenty bucks. Go up to the sporting goods store on 161st Street and River Avenue and buy two—a left-handed one for Mattingly and a right-handed one for us—and then bring me back the change." He gives me the $20. I put it in my pocket. I run upstairs.

By now, it's an hour before first pitch on Opening Day. Fifty thousand fans are coming down from the subway in the opposite direction that I'm walking. I'm the only person in the world who knows that if I don't come through on this mission, Mattingly's gonna go up there against Roger Clemens and the Red Sox on Opening Day at Yankee Stadium with a toothpick in his hand, basically.

So I'm fighting against the crowd and feeling so much weight on my shoulders. I'm making my way through, and I'm about to cross the threshold of Stan's Sporting Goods, when it dawns on me . . . I've played a lot of baseball in my life, and I've been a big fan for a while, and I don't even know what a bat stretcher looks like.

At that moment it dawns on me for the first time: *Is this a joke? Could this possibly be a joke?*

But I had so much fear, because if I go back, and I tell Don Mattingly, "I'm too smart to fall for your BS bat stretcher story," and I'm wrong, I'm gonna be back in the bleachers before my first game and lose my dream job.

So I take three laps around the stadium, convincing myself, *It's gotta be a joke. It's gotta be. It's gotta be a joke.* Then I walk back in. I go down the stairs. I walk into the clubhouse. Mattingly winks at me from across the clubhouse, a couple of the other ballplayers laugh.

Mattingly goes three for four that day. Yankees win. It was my first day in pinstripes.

I didn't learn until later on that I was the first kid in anyone's memory to have gotten the job without having a connection, without somebody knowing somebody or their dad knowing somebody. And you know, as naïvely intense as I was in chasing that bat stretcher, I was perhaps as intensely naïve to think I could get a job working with the Yankees. But the lesson to me is that with a great deal of persistence and a little bit of common sense, even if the thing you're chasing may not exist, you can sometimes will it into being.

Matthew McGough is the author of *Bat Boy: Coming of Age with the New York Yankees* (Doubleday, 2005). From 2006 to 2010, he was a writer for NBC's *Law & Order*. His next book, about the Stephanie Lazarus cold case and the Los Angeles Police Department, is forthcoming from Times Books. His author website is www.matthewmcgough.com.

Under the Influence

In all honesty I admit I sometimes lie. Occasionally I will include a tiny lie in a story I'm telling if I think it will make the story better. I don't do it to protect the innocent, because I don't know any stories where the people in them are innocent. I don't do it to be shocking either, though I admit to once telling a story where I exaggerated the length of my penis. In my own defense I exaggerated down and not up, and I did it for the laugh.

The story I'm telling you tonight does not have a lie in it, or many laughs for that matter. When I'm done telling you this story, you may think it's nothing but a lie, but I'd ask you to trust me on this.

At the age of nineteen I fell prey to a powerful and deeply corrupting influence. It dogged me for six years, costing me many a friend and in the process bringing my family to ruin. It crippled me to such an extent that I have spent the intervening years recovering from it.

The influence I speak of is Hope.

You should know from the get-go, there was nothing in my childhood to suggest I might find myself on such a wayward path. My parents loved me terribly. They taught me right from wrong. They taught me to be courageous in the face of bullies. They taught me patience and forgiveness. They taught me that love would see me through any misfortune.

My trouble began on Independence Day. Not *the* Independence Day but *my* Independence Day. My Independence Day occurred on Memorial Day 1982. That was the day I told my family I was gay. The act itself—"Mom, Dad, I'm gay"—was relatively unexceptional. In fact, it should have been more exceptional, and I've always wished that it had been. However, subsequent events overshadowed it, and it pales by comparison.

The subsequent events took place in my absence, after the fact, as I was in my car driving back to college to take my final freshman exams. I remember being on the highway and thinking how I had expected my parents to sort of freak out and how, much to my surprise, they had not freaked out. They'd been calm and cool—oddly calm and cool. Still, I was happy as I drove back to college. Meanwhile, subsequent events were busy unfolding back home.

My mother was going through the house where I grew up and was gathering things I had made for her: a jewelry box when I was in 4-H, a painting when I was sixteen, a box containing all the letters I'd written from camp and from college. She was removing photographs from the walls and placing them in piles. She was directing my father, who never dared *not* follow her direction, to take my bed and lamp, my desk and chair, the Smith Corona—my Smith Corona even!—and put them all in the front yard, next to the rock garden, not too close to the maple tree. My clothes, my books, my bookcases, my report cards, my Farrah Fawcett posters, my shoes, three years' worth of *Interview* magazines—the good ones with the Andy Warhol covers—everything.

Then, with my brother and my sister and my grandparents watching, my mother removed a cigarette from a tiny crocheted case she always kept them in, lit the cigarette, and then put the match to the pile of items, there in the front yard, that contained the sole and complete record of my existence in my family.

It burned for seven and a half hours, thanks in part to the addition of some lighter fluid to help get the larger pieces of furniture going. All of it, all of what was me and mine prior to that memorable Memorial Day, up in flames. According to my sister, who years later related these details to me, it was a mighty impressive blaze. In their eagerness to feed the fire, and due to an unexpected wind off the fields around the house, the sugar maple that was older than my great-grandfather caught a spark in its branches and was sacrificed.

They cut off all communication with me. They emptied and closed our joint bank account: poof, there goes college. They barred the door. They stopped talking, stopped answering my letters, stopped taking my calls. They stopped everything with me. They just stopped.

I was completely disbelieving. This didn't make sense. My friends all had stories about telling their parents they were gay, and they all ended the same way; sooner or later everything worked out fine. My friend Michael's parents had reacted harshly at first, but within a year they were inviting his new boyfriend to come home with him for the holidays. Everyone counseled me to have a little patience and have a little hope.

And this is how it starts, slowly, just a little hope, just enough to get you through. But hope is cumulative. A little bit here and a little bit there, builds up in the system until it becomes something toxic: denial. I grant you their reaction had been, yes, extreme, but not the *worst* that could happen. The thing for me to do, I thought, was to be a good son, to make them proud, to somehow earn back their love.

So I got a job, then another, then a third: three shifts, three restaurants, six days a week. That would show them, I thought. But they weren't watching. I wrote them letters, lots of letters, about nothing: It's Tuesday, and it's hot; my new roommate is named Cathy; my friends took me out for my birthday yesterday. They didn't write back.

Living, for me, sort of ground to a halt despite the fact that my life just went on and on. I didn't think about my future. I didn't think about my needs. I didn't think about my sadness. I didn't have to, because I had Hope, every day, whispering in my ear: *Don't give up, don't walk away, you're almost there. Don't grow, don't develop. Don't make any sudden movements or you'll never get them back!*

Six years went by like this without a word from them. Finally, hurt and confused beyond my ability to hold it in, and frankly finding it difficult to maintain the illusion that this was temporary, I decided to make one last attempt to force the issue. I flew home and showed up, unannounced, at my mother's office.

It was an amazing visit.

I asked the receptionist to page my mother and tell her that she had a surprise visitor. Then I stood in the lobby and watched as my mom walked down this long hallway toward me. Halfway down the hall she looked up, she saw me, then recognized who I was, then turned and walked away again. It was an amazing ninety-second visit.

Two and a half weeks later, a black funeral wreath was delivered to me at my office with a note that read, "In memory of our son." Clearly it was time to give up Hope and take up therapy.

I talked to a counselor who asked me why I had "invited this turmoil into my life." I talked to a minister who suggested a Christian Youth Camp. I talked to a lesbian who offered to slash my mother's tires if I'd pay for her flight there. I signed up for scream therapy where I beat pillows with a tennis racket and screamed obscenities—and tore my rotator cuff. Mostly I talked to friends. Mostly the pain persisted.

The sheer weight of it threatened to crush me, or at least that's how it felt. Since it was my constant companion, I spent most of my time turning it over in my mind, fingering it like some sort of psychological worry stone. Over the years it's been eroded by so much handling. All that remains now is a small, hard, nearly weightless pebble, really. Worn away is most of the anger and much of the hurt, yet one question remains: how is it my parents taught me love and loyalty in excess of what they, themselves, possessed?

I have come to believe that it's not possible to understand what they did. Not possible for me, anyway. To understand it would mean there was some justification for it, and I know for certain that there is not.

Still, there is no escaping my parents. This thing they did, this extreme and unfathomable and many-layered thing they did, tore a hole in the middle of my life. I have spent years, and a lot of money, darning that hole while trying to keep the rest of my world from unraveling.

And yet their influence on me is enduring. My parents loved

me, terribly. I have been courageous in the face of bullies. I now know there is such a thing as too much patience, but no such thing as too much forgiveness. And love? Love has seen me through every misfortune.

Jeffery Rudell is a graphic designer and writer. His work has appeared in window displays, magazines, and advertisements. His wide-ranging clients include Tiffany & Company, the New York Botanical Garden, and the Johannesburg Stock Exchange. He is also the author of three books of paper crafts. As a writer, his stories have been featured on NPR's *All Things Considered*, the National Storytelling Tour, and on stages from the New York Public Library in New York to the Newseum in Washington, DC. In 2005 he was a candidate on the television show *The Apprentice: Martha Stewart*. He did not win. He lives in New York City with his partner, Albert. More information at jeffrudell.com.

Yes Means Yes?

So I am twenty-four years old, and I've never had sex. I also don't drink. I don't smoke. I don't do drugs, and I don't drink coffee.

I'm a Mormon.

And I've lived in New York City for six years as a Mormon, and it is hard to be a Mormon here if you don't drink or if you don't do drugs, but it is especially hard to live in New York City if you don't have sex. Because I'm young and I wanna have relationships, and I wanna play too and like, date and stuff. But unfortunately, because I don't have sex, the longest relationship I've ever been able to sustain is four weeks . . . and that was only because for two of them he was out of town.

There's this huge part of me that wants to be considered sexy. But if you're not selling sex, you really shouldn't advertise, and so I don't really ever get to come across as sexy. But one time I was at this vintage boutique, and I came across this 1940s slip. It was dark navy blue—lacy at the top and then silk—and it was the sexiest thing I'd ever seen. I tried it on, and

I looked in the mirror, and I thought, *Oh my gosh! I am sexy! Wow! Who knew I could be sexy?*

And so I bought it. I took it home, and I put it in a drawer, and no guy has ever seen me in it. But occasionally late at night I'll try it on and look in the mirror and think, *I'm sexy!*

And I know that Mormons are notorious for saying no to things, and you would think as a person who says no to a lot of things, I wouldn't be any fun. But while I say no to some things, I try to say yes to everything else, which makes me a really enjoyable person.

I learned the power of saying yes when I was going to NYU. They used to have these career fairs, and I was a drama student, so they wouldn't even set up booths for us. But for all the business school students, they had tons and tons of booths with the coolest trinkets they would give away. And I discovered that if I said yes to all the questions they asked, I could get presents.

They would ask, "Are you a Stern student?"

"Yes."

"Are you interested in a job at Morgan Stanley Dean Witter?"

"Yes."

And if I answered yes enough, I would get a cool triangle highlighter with three different colors. And I know that technically that's lying, and Mormons aren't supposed to lie by any means, but I figure I do everything else right so I can do that.

And then another time I was walking by the Javits Center and someone said, "Are you looking for the paper convention?"

And I immediately was like, "Yes!" I walked in and there were all these booths, and I just said yes to everything people asked me, and I left with a bag full of amazing stationery. I thought, *This is awesome!*

It all led up to the mother of all conventions. I had some

friends in town at the Marriott, and we had breakfast. I glanced under the table and saw a badge, and it said, "Bob Barnett, 7-Eleven Convention."

And I was like, "YES!" So I put the badge on, and we went down to this banquet hall, and they were celebrating seventy-five years of 7-Eleven. So I start mingling with people. I'm making friends, taking free samples. And I end up meeting the woman who's running the whole convention. And I was like, "I go to conventions all the time, and this is so well organized."

And she said, "Did you need tickets for today's events?"

And I said, "Yes." And so she gave me four tickets to Madame Tussauds, four tickets on a bus tour, four tickets to Radio City Music Hall, and then she said, "Will I be seeing you on tonight's cruise?"

And I said, "Yes, but, you know, I sent all that stuff in, and they never mailed me anything back."

And she was like, "What?!" And she ran off and came back with four tickets worth $150 each on a dinner cruise around Manhattan.

So that night I got all dressed up, and me and my three friends went on this cruise. It was fifteen hundred 7-Eleven employees and us. And we start mingling. We dance. We get going in karaoke. And then they serve this four-course meal. And at the end of dinner my friend turns to me, and he says, "Elna, I dare you to make a toast." I don't even drink, so I've never made a toast before, but I've seen movies, so I took a knife, and I was like, *tink-tink-tink* on my glass. Everybody shut up, and I said, "I'd like to make a toast to 7-Eleven for redefining convenience." And they cheered.

And the thing that I love so much about saying yes is that where you start at the beginning of the day and where you end up can be two totally different places based on all the things that you say yes to.

But then there's this other side of my life, which is that I do say no to a lot of things. And with sex, the thing I've learned is it's one thing to say no to having sex with someone you've dated for two weeks. It's actually pretty easy 'cause for me that would be kinda slutty to just say yes after two weeks.

But it's a whole other experience to say no to having sex with someone when you feel like you're in love. I met my yes counterpart a year ago, and his name was Nick. And when I met him, immediately I was like, "You!" And he was like, "You!" And we were like, "YESSSS!"

Our first date was amazing. We were walking by a movie set, and we decided to sneak on and pretend we were extras. And so we were extras in the back of all these scenes, and we ended up in the makeup department. And they asked us what we needed, and at the same time we both said, "Black eyes!" So they gave us these huge black eyes, and we spent the rest of the day going around New York City with black eyes.

We had so much fun. We just kept going on adventures. And we were dating. I didn't tell him I was Mormon, 'cause I thought, *You know what? In addition to being Mormon, I am a lot of other things.* But I really, truthfully didn't wanna tell him I was Mormon because I wanted to get to date him, and I knew that it probably wouldn't work out if he knew I was Mormon.

And so as casually as you can bring that up, a couple of weeks into dating him I said, "Oh, by the way . . . I'm Mormon."

And he was like, "Oh, um . . . I'm an atheist. Can you be with an atheist?"

And I was like, "Yes. Can you be with a Mormon?"

And he said, "Yes." So we kept dating. And we kept going on

adventures, and it was really, really wonderful. But then there were these grander things than we were that kept interfering, as much as we tried to ignore them. And I remember one of the bigger ones was when I found out he didn't believe people had souls.

I was like, "What? What!?!? Doesn't everyone believe that? I mean, religious or not, doesn't *everyone* believe people have souls?"

And he said, "No. I don't believe people have souls." I grabbed him by the shoulders, and I looked him in the eyes, and he was like, "What are you doing?"

I said, "I'm looking at your soul. I can see it. I can hear it. I know it's there."

And he was like, "Really? And what does my soul have to say?"

And I listened really close and said, "It says . . . 'Fuck you. I've been inside you for twenty-nine years, and you've been ignoring me the entire time. Argh!'"

So we kept dating, even though at this point I realized my soul mate didn't actually believe in souls. But I was willing to be okay with that. And then the sex thing came up, and he asked, "Are we gonna have sex?"

And I said, "No." And then he did that thing where like, he started to pull away. And I could tell he was starting to phase me out. It's so interesting because every girl knows when a guy starts to phase her out, even if it's just a coincidence that he didn't pick up his phone. You feel it and you know. And so I started thinking, *Why would he wanna phase me out? It's because I'm Mormon and it's because I won't have sex.*

And then I started thinking, *What if he's the love of my life, and I end up marrying a Mormon guy that I like okay, and I spend the rest of my life regretting this decision? What if he's right, and what if God doesn't exist, and then I'm making this sacrifice for this totally imaginary reason.*

And then I started thinking about sex, and how when you're in love sex is totally different. It almost feels like a natural progression of things. And I thought, *You know, maybe I could have sex.*

And then we went out again, and I sensed it was one of the last times we would get to go out with each other. We were supposed to go to this outdoor exhibit, but it got rained out, so we ended up back at my apartment. It was the middle of the afternoon on a Tuesday. We made grilled cheese sandwiches and put on a movie. I was still wet from the rain, so I said, "I'm just gonna change into something else."

I walked into my bedroom. I was just gonna put a T-shirt on. I opened the drawer, and I saw that blue slip. And I thought, *What if I put that on?* I was like, *Why would you do that? It's the middle of the afternoon on a Tuesday.* I thought, *Well, I own that, and I've never worn it. And what is this sex thing? I can do that. I can say yes to having sex.*

And what I love about saying yes is when you do say yes, everything can change. And so I took that slip out, and I put it on. And I walked into the living room, and he said, "What are you trying to do to me?" And I was like, "Shh." And we started kissing. And we lay down on the couch. And the moment was building, and we were kissing. And I leaned into his ear, and I heard myself say, "You need to pray and find out if God exists."

And he was like, "What?"

So I was like, "Never mind." And we started kissing again. And the moment started to build again. And it was all going well again. And it happened again. I leaned to his ear, and I heard myself say, "How can you know if God exists unless you've prayed?"

And he was like, "WHAT?!?!"

And I thought, *What am I doing?! All I wanna do is have sex right now, and instead I have God Tourette's syndrome!*

And he sat up, and I sat up, and he asked, "What are you trying to say?"

And I said, "Well, it's just the only reason I believe in God is because I prayed, and I asked, and I got an answer. And so all these choices that I make are a result of that feeling."

And he asked, "Do you want me to pray?"

And I said, "Yes."

And he said, "Okay. I can do that."

And I was like, "Really? Okay." And so we said good-bye and he left. And the minute he left, I said a prayer. I said, "God, I know I pray a lot, but can this one count for a whole lot more than the other ones? And you don't even have to listen to anything else I ever say, but if Nick prays, will you answer him?"

And then I called my mom and dad, and I was like, "Can you pray?" And they said they would. And then my parents called my grandparents. And literally there was a Mormon family tree across the United States, praying for me that if he prayed, he would get an answer.

I didn't hear from him for two weeks. When I did, we agreed to meet up. And we met up and sat on a bench, and we were just small talking. And finally I just broke through and asked the question that I really wanted to ask.

I said, "Did you pray?"

And he said, "Yes."

I thought, *Wow*, because he's twenty-nine, and his whole life he's never once tried to pray.

I said, "What happened?" And he told me that he sat in his

room in silence, and that he prayed, and he asked if God existed. And he sat there for a long time, and he listened. And he realized that even if he did hear an answer, it would just be him telling himself that he had heard an answer because he wanted to be with me, and that it wouldn't be real.

And that was it. We broke up. And upset as I was that he didn't get the answer I wanted him to get, I totally understood where he was coming from, because he tried as hard as he possibly could to find God for me, and I tried as hard as I possibly could to have sex for him. But in the heat of the moment, all I could do was bring up God.

You know, my whole life I'd thought that I didn't have sex because I was Mormon, but I realized in that moment that I don't have sex because I don't want to. And sometimes saying no can actually be saying yes.

Elna Baker is a writer and comedic storyteller. She's appeared on *The Moth Radio Hour*, *This American Life*, BBC Radio 4, *All Things Considered*, *WTF with Marc Maron*, *Studio 360*, *The Sound of Young America*, *The Joy Behar Show*, and at the Upright Citizens Brigade Theatre. She's written for *ELLE*, *Glamour*, *Men's Journal*, *O, The Oprah Magazine*, *More*, *Five Dials* literary journal, and xo Jane.com. Her memoir, *The New York Regional Mormon Singles Halloween Dance*, was published by Penguin, earning four stars in *People* and the 2010 AML award for best humor writing. She's also the co-host and co-creator of *The Talent Show*, recently named best variety show by *New York Magazine*. Her upcoming novel, *You Are My Revenge*, co-written with Kevin Townley, will be published by Scholastic in 2014.

One Last
Family Photo

I am sitting on a little wooden visitor stool in room 202 of the Houston Hospice holding my sister Kathy's hand, telling her how much I love her. She is on her back in bed in a nightgown and, compared to the hospital we were just at, not much more. Just an oxygen mask and an IV connected to a drug pump that every ten minutes injects her with Dilaudid, a painkiller so powerful and potentially deadly the hospital wouldn't give it to her.

Evidently Dilaudid's what you get when there's no reason to be afraid of dying anymore—when dying is what you're supposed to do.

And so unlike the hospital, which was full of beeps and monitors and people trying to keep Kathy alive, the hospice is very still and quiet. The only sounds are the hiss from the oxygen and every ten minutes the *zzzt* from the drug pump followed by "Ahh" if Kathy happens to be awake, as she is now, looking *out there* through faraway, Dilaudid eyes. When she turns to me and lifts up her oxygen mask and says, "Do you love me enough to trade places?"

Now, I love Kathy more than anyone I've ever known, apart from my little boys, Julian and Ben, and my wife, Jane—on good days.

So I start crying as I look at Kathy thinking, *Are you nuts? Yeah I'm your brother but come on.*

But I'm ashamed to say that to Kathy, so I say, "Well, would you want to be married to Jane?" (a teetotaling Dr. Jekyll to Kathy's party-animal Mr. Hyde), "and would you want to raise Julian and Ben with her?" (Jane continues to breast-feed the boys over my objections, at six and four years, turning me into Mr. Hyde every time I see it.)

Kathy says, "When you put it like that, I don't think so."

And she starts laughing until she falls asleep, having chosen death over life in my marriage, which I totally understand because I feel that way too a lot of times. But the main thing is, everything's under control.

When we first checked Kathy into the hospice, I had a private meeting with the counselor.

I told her, "I'm gonna need your help. My family does not know how to function as a family. We haven't been in the same room in forty years, since my parents were divorced when I was a little boy. Nobody gets along. Everybody suspects each other of some kind of conspiracy—usually of stealing their money— which is frequently true. They hate Kathy's boyfriend, Roger. Roger hates them. I want Kathy's last days filled with peace and love."

And the counselor said, "That's a very nice thought. That's a very noble thought. But in my experience, people usually die the way they lived. So maybe it's not your job to make things right."

Which I thought was a very good piece of advice, except that my job—leading my life, living in my marriage—is infinitely more complicated and painful than trying to lead my family, all of whom have descended on Houston Hospice to be with Kathy.

My dad, a decorated bomber pilot who has transferred his ferociousness from North Korean bombing runs to the ice cream aisle in his local supermarket and is now so massive his knees can't support his body. My bird-like mom (his first ex-wife) in the brand-new face she gave herself for her seventy-fifth birthday. Her gigantic muumuu-wearing but otherwise identical twin sister in her old face—together looking like this before-and-after advertisement for plastic surgery and liposuction. My big sister Corinne, who runs a makeup shop called Façade (without irony). My older brother Earl, who the last time I saw him was subscribing to *Mafia Magazine* (also without irony). And me, the gray-haired baby brother and family emissary to Kathy's boyfriend, Roger, who the men call "Long Hair," the women call "the moron," and everyone calls "the Aborigine," because he's a long-haired moron from Australia, who as I'm sitting there on the stool suddenly walks into the room and past me to Kathy's bed, grabs her by the shoulders, shakes her awake, and says, "Wake up, rabbit girl! I got the license. We're gonna be married."

Kathy opens her eyes and says, "When?"

He says, "Tonight, at ten." They hug, and she falls back asleep, and he turns to me and says, "Just so there won't be any misunderstanding." Meaning he'll be Kathy's legal next of kin, giving him legal control of the heirloom china and silver in their apartment, which my sister Corinne thinks are hers. And legal control of Kathy's body, which my mom thinks is hers.

And he says, "If Corinne wants to have me arrested"—which she does—"it's gonna be about a lot more than silver. If she doesn't leave me alone, I will kill her. I will step on her head, mate,"—he's Australian—"I am over it." And he walks back out of the room, leaving me feeling once again that things are out of control.

So when Kathy wakes up, I say, "Are you sure you want to marry this guy? I'm not here to judge, I just want you to make sure you know what's going on."

Kathy says, "They may have me on a lot of drugs, but I know what I'm doing. I'm not done partying yet."

I say, "OK, who's invited?" Roger has the medical power of attorney, so he's used that to quarantine everybody else in my family down the hall in a family room.

Kathy says, "I want everybody there. Tell Daddy I want him to give me away," which he has never done, at either of her previous weddings.

He's never even *been* to any family wedding, because as he told me when I invited him to my wedding with Jane, "If your mother's gonna be there, I think I'll pass."

I say, "OK."

She says, "I can't look at you, Hunt." My middle name, Kathy's nickname for me. "It makes me laugh. There are grapes around your head."

And she falls back asleep.

So I get up and go down to the family room and tell my mom, dad, brother, sister, and aunt. "They're getting married."

My dad says, "Can't be, she's unconscious, son."

"Evidently not, Dad. Tonight at ten o'clock. She wants you to give her away."

"How did Long Hair get a marriage license? The preacher!" The fundamentalist minister who's been coming around every night trying to get Kathy's deathbed conversion. "That son of a bitch."

My brother Earl says, "Maybe he's trying to adopt a baby, Dad." So that he could legally inherit Kathy's share of the family trust, which cannot go to a boyfriend. Or a childless husband.

My dad says, "I didn't think of that, son!" proud that his offspring has discovered a conspiracy that he himself has overlooked.

My aunt says, "What adoption agency would let a baby go to a drug addict dying of cancer and a moron? I think it's going to be hilarious when the Creature finds out he's not inheriting a thing."

My mom, her twin sister, says, "He's too stupid to figure that out."

My sister says, "I don't care if you're a hideous moron, you can't help it if you're born stupid and ugly. What matters is what's inside"—she's the president of Façade—"and what's inside, I assure you, is pure evil."

I say finally, "Whatever we may think of Roger, and I'm not crazy about the guy, I think he's marrying Kathy because he loves her, and he wants control. Her ashes mean more to him than they do to us."

My dad says, "He doesn't love her any more than my cat, son. It's all about the money. You put your antennae out just a little bit further, and see what you pick up. Now, how are you and Jane getting along?"

"Fine, Dad, we're getting along fine."

I get up and go outside to the garden. The hospice is in a converted Tudor mansion that used to belong to an oil baron, and I sit on a stone bench next to a meditation fountain by an apple tree and call home.

Jane answers and says, "How are you feeling?"

I say, "Fine, I'm doing fine," because I can't tell Jane how I'm feeling, because that will bring me closer to the marriage, us closer to each other, and I don't want to be closer to the marriage. I want to think about Kathy's marriage, somebody else's intractable personal problem–filled life, which is about to end. And so when I finish telling Jane about the chaos, I am completely numb, like *I'm* on drugs.

That night, after changing into the dark suit I had reluctantly packed in New York thinking I might have to wear it once, I walk into Kathy's room for the wedding. Kathy is in the corner, asleep as usual. So we sit around and wait for Roger and the preacher to arrive. And for Roger's mom, Betty, and her lover BJ—Betty Jane—who have flown here for the wedding and, in my mom's book worse than being lesbians, are late.

"Where are Betty and her rodent?" she says.

My sister Corinne says, "Maybe the black flapping vultures flew home?"

My dad wheels over and says, "Let me tell you something about Long Hair. His mother—she is a *he* wearing a wig."

I say, "I don't know, Dad. She is a little mannish, but—"

"She is not a woman, son. Maybe she's a *hermaphrodite*. At the least she's a major oddball."

I get up and try to get away from him, but he rumbles over and continues. "Your day and your garage have something important in common. They both need to be filled"—my dad frequently speaks in aphorisms, some of which have no apparent connection to observable phenomena—"and it doesn't matter how big you build your garage. You can build a ten-car garage, and one day you'll come home with your eleventh car with no place to put it. It's just how it is."

I walk away from him. I'm trying to feel just what I feel for Kathy.

Roger and the preacher walk into the room followed by Betty and BJ. The preacher wakes Kathy up. Corinne does Kathy's makeup, as only the president of Façade can. Kathy looks beautiful, in a burgundy shawl embroidered around the edges, framing her face to look like a Madonna. Corinne gives her a wedding bouquet.

My dad stands up. The nurse walks in to make sure Kathy's not being coerced. Roger walks over to the corner and takes Kathy's hand, and the preacher opens the Bible and begins [*speaking very quickly*], "Dearlybeloved, wearegatheredhereto jointhismanandthiswomaninholymatrimony"—like an auctioneer. Because he needs to finish before Kathy falls back asleep.

Kathy says, "I do." My dad looks at Roger, and they shake hands.

My mom says, "Congratulations," and gives Roger one of her bony osteoporosis hugs. I pop open the champagne and pour it in the paper cups from the water cooler.

And everybody is drinking a toast to the bride and groom when someone says, "How about a picture of the kids?"

So I walk over to the corner and stand on one side of Kathy's bed, and my brother and sister stand on the other, and we pose for a photograph. We're looking out at a giant poster of the same pose, taken twenty years ago at my sister Corinne's wedding, the only photograph of the four of us together ever taken. Corinne had it enlarged and put on Kathy's wall to remind her of home. So I stand there staring at how we used to look: Kathy in a red dress, full of life; me, just home from college, thrilled, really thrilled to tell my family about my new girlfriend, Jane—posing for the last photograph we'll ever take. My mom and dad looking on, all of us together in a room for the first time I can ever remember, and probably the last, because of Kathy who, in the end, is showing us all how hard it is, but how beautiful it can be, to let go.

James Braly is the author of *Life in a Marital Institution: 20 Years of Monogamy in One Terrifying Memoir*, published in 2013 by St. Martin's Press. The first two-time winner of The Moth Grand-SLAM, a contributor to *This American Life*, and the writer and performer of *The New York Times*' Critics Pick Off Broadway monologue *Life in a Marital Institution: 20 Years of Monogamy in One Terrifying Hour* (much of which was developed at The Moth with years of support from Catherine Burns, Jenifer Hixson, Sarah Austin Jenness, Lea Thau, and the amazing Moth community), James has performed at the Whitney Museum, Symphony Space, and on a fourteen-city national tour presented by Meredith Vieira Productions. His autobiographical stories have been broadcast nationally on NPR, *Marketplace*, and *Selected Shorts*, and his personal essays have been published in *The New York Times* and *Redbook*. James teaches storytelling at Fordham University and is developing a television series based on *Life in a Marital Institution* with Meredith Vieira Productions.

TRISTAN JIMERSON

A Dish Best Served Cold

When I first transferred to a small art school and moved to Minneapolis, everything in my life went horribly wrong. My girlfriend wrecked my car. Said girlfriend became an ex-girlfriend. And the house I was living in was condemned. I was working for minimum wage at a comic book store during the day and going to my night classes at art school.

It was not a high point in my life. The only thing that kept me going was the thought of spring break, just one week back home with my parents and friends and away from this life. I had been saving for six months for this trip, because when you make minimum wage, saving for anything takes a really long time.

I finished my last final at school, and I went home and celebrated my new bachelorhood by ordering a Domino's Pizza, eating it off napkins, and playing video games all night. Two days later I was packed, and I was ready to go home. All I had to do was drop my last paycheck off at the bank.

I went into the bank, and I handed the teller my check. I got the receipt, and I flipped it over, and on the back it said my account balance was negative $536.

And I felt all the life just drain out of me, because I just couldn't catch a break.

And so I asked to see my balance statement, and there they were: two $600 Western Union money transfers, a bunch of random delivery orders, and a $400 charge to a website called InmateCanteen.com. I sat down with the banker, and she saw that the charges were false and went about trying to reverse them.

While she was doing that, I went and sat in the lobby, and I started thinking about how unfair identity theft is, because when somebody steals your identity, they only take the good parts. You know? They don't take the rattrap apartment and the depression and the shitty job.

No. They just take the one thing that I had been looking forward to for the past six months. Because while I'm mulling this over, the banker comes back and she tells me that the bank is gonna give me all my money back, but it's gonna take about a week of processing.

So I go home, and I can't get it out of my head. Because the bank wasn't gonna do anything about this, and the police weren't gonna do anything about this, and so these people who rob you, they don't get caught. Nobody cares enough.

But this identity theft was different, because this person had messed with the most dangerous type of person that exists, which is someone with limited options and a lot of free time.

And so I decided to start my own investigation. I took my bank records, and I started going through them, and I called Western Union, and they were no help. And I went to Inmate Canteen.com, and I called the support number, but it was disconnected.

So all I had were these delivery charges, and I noticed something, which was that they were local. And then it hit me: The last charge that I had made on my own account was the last night of my finals—the night that I ordered that Domino's Pizza. I realized that when I read my credit card number over the phone, the woman at Domino's must've written it down and used it again.

The woman at Domino's robbed me.

This was more upsetting, because this was someone who could live six blocks from me, who spoke to me on the phone and heard my voice. Someone who I trusted. I mean, I trusted Domino's! Out of all the people or things in my life that could betray me, Domino's was not on the list. And because I'd spent years as a delivery driver, this broke the code of ethics. So this wasn't just a theft; this felt personal.

And so I had a suspect, and the next day I marched into that Domino's, and I demanded to know who was working the night my identity was stolen.

The manager on duty passed me to his manager, who passed me to *his* manager, and eventually they told me to come back later, and they would have the names for me. So I continued my investigation, and I went to a place called the Green Mill, which was a restaurant where some of the false delivery charges had taken place.

The manager there was really helpful because there was nothing else to do, and he gave me a week's worth of delivery tickets, and I started digging through them looking for a match. After about thirty minutes, the phone rang, and he picked it up and started taking down an order, and then he picks up a piece of paper and starts waving it back and forth, and I come over, and on the paper is a credit card number, and it's *my* credit card number.

The person who stole my credit card is on the other end of that phone! And the manager is looking at me like, *Well, what do we do now?* And I look him straight in the eyes, and I say, "Give me a topper, a hat, and I will take that delivery."

And he looks at me, and he says, "And that will get me fired." And I say, "Okay, maybe that wasn't the best idea. Tell them that your driver is out sick and that it's pickup only," and so he does, and he hangs up, and he looks at me, and he says, "They'll be here in fifteen minutes."

So I grab a newspaper, and I sit down for my very first stakeout.

An agonizing seventeen minutes later, a car pulls in, and a woman gets out and comes inside and asks for her pickup order. I start writing down every detail. The fact that it's a white lifted Chevy Tahoe, the license plate number, what she's wearing, and what she looks like. Meanwhile, she's having a conversation with the manager, and he's saying that the card was declined, and he needs to run it again. She says she doesn't have it on her, it's in her car, and she leaves the restaurant and doesn't come back.

I ask the manager to do me one more favor: I ask him to *69 the number she called from, and I add that cell phone number to my growing list of evidence.

A couple hours later I received a call from a man who introduced himself as the head of Domino's security. He was calling to apologize, to thank me for my help in the investigation, and to let me know that once I filed a police report, Domino's had my back. He had also pulled the hours I wanted and had them waiting at the original Domino's shop.

So I went back and picked 'em up, and I started asking questions there. I asked if anyone there drove a white lifted Chevy Tahoe. The daytime driver said that a girl who worked the night shift did, a girl who matched the description of the person who came into the Green Mill, who was also working the night that my identity was stolen.

I took the cell phone number and gave it to the manager, because I didn't want to call it myself and arouse suspicion. So he called it, and she answered and confirmed her identity, condemning herself.

Next I asked to see her application, because those places always keep those things on file. And at first the manager was wary of the legal things with that. But once I assured him that this was for the police report, he relented.

And so after I've copied down this information, now I have her first, middle, and last name, her date of birth, her Social Security number, her driver's license number. I know her car make and model and the license plate number. I know where and when she works, where she lives, her previous job references, and her e-mail address.

And so I go home, and I'm in a frenzy. I can't stop. I Google her e-mail address, and when you do that, you can pull up all of the accounts that have been created with that email address. And so I found her eBay account, her Flickr account, and her MySpace. Her MySpace was set to public, and I could see her pictures and her comments and her blogs, and I realized that I was going crazy.

But the thing about going crazy is you can't stop. And so I open one of her blogs called "50 Things About Me," and the very first question is "What is my favorite food?" and she wrote "pizza." And by the time I'm at the end of this list, I realize that I know more about this woman, probably, than most of her co-workers and friends, and that this is a real person that I would be sending to jail.

But she broke the code, and so I call the cops. And the next day they send out a police officer to take my report, and the fraud report starts out normal, it's just "How much money was stolen and when was it stolen, and is the bank reimbursing you?"

And then the last question, almost as an afterthought, was "Do you have any additional information which might benefit the case?"

And I said, "Why, yes I do."

And I start listing things. And the confusion on the officer's face turns to laughter once she hears the full story, and she says, "Well, you've done my job for me." And I agree.

Later on that day I receive a call from the detective now working this case. He says that he cross-checked all my information with D.O.T. records and the criminal database, and that it all checks out, and that by the end of the day there will be a warrant out for this woman's arrest.

I tell him that she's going to work tomorrow at Domino's at five. And after a pause, he says that he'll have a squad car waiting for her.

Then I ask the detective if I can be there. Because I've done a lotta work on this, and I kinda want to see the look on her face—that same look of shock and horror that I had when I was standing in that bank and I flipped that receipt over and saw everything I'd saved, gone.

He said that was impossible. But he did say that if I happened to be walking across the street at around five o'clock, no one would probably be the wiser.

So I gotta go undercover one last time, and I found myself standing across the street from that Domino's at five o'clock, squad car parked in back and two officers inside, and I saw that white lifted Chevy Tahoe come around the corner and park, and her get out, and go through the front door. And I could see her back arch up as she froze and saw the officers, because she knew she was caught.

Then they handcuffed her and put her in the back of the squad car, and they drove away. Case closed.

But then a couple hours later I received one of the most surreal phone calls I've ever gotten in my entire life. The man on the other end of the line introduced himself as the CEO of Domino's. He was calling to personally apologize, thank me for my help in the investigation, and, I assume, avoid a giant lawsuit. He asked me how much money was stolen and told me that Domino's would reimburse me for everything. And I told him that the bank was already doing that, and it wasn't about the money.

And so he asked me what I wanted. And up until this point, I hadn't really thought about it, but what do you say? I mean, free pizza for life? A pizza named after me? No, I'd lost my taste for pizza at this point.

I told him I didn't want this to happen to anyone else, that I wanted him to pursue this to the furthest extent of the law, and that every new Domino's employee that got hired would hear this story: that if you fuck with credit card information of customers, you will go to jail.

He said he could do that. And later I received two letters in the mail. The first was a letter that said the woman had pleaded guilty to all charges and would be serving a short prison sentence. The second was a personal thank-you letter from the CEO of Domino's, a check for the exact amount of money stolen, and 500 Domino's bucks. And I realized that I actually did get everything back that was stolen. The money, yes. But for that week, I wasn't the pathetic, depressed art student. No, for that week, I was Tristan Jimerson, private eye. The gumshoe that knows that revenge, like delivery pizza, is best served cold.

Tristan Jimerson is a storyteller, which is a nice way of saying that he doesn't have a real job. He has stumbled through life working as a bartender, copywriter, radio DJ, local TV news editor, delivery driver, and a handful of other odd jobs. He is currently opening a restaurant of his own. Tristan grew up on the rolling plains of rural Iowa, and after deciding that it wasn't cold enough, moved to Minnesota.

A Work in Progress

So two weeks ago I was a bridesmaid, and the reception was actually here at the New York Public Library, and I will never forget this wedding. Yes, it was very beautiful. But more importantly, I survived the slick marble floors that are all over this building. Tile and marble floors are public enemy number one to a stiletto-loving girl like me. And I had five-inch heels on that night.

Most people learn to walk in very high heels. They bend their ankle so that the ball of the foot touches the ground first; you have more stability.

I don't have ankles, so I hit each step on the stiletto, which makes the possibility of the banana peel wipeout very likely. But given the choice between practicality and theatricality, I say, "Go big or go home, man. Go down in flames if you're gonna go."

I guess I'm a bit of a daredevil. I think that the nurses at DuPont Institute would agree. I spent a lot of time there as a child. Doctors amputated both of my legs below the knee when I was an infant, and then when I was five, I had a major surgery to correct the wonky direction in which my tibia was growing. So I had two metal pins to hold that—full plaster casts on both legs. I had to use a wheelchair because I couldn't wear prosthetics.

One of the best things about getting out of the hospital is the anticipation of the day you return to school—I had missed so much class, I just couldn't wait to get back and see all my friends. But my teacher had a different idea about that. She tried to prevent me from returning to class, because she said that in the condition I was in, I was "inappropriate," and that I would be a distraction to the other students (which of course I was, but not because of the casts and the wheelchair).

Clearly she needed to make my difference invisible because she wanted to control her environment and make it fit into her idea of what "normal" looked like.

And it would've been a lot easier for me to fit into what "normal" looked like. I know I wanted that back then. But instead I had these wooden legs with a rubber foot that the toes broke off of, and they were held on with a big bolt that rusted out because I swam in the wooden legs.

You're not supposed to swim in the wooden legs, because, you know, the wood rots out.

So there I was in second grade music class, doing the twist, and mid-twist I hear this [*makes loud cracking sound*]. And I'm on the floor, and the lower half of my left leg is in splinters across the room. The teacher faints on the piano, and the kids are screaming. And all I'm thinking is, *My parents are gonna kill me. I broke my leg!*

It's a mess.

But then a few years later, my prosthetist tells me, "Aimee, we got waterproof legs for you. No more rusty bolts!"

This is a revelation, right? This is gonna change my life. I was so excited to get these legs . . . until I saw them.

They were made of polypropylene, which is that white plastic "milk jug" material. And when I say "white," I'm not talking about skin color; I'm talking about *the color white*. The "skin color" was the rubber foam foot painted "Caucasian," which is the nastiest shade of nuclear peach that you've ever seen in your life. It has nothing to do with any human skin tone on the planet. And these legs were so good at being waterproof that they were *buoyant*. So when I'd go off the high dive, I'd go down and come straight back up feet first. They were the bane of my existence.

But then we're at the Jersey Shore one summer. By the time we get there, there's three hundred yards of towels between me and the sea. And I know this is where I first honed my ability to run really fast. I was the white flash. I didn't wanna feel hundreds of pairs of eyes staring at me. And so I'd get myself into the ocean, and I was a good swimmer, but no amount of swimming technique can control buoyant legs.

So at some point I get caught in a rip current, and I'm migrating from my vantage point of where I could see my parents' towel. And I'm taking in water, and I'm fighting, fighting, fighting. And all I could think to do was pop off these legs and put one under each armpit, with the peach feet sticking up, and just bob, thinking, *Someone's gotta find me.*

And a lifeguard did. And I'm sure he will collect for therapy bills. You know? Like, they don't show that on *Baywatch*.

But they saved my life, those legs.

And then when I was fourteen it was Easter Sunday, and I was gonna be wearing a dress that I had purchased with my own money—the first thing I ever bought that wasn't on sale.

Momentous event; you never forget it. I'd had a paper route since I was twelve, and I went to The Limited, and I bought this dress that I thought was the height of sophistication—sleeveless safari dress, belted, hits at the knee.

Coming downstairs into the living room, I see my father waiting to take us to church. He takes one look at me, and he says, "That doesn't look right. Go upstairs and change."

I was like, "What? My super-classy dress? What are you talking about? It's the best thing I own."

He said, "No, you can see the knee joint when you walk. It doesn't look right. It's inappropriate to go out like that. Go change."

And I think something snapped in me. I refused to change. And it was the first time I defied my father. I refused to hide something about myself that was true, and I refused to be embarrassed about something so that other people could feel more comfortable.

I was grounded for that defiance.

So after church the extended family convenes at my grandmother's house, and everybody's complimenting me on how nice I look in this dress, and I'm like, "Really? You think I look nice? Because my parents think I look inappropriate."

I outed them (kinda mean, really).

But I think the public utterance of this idea that I should somehow hide myself was so shocking to hear that it changed their mind about why they were doing it.

And I had always managed to get through life with somewhat of a positive attitude, but I think this was the start of me being able to accept myself. You know, okay, I'm not normal. I have strengths. I've got weaknesses. It is what it is.

And I had always been athletic, but it wasn't until college

that I started this adventure in Track and Field. I had gone through a lifetime of being given legs that just barely got me by. And I thought, *Well, maybe I'm just having the wrong conversations with the wrong people. Maybe I need to go find people who say, "Yes, we can create* anything *for you in the space between where your leg ends and the ground."*

And so I started working with engineers, fashion designers, sculptors, Hollywood prosthetic makeup artists, wax museum designers to build legs for me.

I decided I wanted to be the fastest woman in the world on artificial legs, and I was lucky enough to arrive in track at just the right time to be the first person to get these radical sprinting legs modeled after the hind leg of a cheetah, the fastest thing that runs—woven carbon fiber. I was able to set three world records with those legs. And they made no attempt at approximating humanness.

Then I get these incredibly lifelike silicon legs—hand-painted, capillaries, veins. And, hey, I can be as tall as I wanna be, so I get different legs for different heights. I don't have to shave. I can wear open-toed shoes in the winter. And most importantly, I can opt out of the cankles I most certainly would've inherited genetically.

And then I get these legs made for me by the late, great Alexander McQueen, and they were hand-carved of solid ash with grapevines and magnolias all over them and a six-inch heel. And I was able to walk the runways of the world with supermodels. I was suddenly in this whirlwind of adventure and excitement. I was being invited to go around the world and speak about these adventures, and how I had legs that looked like glass, legs covered in feathers, porcelain legs, jellyfish legs—all wearable sculpture.

And I get this call from a guy who had seen me speak years ago, when I was at the beginning of my track career, and he says, "We loved it. We want you to come back." And it was clear to me he didn't know all these amazing things that had happened to me since my sports career.

So as I'm telling him, he says, "Whoa, whoa, whoa. Hold on, Aimee. The reason everybody liked you all those years ago was because you were this sweet, vulnerable, naïve girl, and if you walk onstage today, and you are this polished young woman with too many accomplishments, I'm afraid they won't like you."

For real, he said that. Wow.

He apparently didn't think I was vulnerable enough now. He was asking me to be *less than*, a little more downtrodden. He was asking me to disable myself for him and his audience.

And what was so shocking to me about that was that I realized I had moved past mere acceptance of my difference. I was having *fun* with my difference. Thank *God* I'm not normal. I get to be *extraordinary*. And I'll decide what is a weakness and what is a strength.

And so I refused his request.

And a few days later, I'm walking in downtown Manhattan at a street fair, and I get this tug on my shirt, and I look down. It's this little girl I met a year earlier when she was at a pivotal moment in her life. She had been born with a brittle bone disease that resulted in her left leg being seven centimeters shorter than her right. She wore a brace and orthopedic shoes and they got her by, but she wanted to do more.

And like all Internet-savvy kindergarteners, she gets on the computer and Googles "new leg," and she comes up with dozens of images of prosthetics, many of them mine. And she prints them out, goes to school, does show-and-tell on it, comes home, and makes a startling pronouncement to her parents:

"I wanna get rid of my bad leg," she says. "When can I get a new leg?"

And ultimately that was the decision her parents and doctors made for her. So here she was, six months after the amputation, and right there in the middle of the street fair she hikes up her jeans leg to show me her cool new leg. And it's pink, and it's tattooed with the characters of *High School Musical 3*, replete with red, sequined Mary Janes on her feet.

And she was proud of it. She was proud of herself. And the marvelous thing was that this six-year-old understood something that it took me twenty-something years to get, but that we both did discover—that when we can celebrate and truly own what it is that makes us different, we're able to find the source of our greatest creative power.

Aimee Mullins has built a career as an athlete, model, actor, and advocate for women, sports, and the next generation of prosthetics. Mullins was born without fibular bones and had both of her legs amputated below the knee when she was an infant. She learned to walk on prosthetics, then to run—competing at national and international levels as a champion sprinter, setting world records at the 1996 Paralympics in Atlanta. In 1999, Aimee made her runway debut in London at the invitation of Alexander McQueen. She's a passionate voice heralding a new kind of thinking about bodies and identities. Aimee also has received accolades for her work as an actor, debuting in the art epic *Cremaster 3*. She is currently starring as Isis in Matthew Barney's *Ancient Evenings* project, an adaptation of the novel by Norman Mailer.

NATHAN ENGLANDER

Unhooked

For those of you who are less than a hundred years old, I want to tell you there used to be something called the Soviet Union. They were our archenemy, and we were locked in a perpetual state of Cold War with them until I was an adult.

To contrast that to the perpetual War on Terror that we're in now—where going around the city, we're all afraid *something*'s going to blow up. Back then, we were afraid *everything* was going to blow up. We were going to melt the whole world into a tiny glass marble.

The symbol of the split between East and West was the Berlin Wall, which not only divided that city, it divided the planet. People would die trying to cross. They were literally trapped, and they would dream of freedom, and they would hide in trunks of cars or try to dig under or hang glide over. And they would be shot dead. That's how serious it was.

So in 1989, I'm on my junior year in Jerusalem, studying abroad, and suddenly word comes out of nowhere that the wall has been breached. It's open. There's a crossing between East and West. People can move freely between. And it's not like today, where Halliburton would, for a hundred million dollars, pull the thing down. People are literally ripping it down with their bare hands, with hammers and chisels. This is just unbelievable.

The only thing I can think of, in terms of today, is if I announced right now onstage that there's peace in the Middle East, and you can take an Al Qaeda bus tour of Kabul—you know, go see Osama bin Laden's coffee shop.

It was *mind-boggling*.

Within two seconds people start showing up in Jerusalem with pieces of the wall. They're going over there and chipping at it. They're helping put the world back together. They're a part of history.

And this girl I have a crush on shows up, and she gives me a piece of the wall. It's got graffiti on it. I'm holding it, and it's like holding moon rock. I mean, I'm holding it! I just can't believe I'm holding it. It's such an amazing thing to be a part of.

Except I *ain't*.

It's clear to me in an instant. I need to go be a part of this. So I grab my buddy Joel, who dragged me to Jerusalem, and we set the plan in order. We're gonna do it Jewish-boy style. We're going to do a sort of Passover slavery-to-freedom route. So we fly into Warsaw, and we do Auschwitz, Majdanek, Treblinka. We hit all our favorite concentration camps. And we end up in Prague, where we're going to take a night train to Berlin. That's the end of this heroic journey for us. We're going to get to Berlin in the morning, chip at the wall, cross to the West, and go back home.

Well, we thought this was a grand plan. But nobody else seems to have thought so, 'cause we are alone on this platform at night. It is pitch-dark, and there's nobody else there. But here comes our train. At least we think it's our train. It starts rolling through the station, but it doesn't stop. It just keeps rolling. And what it is is an old freight train.

Now, I grew up religious on Long Island. I had been raised on a full-on diet of the Holocaust. And this instantly sets off the Holocaust PTSD in my head. You know what I'm saying?

I'm a Yeshiva boy. We didn't do *The Diary of Anne Frank*. We went *Clockwork Orange*–style. From a way too young age, they would sit us down and play tapes that flashed images—big black jackboots and piles of bodies, teeth, hair—just these really unbelievably dark images.

And there's no greater symbol of the Holocaust than the trains. I mean, these are the trains that annihilated our people. They would stuff them full of Jews, and when there was no more room, they would stuff babies in over the people's heads.

And there we are, standing on the same platform. It's not like it's changed. We're on *the same platform*. These are the *same tracks*. This could be the same train that took our people to their destruction. And we're standing there, dead silent. But the next train is our train, and we get on it.

And back to growing up on Long Island, I know trains. And I know when something doesn't feel right. And I step into the train car, and this feels bad. It's too hot and already overpacked. We're looking for our seats, and we go over to our assigned compartment, and we open it, and we expect, like, two British people drinking tea. But instead the beds are open, and it's six guys laid out head to toe like sardines. And honestly, it smells of piss. It smells of beer. And most of all, it just smells of sadness. These are refugees. Joel and I are on some sort of freedom adventure, but these people have been trapped behind the Iron Curtain, and the wall has come down, and these are refugees on the move. We don't want our seats anymore, and they ain't giving 'em up. So we look around in the packed car, and this nice family makes room for us. We take off our backpacks, and they slide their kids over, and they let us in their compartment. And I could cry telling this to you right now: these people with nothing, they offered to share their food with us. We settle in. And we're rolling. We're on our way to Berlin.

And then the train stops. And we hear voices yelling.

I don't speak the language, and I don't know what's happening, what's getting screamed. But suddenly, *bedlam*! The family is grabbing their stuff. Everybody has to get off the train.

And there we are with our big packs. We're like turtles getting jostled. We are out of the train, and we're down the ladder. We're not at a station, we're on the dirt, in the middle of the night, running with these refugees that are going this way and that. We don't know if there's a fire, or what's going on.

We are just *terrified*. I'm kind of a coward, and it suddenly seems like a nightmare of a bad idea, what we've done in coming here.

But eventually there seems to be a dominant stream. They're sending the whole front of the train to the back of the train. The train is being split in the night. We climb back up, and, well, if it was packed before, there is now no room at all. It's really panicky. I just want some space, somewhere to be. I want to get safely to Berlin, and I want to cross that wall. We're pushing, and the compartments are overflowing. We make our way to the end of the car, and the last compartment at the end of the car has the curtains drawn.

So we give it a yank, and we hear someone scream, "Fuck!"

Now I have to tell you, you cannot learn to curse like an American. You know what I'm saying?

THE MOTH

I have an Israeli friend, Motti, and I remember he would always be like, [*Israeli accent*] "Nathan, I give a shit."

I'd be like, "No, no, Motti, you *don't* give a shit." You know? He still can't learn it.

Point is, that is a *pitch-perfect* "fuck" that I get.

So we're like, "Fuck, did *you* say 'fuck'? *We* say 'fuck'!"

It's this chorus of joyous "fucks."

And then the door flies open. We jump in. It slams shut.

There are two American frat boy types in there, and the dudes have eyes like saucers. They are as scared and panicked as we are.

And this is the embarrassing part of the story, but any of you who are my age who backpacked back then can bear witness: we honestly all deeply believed that Europe was filled with small bands of ninja robbers who were trained solely to rob nineteen-year-old Americans. Like, they wanted the bounty of half a joint and a Cowboy Junkies mix tape. As if on the black market you could feed a family off such a prize.

The even more embarrassing part of the story is we also honestly believed—it's so stupid—but we told each other that they would gas you. That they would have tanks of sleeping gas, and they would knock you out, and then take your stuff. So we all traveled with ropes or bicycle chains, and we'd lock the train doors.

Well, guess what? These guys have a bicycle chain, and we are thankful for it, because people are screaming and pulling and yanking and banging at that door. But the train starts moving on, and the banging sort of subsides. Every once in a while, there's more banging and screaming outside, but that door's not coming open for anyone.

And in the way you can make a home anywhere, the four of us are now a team. We're a group. We're safe. The adrenaline drains out, and we pass out.

We wake up in the morning, and it is beautiful. I've never been so overjoyed at seeing a morning like that. Sun streaming in. It is lovely. It's bucolic. And it's dead silent. There's just trees outside the train. And we're waiting, and we're not moving, so I go to check what's going on. And I go out into the corridor, and I suddenly very much understand why it's so silent.

There's nobody else in the car. Our car is completely empty. So I look into the next car, and then I understand why it's empty. Because there *is no* next car. There's no locomotive. There's no train.

I look behind us, same difference. We're a car alone. We've been unhooked. At some point in the night, we'd lost our train. I also then understand that maybe one of those people banging and pulling and screaming in the night was a friendly conductor trying to tell us there was a second switch.

So I go back into that compartment, and, honestly, we'd had a very bad night. And this is very difficult information to relay.

You know: *"There's no train."*

"What do you mean there's no train? Where are we?"

"I don't know."

"You don't know what station?"

"I don't know what *country*."

So they come out and see that we've, indeed, lost the train. And we don't have iPhones; there's no compass. We only know which way our bodies were hurtling through space last night. So we put on our packs, and we step down onto the tracks, and we hike.

We see a station in the distance, which is good, and we hike towards the station. And there's another fact that I have not forgotten in the twenty years since, which is when you show up at the station without the train, the platform is *so much higher* than you would think.

But they hop up. Joel pulls me up. It's six in the morning. And there's just one drunken blond dude about our age with a bottle of vodka, sort of stumbling around on the platform—looking happy, not scary.

We go up to him to inquire:

"Do you speak English? And what country are we in?"

He does speak English. He's been out partying. He's just finished his degree. He's been celebrating drunkenly all night. We are in the German Democratic Republic, in East Germany. We are in the city of Dresden. And guess where he's going home to? He is headed home to *Berlin*. So our group of four is now five strong. And our train is coming. It's joyous.

I really just want to get to the wall at this point, and we get on the train. We take our seats. In comes this big, strong East German woman, out of central casting, in this very serious conductor uniform. And she takes our tickets, but our tickets are no good. I mean, try showing up at O'Hare with a ticket from LaGuardia. Our tickets aren't even from the same country. We have Czech tickets. We did not originate in East Germany. So the tickets are *no good*.

So we pull out Eurail passes, which are good everywhere. But she looks at them, and she doesn't know them, and they're also no good. And she makes it very clear that we are being turned off at the next stop.

Now, you know what? I held it together through Israel and

the Intifada, and I held it together through the trip and the night. But now I'm actually terrified.

Because I remember my mother talking about my grand-parents, saying, "Oh, yes. These relatives used to write them from across the ocean, and then one day they stopped writing."

You know what I'm saying? Then they were just *gone*. This is a part of the world that swallows Jews.

And you know what? Those refugees back in our compart-ment, that's serious. There's a reason they're racing to get away. That wall came down in a day; it could go back up in a day. Half the world was trapped behind it for all those years.

And I just think: *What have we done?* And as I tell you now, back to that Al Qaeda bus tour idea, it's like: *Did we have to be on the* first bus? *What have we DONE?* So I'm having a panic at-tack, and Joel's trying to keep me under control, when I see our German friend—he's up on his feet, and he's talking to the conductor. And he's gesticulating. He's delivering a sort of Get-tysburg Address there. And I mean, honestly, with the morning light streaming in through the windows, he looks almost sober. It's beautiful. Whatever he's doing, it's beautiful.

And when he's done, this conductor's hard face goes soft, and out of nowhere she reaches out and punches our Eurail passes, and she welcomes us on the train to Berlin.

We ask our new friend, "What did you tell her?"

And he says, "I told her this. These people have come from America to our country. They've come to *see* our country. Are you going to tell them that a ticket that is good in Madrid, that is good in Rome, that is good in Paris, is no good here?

"The great conflict is *over*.

"We are *one world* now. We are, all of us, brothers."

THE MOTH

Nathan Englander is the author of the story collections *What We Talk About When We Talk About Anne Frank* and *For the Relief of Unbearable Urges*, as well as the novel *The Ministry of Special Cases*. He is the translator of *New American Haggadah*, edited by Jonathan Safran Foer. His play, *The Twenty-Seventh Man*, premiered at the Public Theater in 2012.

The Small Town Prisoner

I'm going to tell you a story about my dad. His name was George Bullard. He was born in a rural area, right up the northeast corner of Mississippi that most folks call British County, and the locals just call paradise.

He grew up with eight other siblings on a farm. He married when he was twenty, had two daughters, and his wife died so he raised those two daughters. And after they were grown, he married my mother, who was about twenty years younger, and they had another family, so I'm the last of the last.

My dad was about fifty years old when I was born, but I was very fortunate to be raised by him.

He raised and trained bird dogs all of his life, and that's how he made a living. If the bird dog business got a little slow, he'd paint a house or two and do some things like that, but after he got up in his sixties someone convinced him to get into politics. He ran for Board of Aldermen, which is like the city council, and he was elected by a landslide. Everybody loved him.

His assignment was fire commissioner. Now, all the previous

fire commissioners did was go to meetings and make political decisions, but my father liked to get involved, so he went to the telephone company and said, "Can't y'all hook my telephone up with the one at the fire department?"

So they did, and every time the fire department telephone rang, our phone rang—one long continuous ring until you picked it up—and then you didn't talk, you just listened to see where the fire was so he could go. And he went to all the fires, day or night. He knew almost nothing about firefighting, but he knew how to encourage young men, so he'd go and encourage 'em.

I got involved because my father had almost stopped driving at night because of his age, and as a teenager I had a driver's license, so I kept jeans and tennis shoes right there, and I drove him at three o'clock in the morning.

Well, after a few turns as board alderman, several people, myself included, convinced him not to do that anymore, but he found that he missed the camaraderie he had formed with all the firemen, and because the firemen and the police department were in the same building, he missed all the policemen too. So he would just go down there to visit every now and again. And this being a small town, they worked out something which might not have been real legal, but they taught him how to operate the police radio, and anytime anybody wanted a day off or was sick, he'd go in and work an eight-hour shift. Somehow they managed to pay him, I don't know how.

But one day he got to his job down at the police department, and he discovered, to his amazement, they had a prisoner!

I did say it was a small town. It was most unusual.

And that morning he really didn't have much to do. He'd wander back and talk to this young man, and when he went out for lunch he brought a couple hamburgers back for him. Well, by one or two o'clock, he had made a decision about this young man, and he always trusted his instincts about people. He had decided that in spite of being long-haired—way down to here, which my father hated—that he was a decent young man, so he'd see if he could help him.

He started to inquire of him, "Why are you still here? You seem like such a nice young man. Won't anybody come get you out of jail?"

And the young man told him, "Well, I had a little too much to drink last night, and they arrested me for drunken disorder and here I am."

My dad said, "Well what would it take to get you out?"

And he said, "Well, I have to pay a two-hundred-dollar fine."

My dad said, "Well, why can't your family pay the two-hundred-dollar fine?"

He said, "Well, I think if I could talk to my father face-to-face I could get the two hundred dollars from him, but I don't know how he's going to react to a collect call from the Boonville jail."

Well, my dad mulled this over a little while, and he said, "Well, do you think if I turned you loose, you could go find your father and get two hundred dollars and come back?"

I'm going to remind you that my father's only duty was operating the police radio that talked back and forth with the cars.

So the young man said, "Well, see, I'm from Corinth, Mississippi, and that's about twenty miles north of Boonville. You know they impounded my car. I think I could get the money from my dad, but I got no way to get up there."

My dad said, "What would you say if I gave you your car?"

He said, "They impounded it."

And my daddy said, "Well, is it a blue Chevrolet?"

And he said, "Yes, sir."

And then my daddy said, "It's parked out in the parking lot. I can probably find the keys."

So he scrounges around in the desk drawers, and he finds the keys, and he not only releases the prisoner, over whom he has no authority, he gives him a getaway car.

Well, as the kid leaves, my father says, "Now, son, I believe if I could borrow two hundred dollars from my daddy, I'd borrow another five to get me a darn haircut."

At about four o'clock the policemen started coming back to change shifts, and as they came in, they went to the back to check on the prisoner. And they discovered, to their dismay, that they didn't have one.

And they said, "Mr. George, what happened to the prisoner?"

My daddy was busy doing his little closing up paperwork, and he said, "Oh yeah. I turned him loose."

And the police officer said, "You did what?"

"Turned him loose."

He said, "Mr. George, why did you do that?"

Daddy said, "Well, he just seemed like a nice young man, and he'll be back in a little while with his two hundred dollars."

And the police officer was kind of taken aback. He'd known my father all his life, my father was like a grandfather to most of those guys.

He said, "Okay, well, we'll take care of this," and he went back to the other policemen to try to figure out how they were gonna get out of this without my father losing his unofficial job, and one of them says, "Well, we ought to remind the chief that George Bullard helped get him elected." But another of 'em said, "Oh, I got a better idea. Let's just tear up the paperwork, and we'll just pretend we never arrested that boy."

Well, my father wouldn't hear of it. He said, "Oh no. I know that boy's coming back. I know he is."

And the police officer said, "How can you be so sure? You don't even know him."

And my father's answer was simple: "He told me that he would." Well, they didn't know what to say to that, so they just didn't say anything.

They waited around and four-thirty came and five o'clock, and of course no young man returned. And at about five-fifteen they're trying to get my dad to go home, 'cause his shift ended at five.

He's kind of stoic, and he says, "No, I'm gonna wait around until he comes back."

One of 'em observed, "Might be kind of a long wait." But no, my dad didn't get discouraged.

And all of a sudden the door opens, and the young man walks in—plain cut, shaven, short hair—walks up to the counter, and they don't even acknowledge him 'cause they're still mulling over what they're gonna do to save my dad, and finally the young man says, "Excuse me, I'd like to pay my fine."

And that kinda got their attention, but they still didn't recognize him, and one of 'em walked to the counter and said, "What fine is that you're talking 'bout?"

He said, "Well, you guys arrested me last night—locked me up. I owe two hundred, and I'm here to pay it." Started counting out twenty-dollar bills. When he got to two hundred, the police didn't say a word, but they got out the book and wrote him out a receipt. They thanked him. The boy started to leave. When he got to the door to go out, he turned around and—almost as if he knew what the situation was like there in that office with my dad—said, "Oh, by the way, Mr. Bullard, I'm sorry I was late getting back, but I had to wait in the line at the barbershop."

Wanda Bullard grew up in Booneville, Mississippi, but lived on St. Simon's Island, Georgia, for thirty-four years. A teacher for more than forty-two years, she worked with emotionally disordered sixth, seventh, and eighth-grade students in Brunswick, Georgia. Most Sunday afternoons she hosted a cookout in her backyard for all comers, including The Moth's founder, George Dawes Green. Telling stories on Wanda's porch was his inspiration to begin The Moth. Wanda died in 2011, and we miss her terribly.

Save Me

The Past Wasn't Done with Me

The first time that I passed out on the Chicago L train, I just knew that I was dying from mad cow disease. At least that's what I told my doctor when I was trying to self-diagnose in his office, and he was pretty impressed by the depths of my neurosis. Understand, this was before WebMD when everyone could do it. But he assured me that despite the fact that I had been to Europe and eaten several steaks, I wasn't suffering from mad cow. I had anxiety. And he asked me if there was anything that had happened recently that had been causing stress, and I had to think about the question for a little while.

I said, "You know, I haven't been adjusting well to my move to Chicago," and he nodded his head and said, "You know, a transition like that into a new city can cause a lot of stress."

I said, "My father's dying of cancer, and I can't convince him to take better care of himself." He nodded again; this was obviously a story he'd heard a lot of times before.

Then I said, "My daughter almost died last year from febrile seizures, and I'm pretty much terrified to be left alone with her." Now, this raised his eyebrows. He wrote me a prescription for Xanax and gave me the name of a therapist he wanted me to see right away to delve into this further.

Now, I don't know what prompted me to say what I said next, but as he handed me the prescription, I just blurted it out: "There's one more thing: When I was fourteen years old, I shot my best friend in the face accidentally, and I watched him die."

Henry was one of seven people to die that day in New York City, 1988. At fourteen he wasn't even the youngest—a twelve-year-old kid from Queens had that dubious distinction. But his was the death that I saw with my own eyes. The one that I was responsible for with my own hands, and the one I'm going to carry with me for the rest of my life.

Now, home back then was a two-bedroom co-op in the Kensington section of Brooklyn. It was a big source of pride for my mom, who had raised my three older sisters and me almost single-handedly since splitting from my dad when I was four years old. This was the first place that she owned, after what had seemed like an annual ritual of moving. Now, for those who don't know, New York was really violent and dangerous back then. Like Detroit, New Orleans, and Gary, Indiana–rolled-into-one dangerous. You know, two-thousand-murders-a-year violent. But I never let the violence swirling around in the world outside ever impact me.

I was actually an honor roll student all the way. And when Henry and I met in the seventh grade, we got along immediately. The physical contrast couldn't have been more extreme. He was unusually muscular and well built for a twelve-year-old, and I was just as oddly tall and lanky for a kid the same age. But that's pretty much where our differences ended. We both were into all the same things. We shared all of the same fears. We

walked together every day after school to the Carroll Street
subway station in South Brooklyn. And we both hated the older
boys from John Jay High School nearby, who'd show up every
Halloween and rain rotten eggs, D-cell batteries, and of course
water balloons filled with Nair on our heads, which gave you a
nice surprise when you got home and tried to clean up.

He was my first and best friend. Now on the afternoon of
April 14, 1988, Henry and Chris, another friend of mine,
came by my apartment like they had many times before. They
dropped their book bags and plopped down on my bed. My
mother was a captain in the Army Reserves at this time; we had
three guns in the house. The .38-caliber revolver was my favorite, not just because it was the one that was kept loaded. It was
just the most interesting. It looked like a gun from the movies,
and it was the one I always showed to my friends, even though
my mom never knew about it. And this day was no different.

I started off by emptying the gun, made sure all the bullets
were out. Then I demonstrated my index finger spin—the cowboy move that I'd been working on. Then I took a single bullet,
pretended to insert it into the cylinder, and pointed the gun at
my friends. I can actually remember smiling as I pulled the trigger, ready to shout, "Gotcha!" when I made them jump.

But instead of the dull click of a hammer followed by laughter, there was a muzzle flash, an explosion, and shock. Both of
my friends, Chris and Henry, had turned their backs to me, and
I remember being overcome with confusion. *How did the fuckin'
bullet get into the chamber?*

Chris turned and looked at me, and my heart started racing,
and we both looked over at Henry. I guess we were waiting for
him to turn around, say, "Oh shit," and then tell me how much
trouble I was gonna get into when my mother got home.

Now, whenever we're faced with something horrific, I think it's human instinct to want to run, and mentally that's what I did. I just fled into my own psyche. I went back years to being with my father at Coney Island on the pier, trying to catch a bluefish with my piece-of-shit rod and reel, and then the next thing you know, I was back there in the hallway, and it was full of people.

My mom was there now, sobbing. The paramedics were there. Of course, the cops were there. When one of the paramedics came out of the apartment, I remember begging him, "Please tell me he's okay, please tell me he's okay," and even though I knew what he was gonna say, I just wasn't prepared for the words.

He just said, "He's gone."

That night in the police station I had to recount in detail everything that had happened. I didn't want to. I wanted to crawl under that table and hide. But I did, slowly, methodically, choking back tears when I looked down and realized that my sweatshirt was covered in blood.

My dad was there—I almost never saw him at that time—but he was there with my mom, with the same forlorn look on his face.

The wake came about a week later, and I didn't think Henry's family would have any interest in me attending, but my mom insisted we go. So when we got to the funeral home, there was a huge crowd gathered around the coffin, and I made my way over to Henry. He looked really nice. They had him in a really nice blue suit. But I remember the coffin making him look so small. And I just stood there and stared at him while everyone else around me wailed. That's when I suddenly heard this woman's voice. She said, "I JUST WANT TO SEE HIM!" and I remember it made me jump, because I didn't know whether she was talking about Henry lying there in a coffin, or me, his killer, standing over him, crying onto his jacket. I knew every eye in the funeral home was on me, and all I could do was just close my eyes and wish that I was someplace else.

Now, miraculously, Henry's family did not want to press charges. They embraced me and offered their forgiveness, and when the Brooklyn DA hit me with a long list of charges, ranging from manslaughter to assault with a deadly weapon—I think it was seventeen charges total—they were the ones who stood up and said they didn't want to destroy two young lives instead of one.

They're the reason that, instead of going to jail, I got one year of counseling. That was my sentence. I remember thanking them profusely outside of the courthouse that day for giving me a second chance when I didn't think I deserved one.

In the years that followed, I thought it was odd that no one—none of my friends, none of my family—ever said a single word about Henry. Everyone went about their lives as though he had never existed. The entire incident was wiped from my record when I was sixteen, so it hadn't even existed in a legal sense, and if I never mentioned it again, it would never come up.

But I thought about it, the shooting and Henry, almost every fuckin' day. And oddly enough, it's what drove me for a number of years. Ask any friend of mine in college; I was the most anal-retentive dude they ever met. I wouldn't touch alcohol. I wouldn't smoke a cigarette. Don't get me wrong, I made up for it years later. But I just felt like I had to do him proud. I had to be perfect. And for a long period of time, I thought I was doing it. Successful career. Faithful husband. Doting father to my daughter, who I watched grow from an infant into a toddler.

When my daughter got sick at eighteen months, it pretty much derailed all of it. We rushed her to the hospital, her body was convulsing, and all of a sudden all of these emotions and feelings I hadn't felt since I was fourteen came rushing back. The feeling of panic, the feeling of helplessness. And that's when it dawned on me, *Maybe this is it. Maybe this is gonna be my sentence, that I'm gonna have to see what it's like to lose a child.* And, you know, miraculously, she did survive, and the doctor assured me that some children just have a really low tolerance for fever, and it's something that she would almost certainly grow out of. But the damage was done, and when we got back home, everything was just completely different. I was terrified to be left alone with her. I felt like this marked man, and the second it was just me and her, something was gonna go wrong.

It didn't help that after she got sick, a recurring dream I was having about Henry began to repeat itself with disturbing frequency. And it was always the same dream: In the dream I'd be asleep, I'd wake up, sit up in my bed, and he'd be sitting there on the edge of my bed, staring at me, with the bullet hole still in his chin, about the size of a nickel.

I'd start talking to him. I'd say, "Hey, how are you doing?" and his blank face would just show no expression. And after a while, I'd start getting desperate and pleading with him. I'd start asking him if he knew how sorry I was. I'd ask him if he knew that it was an accident. I'd ask him if he knew how much I missed him. Then finally he would open his mouth and try to respond, but just like on that day, the bullet stopped him from speaking, and he just gasped for air. I'd break down in tears, and I'd wake up crying in bed.

And this dream repeated itself for years. Henry always there, staring at me, the same, and me just getting older and older and older. Fourteen, eighteen, twenty-one, twenty-five, thirty, and starting to gray. It took me passing out on the L that day to realize it, but I knew that I needed help.

Now, Henry is dead, and I killed him. No one can absolve you of your sins if you don't believe it in your heart, and I honestly don't believe there's any amount of good I can do in my life that'll absolve me of his death. But my trying to live a life for two people, one of whom I can never bring back, was just a recipe for disaster that was gonna doom me and everyone who cared about me.

It took this chain of events that started with me passing out in public and ended with me having that first tentative conversation with my mother about that day to realize it. And it was an interesting conversation, if uncomfortable. I found out that my mom, of course, had been dealing with a lot of the same feelings of guilt. But more illuminating, she'd been battling anxiety since the day it happened. I think we found some small amount of comfort in learning that little thing about each other.

My marriage died, but I lived on. My daughter's thirteen years old now and healthy. I have an eight-year-old son, and he's healthy as an ox. I hope both of my kids grow up to be wonderful people—the type of people who bring so much joy to everyone around them that their absence would be a tragedy, because that's the type of person that Henry was.

He died twenty-four years ago, and it's still fresh. But I'm no longer miserable. In fact, I am well on my way to becoming one of the happiest people I know, and I think that fact would've made him happy. He also doesn't visit me in my dreams anymore, and I can finally admit that I'm comfortable with never seeing his face ever again, in my dreams or otherwise. Because at the end of the day, what will an old man like me have to say to his fourteen-year-old friend that hasn't been said already?

Kemp Powers is a writer, editor, author, and occasional birdwatcher. He was a very angry and cynical young man who inexplicably grew into a happy and optimistic adult. His Bosc pear obsession has remained consistent throughout. A journalist for almost twenty years, he has told the stories of countless others in the pages of magazines and newspapers ranging from *Esquire* to *Forbes*. Now he also tells tales much closer to home, both as a storyteller and a playwright at Los Angeles's award-winning Rogue Machine Theatre company. His new play, *One Night in Miami . . .* has its world premiere in 2013.

JENNY ALLEN

Hair Today
Gone Tomorrow

A few years ago, I was diagnosed with cancer. And about five minutes later, I had to start chemotherapy. When you have the kind of chemotherapy I had, you lose your hair. This seemed like such a small price to pay, you know? My hair or my life? My hair or my life? I don't know, I think I'll pick *my life*.

I was kind of hoping that after my hair fell out and grew back, I'd get *better hair*. I have this unruly hair, and it has a mind of its own. No matter how expensive my haircut, a lot of the time it looks like I've had it cut by a mental patient.

But no matter how I felt about losing my hair, just the prospect of not having any forced me to reconsider my whole sense of my personal style and, in a way, my whole sense of myself. What kind of cancer person was I going to be? How would I wear my disease? Would I try to hide it, or would I announce it to the whole world?

In other words, was I going to be a *scarf* person or a *wig* person?

Because it seemed to me that if I showed up places suddenly

wearing a scarf all the time, people would know it was because I'd gone bald, and they would probably guess why. But if I showed up wearing a wig, even the people who could tell it was a wig would probably assume that I was wearing it because I didn't want to talk that much about why.

If I wore a wig, I'd be saying to everybody, "Please, just let me blend in."

So I had this dilemma—scarf or a wig, blend in or not blend in? I thought about it, and I decided that my truer self would wear a scarf, because I have a lot of self-righteous integrity. And I thought a wig would be dishonest, and I wasn't ashamed of my disease.

One night I ran into my friend Ruth. Now, I had met Ruth originally because she was my dentist, and she was a wonderful dentist, very kind and generous and understanding about those of us who showed up needing a root canal because we had failed to floss in our twenties.

She used to say, "Oh, Jenny, in terms of evolution, our teeth are only supposed to last us about forty-five years, so you're doing great!"

And she'd become my friend, and our kids had become friends, and they even went to the same school because she had recommended it. And by some horrible coincidence, she and I both had the same kind of cancer, only she was much farther down the chemo path than I was and had already lost her hair.

I'd seen her a few weeks earlier just wearing a scarf, and so I was very surprised when I ran into her at a school play, and there she was with her old hair back, this big corona of dark curls.

And I said to her, "Ruth, I love your hair!"

And she said, "It's a wig! I never thought I'd wear a wig, but it's kind of nice when you go out. It's kind of creepy, but it's dressy."

And I looked at her head, and actually, I could tell that it was a wig if I looked really closely, but I thought: *It looks very nice.* And then I thought: *Well, if Ruth can feel good in a wig, then maybe I could too.* It seemed unlikely, but possible. I thought: *Maybe I should just* consider *wearing a wig.*

Then Ruth said to me, "You know, Jenny, you should get one. Medical insurance pays for the whole thing."

And this seemed so bizarre as to be almost unbelievable, and really reason enough to get a wig. I love free things, particularly when my insurance company pays for them. And I found out that wigs cost hundreds and hundreds of dollars, so this seemed like the ultimate freebie. It was like great swag, even if it was *cancer* swag.

So I thought: *Well, maybe I'll go to the store and get a wig.* So I did.

I went to a wig store right near Columbus Avenue called Bits & Pieces.

My wig fitter was French, and he said, "What do you want?"

And I said, "I want a wig."

"What kind of hair?"

"I don't know. How many kinds do you have?"

And he explained to me that they had synthetic wigs, they had wigs made from the hair of Indian women, and they had wigs made from the hair of Caucasian European women. Now, the synthetic wigs were the cheapest, and the Indian hair wigs were in the middle range—they were $800 to $900. But the wigs made from the hair of Caucasian European women were $4,000 to $5,000.

Now, I thought: *You know, even if my insurance company paid for this, it's just obscene to spend this kind of money on a wig. And why is the hair of Caucasian European women* four times *as expensive as the hair of Indian women?* It was so racist! So I decided to go with the Indian women's hair, even though I felt very uncomfortable knowing they had probably been paid about 22 cents to have it shorn from their heads.

So I took my wig home. The wig fitter put it in a big paper bag, and inside the paper bag was a Styrofoam head with the wig on it. When I got home, I took it out of the bag and put it in the corner of my bedroom to wait until I might consider wearing it.

And it was very unsettling to look at it over there. Sometimes I felt like my wig head, which was so well groomed, was condescending to me.

So a couple of weeks went by, and my hair did fall out. Now, it didn't just fall out all at once. It sort of gradually gave up the ghost. First in these strands in my brush, and then in clumps in my shower drain that made me think that there was a dead mouse down there. And every time I looked in the mirror, my baldness told me how sick I was, in spite of all this optimism and cheerfulness that I was summoning.

And I wasn't completely bald. I had these sort of sad wisps of hair here and there that somehow just made it worse.

My head seemed to be saying to me, "Hello, Sickie. Hello, sick person with cancer."

Every time I went out in my scarves, my head felt very exposed, very uncomfortable. And people would ask me questions about how I was doing and how my chemo was going.

And I didn't like it. I didn't like it when they looked at me as if they were about to cry.

And then one day I realize that my eyebrows have fallen out. And for some reason, this is completely unexpected by me, and makes me feel surprisingly sorry for myself. Having no eyebrows makes me feel very naked, very vulnerable, very exposed.

My hair was part of my head, but my eyebrows were part of my *face*.

I look like a big baby. And every time I look in the mirror, and I see the baby, I feel so bad for her that I wanna cry. And I decide I need more of a buffer between me and the rest of the world. I'm tired of people asking me about my disease. I'm tired of them looking at me like they're about to cry.

I'm ready for my wig.

So it turns out that my friend Martha's daughter Anna is about to graduate from the University of Chicago, and I decide that this might be the perfect occasion to wear my wig.

And so I go to Chicago, and I bring my wig. And the morning of the ceremony, I get up, and I put my wig on my head. First I comb it and brush it, and then I fit it carefully to my head. And I start walking toward the graduation, along with the throngs of other parents and grandparents and friends.

And as soon as I start walking, I know that I should've been practicing wearing my wig all these weeks, first in my bedroom maybe and then around my neighborhood. Because every time I look in a store window I recognize myself, but I look like I'm in disguise. I feel like I've done something really bad, like robbed a bank, and now I'm trying to lose myself in the crowd by going incognito in my wig.

And I'm very self-conscious about the wig itself. I keep tugging at it and fussing with it and imagining that there are strands of hair coming out, even though there aren't. This wig is a stranger to me, and I'm uncomfortable having it in my personal space.

Now, someone at the graduation is selling sun hats. This is a very smart person. They've realized that some of us women here haven't put it together that we're going to be spending about four hours in the scorching Chicago sun, and we might not want to get sunburned.

So I buy one of the hats, in part so I won't get sunburned, but really because I think the hat is going to cover up my wig and make me feel much less self-conscious. I put the hat on over my wig, and I take my place in a folding chair among this ocean of folding chairs, and the ceremony starts.

And it goes on and on. And by the second hour or so, my head is just broiling under my wig and my hat. These little rivulets of sweat are coming down from underneath my wig, onto my neck, and that makes the wig really itch. And the wig itself is so hot and heavy, it feels like I'm wearing my cat on my head. I feel like my head is suffocating in there. It is just so, so very, very hot.

And I think: *God almighty, if I could just take off my hat, maybe my wig could just breathe a little*. So I whip off my hat.

And in one of those nearly free-fall, slow-motion moments, one of those moments that is at the same time like a dream and like the realest thing that has ever happened to you, my wig comes off with my hat. And it is so embarrassing that I can't even be embarrassed, because embarrassment can't even cover it.

I mean, I've lost everything—my hat, my wig, my hair. And yet I feel strangely free. And I start to laugh because it's so funny that I've gone to all this trouble only to end up like this. I feel like I'm in a great *Lucy* episode. But I take my wig and my hat, and I put them back on my head, really for decorum's sake, you know?

I feel so bad for the people behind me. I can't even look at them. And I sit through the rest of the ceremony, and then I go back to New York, and I take my wig, and I put it in a plastic bag, and then I put it way in the back of one of my dresser drawers so I won't ever have to look at it. And I go back to wearing my scarves and bandanas until my hair grows back in—which it does, by the way. It's just the same old hair, but for the first time, I'm kind of glad to see it.

And Ruth's hair grows back too. And for two years, we have just a lot of fun doing the normal things we like to do, like worrying endlessly about our children and eating the delicious food that she cooks at her house, and telling our cancer stories.

She really likes my wig story. And I love it when she does this version of something that happens to you a lot when you have cancer. People come up to you and tell you an inspiring story of their aunt or their grandmother who had terrible cancer, and then it went into remission, and she went out and got her Ph.D., or she took up parasailing, and she had a whole new life.

At the end of these stories, you always ask the people, "How is she doing?"

And they always say, "Oh . . . she died."

And I say to Ruth, "Do it again, Ruth! Tell the inspiring people story again!" We crack each other up with our stories.

And then Ruth's cancer comes back. And after a long time, she dies. And I miss her so much. And in the light of this loss and other losses—one of my editors dies, women I meet in various doctors' waiting rooms die—getting rid of my wig seems so cocky. You know, who am I to say that I'm done with my disease? Who am I to say that there's never going to be an occasion where I might consider wearing that wig again?

And then I read one of those very bossy magazine articles about how to de-clutter your closets, and how you must ask yourself realistically if you are ever gonna wear that bridesmaid dress again or that pair of culottes, and if you answer no you have to throw them away.

And I think to myself, *realistically*? Realistically, I might need chemo drugs again, and I might lose my hair again, but I would never, ever wear that stupid wig again.

Better to go back to the scarves. Better to let people ask me questions. Better to let people look at me like they're about to cry. Better to let the other women out there walking around with no hair see that I'm one of them. So I threw it away.

Jenny Allen's essays and articles have appeared in *The New Yorker*, *The New York Times*, *New York*, *Vogue*, *Esquire*, *More*, *The Huffington Post*, and *Good Housekeeping*, and in anthologies including *Disquiet, Please!*, *In the Fullness of Time*, and *The 50 Funniest American Writers*. She is the author of *The Long Chalkboard*, a collection of fables for grown-ups. Ms. Allen has appeared off-Broadway in Nora and Delia Ephron's *Love, Loss and What I Wore*; in productions of *Jules' Blues*; and in readings of *Spalding Grey: Stories Left to Tell*. Her one-woman show, *I Got Sick Then I Got Better*, directed by James Lapine and Darren Katz, was extended three times at New York Theatre Workshop and is now seen in venues around the country. A similar version of "Hair Today, Gone Tomorrow" appeared in the October 2012 issue of *MORE*. See www.jennyallenwrites.com.

JOYCE MAYNARD

The One Good Man

I was thirty-nine years old, living in a small town in New Hampshire with my three children, writing a syndicated weekly newspaper column about my life.

It was a really bad time in my life. My mother had just died of a brain tumor. My husband had told me he didn't want to be married to me anymore, and our marriage had ended the week that my mother died.

She left me a small amount of money in her will. I was spending most of that money on a lawyer, trying to defend myself against a suit for the custody of our three children. I was under scrutiny by a *guardian ad litem* to see if I was, in fact, a fit mother, and the legal bills were mounting with horrifying speed.

The winter was cold, Christmas was coming, and I was an orphan. And then one day, a letter dropped in the mail slot.

The address was written in pencil, and the return address was followed by a long series of numbers. Even if the city written on the return address corner was not Folsom, California, and even if I'd never bought a single Johnny Cash album, I would have known it came from a man in prison.

So I opened the letter. It began,

"Dear Lady Joyce,

Many of the guys on my cell block wait excitedly for the day that *Penthouse* or *Biker Chick Magazine* is delivered. But the big day in my week is Tuesday afternoon, when I get to read your newspaper columns about your life with your children."

He knew them well, from my columns. He knew that my daughter had just been cast in *Annie* and gotten braces. He knew that my son Charlie played the trumpet and that my son Willy was a would-be pitcher. He knew that I drove a 1966 Plymouth Valiant that was frequently having problems. He signed his letter, "For real, Grizzly."

So I wrote back. "Dear Grizzly, thank you very much for your note." And I enclosed in the envelope the annual Christmas card photograph that I always took of my kids and me—them in their red-and-green holiday sweaters and me in this kind of ridiculous golden dress. And very swiftly I got another letter back.

Now, I should tell you another thing about men in prison. You know all that time that you and I spend on things like going to our jobs, taking care of our children, our houses, our cars, cooking meals, maybe having a relationship (maybe even having sex)? Men in prison don't have to spend time on any of those things, which means they have a lot of time for writing letters. A man in prison who cannot touch a woman often develops a particular kind of brilliance at letter writing.

So when I wrote Grizzly a two-sentence letter, I got back a five-page letter. And when I wrote Grizzly a one-paragraph letter, I got back a ten-page letter. And when I wrote Grizzly a one-page letter, I got back a fifty-page letter.

He was writing back more and more. You're probably thinking—and I won't pretend that this isn't an issue here—that I might be a woman of questionable judgment, and you're right, without a doubt. But one thing I will attest to, and I will stand on this to my last breath, is that I know good writing. And Grizzly knew how to do it.

He never wrote about life in prison. He always wrote about what had happened before, and he'd had a very tragic life. He grew up in the orange groves of Southern California, and he described how his family had very little money, but his mother used to make these little figures for him out of orange peels, and that's what he would play with. Later in life his parents died tragically.

He wrote about the woman that he had loved. And he loved hard, Grizzly. Then his wife died in childbirth. He raised his daughter on his own.

I'm reading all this in his letters, you know, just enthralled. And sometimes actually weeping, he told the story so beautifully.

He fell in love again, but that woman was with him in a terrible motorcycle accident—she was on the back of his Harley—and she was so horribly disfigured that she forbid him to ever see her again. And then one day he sent me a photograph of his daughter in an open casket after *she* had died.

He's sending me advice for my son Will, how to throw a knuckleball. He's drawing diagrams of the inner workings of my Valiant to show me how I can check the plugs and points and change the oil. I could pretend that all of this correspondence was in the name of making a lonely prisoner feel happy, and maybe finding out about the lives of men in prison. But I will admit to you that more and more I was being drawn into this relationship myself.

I have to say in my own defense here that at the point Grizzly came into my life, I had been single and out in the world of dating a little bit. And I know there are women who will understand this: if you have been a single woman out in the world of dating, the fact that somebody's a senior partner in a law firm, or they work for Charles Schwab, or they have tenure at NYU, is absolutely no guarantee that the person won't be a true sociopath.

So I actually came to believe that maybe I had found the one good man. I really believed that I had found the one good heart, just like he signed his letters: "For real, Grizzly." There was something so real about this man. About his language, his stories. His spelling.

He sent me a photograph of himself, and maybe you're picturing a kind of gruffly handsome Tommy Lee Jones kind of person. I've got to tell you, no. This photograph was especially taken for me, and he was standing in front of this cinder-block wall with a guard. He had a bandage over his head—I'm not exactly sure why that was—and he had a big long beard. And he said that he had actually put on his best shirt for this occasion. It was misbuttoned.

And to be honest, I'd have to say that he was an ugly man. But I had been married to a very handsome man, and so I knew the lie of that one too.

And he continued to write these letters and to talk about all of the ways that he would have treated me if he had been with me instead of my husband. He didn't think much of my $125-an-hour lawyer either. He told me very clearly in his rustically authentic language what he would do to my husband if he were around. Which was to make him eat his underwear.

I guess I have to tell you that I was falling in love with Grizzly. I have seldom read stories more powerful than the ones that he spun out in the growing stack of pages that were accumulating on my bedside table. I had started saving these letters till I went to bed on those long, cold, New Hampshire winter nights when I felt so alone in the world, and it seemed like my one friend and protector was this man three thousand miles away in prison.

There were a couple of moments when I recognized that this really didn't make sense, and I'd try to cut it off. Every time that I would send him a letter saying, "You know what? Really, Grizzly, I don't see a future here," he would send back another story that would just break my heart.

Around that time, he wrote back with astonishing news—he was getting out! And in fact his bus could probably make it to New Hampshire by the start of Little League season.

My friend said, "You've got to find out what he was in for."

This seemed like a really rude thing to ask a person. It showed a lack of trust, as if I didn't have the kind of good heart that he did. But when I knew he was coming out, and he was coming to play catch with my sons, I thought I'd better place a call to Folsom Prison.

I went through a whole series of social workers to get to the one who was in charge of Grizzly's case.

I said, "I've got to know what he's in for."

She said, "We don't do that. There are many procedures. Why do you ask?"

I said, "Well, I'm in a relationship with this person, and now that he's getting out on parole, he's coming to visit."

She said, "You know what? I'm gonna break the rules. Sit down, honey.

"Your friend will not be getting out any time in the next

three hundred years," she said. "Do you know why they call him Grizzly? He's in Folsom for the grisly murder of his parents. They were beheaded.

"And I'm going to ask you to please never let him know that I told you this because even in prison he is known as a very violent and dangerous man."

I did not write back to Grizzly. But the letters continued to come to me, of course, dropping through the mail slot. At first he just sounded baffled, then increasingly pleading, and then the tone of the letters changed, and they became angry and fierce, and putrid and violent. If any words I've ever read could have drawn blood, these would have been the ones.

The letters kept showing up for a full year. I stopped reading them.

That was the year that my divorce concluded. The *guardian ad litem* determined that I was fit to maintain custody of my children. Clearly she had not spoken to the social worker at Folsom Prison.

I never could throw Grizzly's letters away, so I put them in a box, and I put the box in the back of my closet. And I'm going to break Moth tradition tonight by reading a short passage from one of those letters:

Now listen up, baby. I don't have much to give you in the way of trinkets and such. I'm betting there's guys out there lining up to take you out to fancy restaurants, and put a ring on your finger—24 karat, who knows? Guys that'll buy you a car, buy you a house, fly you to Gay Paree. Me I can't even plant a kiss on those sweet lips of yours, not that I wouldn't CHEW OFF MY RIGHT ARM TO DO IT.

All I can give you when the day is done is one goddamn

thing, and that's my heart. I see who you are. I know you like I know my blood. I read what you wrote and I read between the lines too, baby.

I'd die for you. I'd kill for you. There isn't words to say it, but if you close your eyes and take a breath, you'll feel it. Someplace in California, there's a man locked up in a concrete box that's got you in his brain right now. Put your hand on your heart, baby, and feel it beating, imagine me inside you. I'm with you now. I'll be with you forever.

And I guess I'm with him too, because even many years later I am haunted by this knowledge: that somewhere in a maximum-security prison in Folsom, California, there is a Christmas photograph of me and my three children taped to a cinder-block wall.

Joyce Maynard is the author of thirteen books, including *To Die For* (adapted for the motion picture directed by Gus Van Sant) and *Labor Day* (soon to be released as a film directed and adapted by Jason Reitman, starring Kate Winslet). Her 1998 memoir, *At Home in the World*, has been translated into fourteen languages, and has just been rereleased with a new introduction by the author. Her newest novel, *After Her*, was published in September 2013.

Life Support

So I got to say, hands down, my twenties were the worst years of my life. I spent most of my young adult life trying to escape southern Indiana, which is where I'm from. And the thing you have to know about southern Indiana is it's highly prejudiced and terribly boring. So one of the things I was looking forward to was going to college.

And I picked—back then we called them Negro colleges, it was part of the Negro colleges consortium—I picked a black school down in Atlanta, Georgia, so I could be with *my people* because I was the only black kid in the middle-income world of Evansville, Indiana. I knew nothing about my people. We didn't have Martin Luther King Day and all those wonderful things yet. I thought it would be great! *I'm moving to Atlanta, I'm going to experience the culture of the African diaspora, and I'm going to change the world with my achievements.*

The trouble started when I first got to school, and the president of the college decided to embezzle funds from the school. And the way he did that was he took loan checks and scholarship money from innocent kids in transition like myself. So that was the first thing that happened.

The second thing that happened was I had an opportunity to work on a film set. The producers of the movie said, "Yes, yes, since you're part of the mass communication classes you can take this and get credit." So I am working on this major motion picture, and about three and a half weeks into it the producers and the directors just up and left. They pulled out their trucks, and they took everything away, and they didn't tell anybody. So, as a result, I lost my college credit for the class, which ruined my GPA. I am an overachiever, and you do not fuck with my GPA, OK? You can take anything from an overachiever, but you *cannot fuck with the GPA.*

So I lost my scholarships, and as a result, I lost my housing, and for two and a half weeks I became homeless. I found a job at a McDonald's, and I slept on the stock room floor until I got my first paycheck, and then I bought a bus ticket and came back to the place that I'd run from, southern Indiana.

So I got home, and I knocked on the door, and my mother said, "Oh, you're here! So sorry, but I've sold your bedroom set to your grandmother. And your bedroom is no longer here either: I've turned it into my sitting area."

There was nowhere for me to stay, so in protest I went to go live out in the garage with the car. It was an unfinished garage, and I was sleeping on the outdoor furniture that Mom had left, and I was terribly, terribly depressed now. I was sleeping something like sixteen hours a day, and this went on for a couple of weeks.

I became clinically depressed, and the thing you have to realize is that when you are clinically depressed, you have absolutely no energy. It's not just like, *I'm sad.* You don't have energy to do anything. So I finally got up the nerve to open up a newspaper to look for a job in southern Indiana. I opened up the paper, and I got excited because this was the 1980s and the new thing was to have home health-care aides—people who would go in and sit with the elderly, help to feed them, give them their medicine and things like that. So when I opened up the page, I saw it, and it was like a hallelujah moment: *Ahh! Sitter! What better job for a depressed person than to have a job just sitting?* That's all I had to do. I thought, *Thank God! I can go do this job.*

So I went to this place called Health Skills, and it was a temp agency. They gave me my first assignment, and one of the things that they did not tell me was that when you're the new kid on the block you get all the worst assignments. So, as a sitter, for the first few assignments that I had, I would have only terminally ill patients—people that were dying.

I take this job. On the first day, I walk up to this door. It's a frame house on cinder blocks with a little front porch in a working-class, all-white neighborhood. So I knock on the door, and the door has a window in it, and I see this woman peer out, and she's this thin, skinny, Sissy Spacek–looking woman. And she looks at me and she says, "Go away!"

And so I say, "Hi, ma'am. I'm here from Health Skills. I'm here because you needed a sitter." I think that will help, but she says, "Go away! I don't want you here!" And so I try to explain this to her again, and she says, "Fine!" So what she does is she goes to the phone, and she calls the company. I'm standing outside. It's hot. It's July, and it's kind of sticky, and I'm waiting on her to get through this phone call, and finally she just slams down the phone, comes to the door, and she opens it and lets me in.

So I am walking through this house, which is a lot like a

railroad apartment in New York. You have to walk through the living room and kitchen to get to the bedroom, and the bathroom is off to the side, so you can see all the way through the house. We make our way to the back of the house, and I get to the bedroom, and I am hit with this horrible stench, and I had to immediately stop my own gag reflex. The air is filled with the smell of bile, and I look on the bed, and there's this man lying on a hospital bed in an otherwise normal-looking bedroom, and he has breathing tubes and IVs and that kind of stuff in him, and he's completely unconscious. And the breathing machine is working, and it's pumping up this brown mousse. It kind of looks like styling foam. It's coming out of his mouth and nose. And what I discover is that this man is dying of cirrhosis of the liver, and in the final stages the liver and the bile are breaking down. It's building up as fluid in the lungs, and the body is trying desperately to get rid of that so that he can breathe. So that's what's coming up out of his mouth and nose. And so every fifteen minutes this process goes through, and I have to stand there and clean it up. So me being an overachiever and wanting this job and wanting to do well, I throw myself into the job, and I'm helping. This woman who let me in is very aggressive. She doesn't say anything, but she's not very kind to me.

So we clean up this man, and there's nothing for me to do but to just wait. So I say, "Maybe I should just sit down." And I look at this woman, and she's staring at me with hate pouring from her eyes. I don't know what the hell I've done. I've just done my job, and I've done it pretty well. So I look at her, and I say, "Look, I can get this, I'm fine now."

She just turns around, doesn't say a word to me, and walks right back down that hallway and goes and sits on the couch. And even though she's sitting across from the TV, she's sitting in profile so she can see down the hallway, and she's staring at me—she's got her eye on me. I try to take all this in.

I sit down, and I'm looking around the room, and it's filled with this nice Shaker furniture, and it's got a floor-to-ceiling Confederate flag behind the man's bed.

And the thing that I have to tell you is that when you are depressed, it takes a little while for the gears to kick in, and that's what happened to me at this moment. So I'm taking in the furniture—there's a lovely armoire, and I'm so Martha Stewart, I'm into decorating and everything—so I'm actually kind of impressed because it's very sparse, but very nice. And they have a little coat tree, and I notice that on the coat tree there's this beautiful robe. Kind of like a church robe except it's white, and it has a round circle with a white cross on it and a hood. But I'm still not grasping what's happening because I am totally amazed by this hood and the buttonhole stitching that is going around the eyes of the hood. So I'm not paying attention. I was like, *You know, maybe I should take up sewing . . .*

And then I looked down the hallway, and the woman is still looking at me. And the way we deal with things socially in Indiana is that we try to normalize things. So that's what I did, I thought, *OK. I'm just going to sit here. And oh! There's a table and there's a book on it. Hooray! I have something to do now.*

So I pick up this book, I'm flipping through the book, and it looks like a Bible because it's got gilt lettering on the outside, and I thought, *Oh great! It's a Bible! I know that! You know, Genesis, Corinthians, Ephesians; Proverbs for wisdom, Psalms if you're sad.* So I open up the book, and I'm trying to look for something peaceful and happy to read, and instead I come across this horrible-looking manifesto that talks about the superiority of the white race and how we need to annihilate everyone but them for their own safety. And I shut the book.

And it finally hits me that I am in the home of an honest-to-god Klansman, and I am a black woman.

And I look down the hallway at this woman, and she's looking back at me like, *Do you get this now?* And I'm like, *Oh shit!*

And then right at this moment, the mousse starts coming up out of this man's mouth and nose again, and I think, *Thank God, thank God! I've got something to do, I've got something to do!*

So I run over to this man, and my brain is racing because I'm wigging out. And I'm cleaning him up, and the stench is awful, and I'm looking at this man, I'm looking very calm and professional—cleaning, cleaning!

But inside my mind, I'm like, *Oh my God! I hope he doesn't wake up. Holy shit! I'm so glad he's not conscious, I am helping to clean him up and he probably hates me and, you know, I don't hate him personally, but my people hate him.* And I'm feeling all of this anxiety, and then I think, *Dude, you cannot do this right now because you need a job, OK? Because you have got to get out of the garage, and you are so depressed you can't do anything else. You do not have time for a Rosa Parks moment. You have to get through with this. OK?*

I think to myself, *You know, I'm an overachiever. I can totally do this. I am not going to let a little racism stand in my way. I am going to get this done, I am going to do it well, I am going to get an A+, I am going to get a check, and I am going to get the fuck up out of here, OK!?!*

And that is exactly what I did. I did that every fifteen minutes for four hours that day. For *four* hours. And I sat there, and I watched him, and after a while the woman went to go get something to eat, and she did get distracted by the TV, and I came back the next day.

I came back, and she opened the door, and we went through the ritual again, and she wasn't quite as unfriendly. I guess she recognized that I was not going to kill the man. So we kept on with this routine, and she did take a little bit of rest. And I came back again a third day, and the third day she was even more tired, and I realized that this woman was not getting any rest unless I was there to take care of him; that nobody would come to save her, or to help her, which I thought was really sad.

And by the fourth day, she just came to the door and immediately lay down, and I did the job, and I had to wake her up at the end of that four hours.

And then on the fifth day, the temp agency called me, and they said, "Steph, we don't need you anymore." The man had passed away. But the lady had called to leave me a message.

She wanted me to know that I'd given him the best care that he'd had since he left the hospital, and the most peace and rest that she got was when I was there, and she wanted to thank me personally.

And I thought, *Man, that is amazing.* And she left me a tip, which the temp agency would not let me keep.

But a few months later, I realized I really did get a tip and it was this: the knowledge that we had come together, she and I, these two incredibly desperate people in a highly charged, highly provocative situation. And it could have been a train wreck; it could have been a mess. But instead, we came together, and our lives touched, and in that touching we changed the trajectory of our lives just a little bit.

I'd like to think that I changed the way that she thought about people of color—that we weren't whatever it was that those people were teaching her, and that she might reconsider the prejudices that she had. And for myself, I got a job that gave me something to do every day, which I desperately needed. I had left Indiana to change the world. And I didn't; I couldn't. But I realized that even if I couldn't change *the* world, I could change a little piece of the world that I was in, and that was enough for me.

Stephanie Summerville is a musical theatre performer living in New York. She is a singer with the Secret City, an Obie Award–winning art salon held monthly at Dixon Place. She is also a proud graduate of Sarah Lawrence College and an alum of the New York Shakespeare Festival Lab at the Joseph Papp Public Theater.

JENIFER HIXSON

Where There's Smoke

I reached over and secretly undid my seat belt. And when his foot hit the brake at the red light, I flung open the door, and I ran. I had no shoes on. I was crying. I had no wallet. But I was okay because I had my cigarettes. And I didn't want any part of freedom if I didn't have my cigarettes.

When you live with someone who has a temper—a very bad temper—a very, very bad temper—you learn to play around that. You learn, *This time, I'll play possum, and next time I'll just be real nice, or I'll say yes to everything.*

Or you make yourself scarce, or you run. And this was one of the times when you just run.

And as I was running, I thought, *This was a great place to jump out*, because there were big lawns and cul-de-sacs.

Sometimes he would come after me and drive and yell at me to "get back in, get back in!"

And I was like, *No, I'm outta here. This is great.* And I went and hid behind a cabana, and he left.

And I had my cigarettes.

I started to walk around this beautiful neighborhood. It was ten-thirty at night, and it was silent and lovely. There was no sound, except for sprinklers. And I was enjoying myself. Enjoying the absence of anger, and enjoying these few hours I knew I'd have of freedom.

Just to perfect it, I thought, *I'll have a smoke.* And then it occurred to me, with horrifying speed, *I don't have a light!*

Just then, as if in answer, I see a figure up ahead. *Who is that? It's not him. Okay. They don't have a dog. What are they doing out on this suburban street?*

And the person comes closer, and I can see it's a woman. Then I can see she has her face in her hands. Oh, she's crying. And then she sees me, and she composes herself. And she gets closer, and I see she has no shoes on. She has no shoes on, and she's crying, and she's out on the street.

I recognize her, though I've never met her.

And just as she passes me, she says, "You got a cigarette?"

And I say, "You got a light?"

And she says, "Damn, I hope so."

And then she digs into her cutoffs in the front. Nothing. Then digs in the back. And then she has this vest on that has fifty million little pockets on it, and she's checking and checking, and it's looking bad. It's looking very bad. She digs back in the front again, deep, deep, and she pulls out a pack of matches that have been laundered at least once.

We open it up, and there is *one match* inside.

Oh my God, it's like NASA now. *How we gonna do it?* And we hunker down. We crouch on the ground. *Where's the wind coming from?* We're stopping. I take out my cigarettes. *Let's get the cigarettes ready.*

"Oh, my brand," she says. Not surprising.

We both have our cigarettes at the ready. She strikes once. Nothing. She strikes again. *Yes!* Fire. Puff. Inhale. Mmmm. The sweet kiss of that cigarette.

And we sit there, and we're loving the nicotine, and we both need this right now, I can tell. The night's been tough.

Immediately we start to reminisce about our thirty-second relationship:

"I didn't think that was gonna happen."

"Me neither."

"Oh, man, that was close."

"I'm so lucky I saw you."

"Yeah."

Then she surprises me by saying, "What was the fight about?"

And I say, "What are they all about?"

And she says, "I know what you mean. Was it a bad one?"

And I say, "You know like, medium."

"Oh."

And we start to trade stories about our lives. We're both from up north. We're both kind of newish to the neighborhood (this is in Florida). We both went to college—not great colleges, but, man, we graduated.

And I'm actually finding myself a little jealous of her because she has this really cool job washing dogs. She had horses back home, and she really loves animals, and she wants to be a vet.

And I'm like, "Man, you're halfway there!"

I'm a waitress at an ice cream parlor. I don't know where I want to be, but I know it's not that.

And then it gets a little deeper, and we share some other stuff about what our lives are like. Things that I can't ever tell people at home. This girl, I can tell her the really ugly stuff, and she understands how it can still be pretty. She understands how nice he's gonna be when I get home, and how sweet that'll be.

We are chain-smoking off each other. "Oh, that's almost out. Come on . . ."

We go through the entire pack until it's gone.

Then I say, "You know what? This is a little funny, but you're gonna have to show me the way to get home." Because although I'm twenty-three years old, I don't have my driver's license, and I just jumped out right when I needed to.

And she says, "Well, why don't you come back to my house, and I'll give you a ride?"

"Okay, great."

We start walking. And we get to this corner with lots of lights, and the roads are getting wider and wider, and there are more cars. I see lots of stores—you know, Laundromats and dollar stores and EmergiCenters.

And then we cross over US-1, and she leads me to some place, and I think, *No*.

But, yes.

Carl's Efficiency Apartments. This girl lives here.

And it's horrible, and it's lit up so bright, just to illuminate the horribleness of it. It's the kind of place where you drive your car right up, and the door's right there, and there are fifty million cigarette butts outside. There are doors one through seven, and you just know behind every single door there's some horrible misery going on. There's someone crying or drunk or lonely or cruel.

And I think, *Oh, God, she lives here. How awful.*

We go to the door—door number four—and she very, very quietly keys in. As soon as the door opens, I hear the blare of a television, and on the blue light of the television, the smoke of a hundred cigarettes in that little crack of light.

I hear a man, and he says, "Where were you?"

She says, "Never mind. I'm back."

And he says, "You all right?"

And she says, "Yeah, I'm all right."

And then she turns to me and says, "You want a beer?"

And he says, "Who the *fuck* is that?"

And she pulls me over, and he sees me, and he says, "Oh. Hey."

I'm not a threat.

Just then he takes a drag off of his cigarette, a very hard drag—the kind that makes the end of it really heat up hot, hot, hot. And long. And it's a little scary. And I follow the cigarette down, 'cause I'm afraid of that head falling off. And I'm surprised when I see, in the crook of his arm, a little boy, sleeping. A toddler. And I think, [*gasps*].

And just then the girl reaches under the bed and takes out a carton, and she taps out the last pack of cigarettes in there. On the way up, she kisses the little boy, and then she kisses the man.

And the man says again, "You all right?"

And she says, "Yeah. I'm just gonna go out and smoke with her."

And so we go outside and sit amongst the cigarette butts and smoke.

I say, "Wow. That's your little boy?"

"Yeah, isn't he beautiful?"

"Yeah, he *is*. He is beautiful."

"He's my light. He keeps me going," she says.

We finish our cigarettes. She finishes her beer. I don't have a beer, 'cause I can't go home with beer on my breath. She goes inside to get the keys. She takes too long in there getting the keys, and I think something must be wrong.

She comes out, and she says, "Look, I'm really sorry but, um, like, we don't have any gas in the car. It's already on 'E,' and he needs to get to work in the morning. I'm gonna walk to work as it is. So what I did was, here, look, I drew out this map for you. You're like a mile and a half from home. If you walk three streets over, you'll be back on that pretty street, and you just take that and you'll be fine."

She also has wrapped up, in toilet paper, seven cigarettes for me—a third of her pack, I note. And a new pack of matches.

And she tells me, "Good-bye," and "that was great to meet you," and "how lucky," and "that was fun," and, you know, "let's be friends."

And I say, "Yeah, okay." And I walk away.

But I kinda know we're not gonna be friends. I might not ever see her again. And I kinda know I don't think she's ever gonna be a vet. And I cross, and I walk away.

And maybe this would have seemed like a visit from my possible future, and scary, but it kinda does the opposite. On the walk home I'm like, *Man, that was really grim over there. And I'm going home now to my nice boyfriend, and he's gonna be so extra-happy to see me. And we have a one-bedroom apartment. And we have two trees, and there's a yard. And we have this jar in the kitchen where there's loose money that we can use for anything. We would never, ever run out of gas. And I don't have a baby, you know? So I can leave whenever I want.*

I smoked all seven cigarettes on the way home. And people who have never smoked cigarettes just think, *Ick, disgusting and poison.* But unless you've had them and held them dear, you don't know how great they can be, and what friends and comfort and kinship they can bring.

It took me a long time to quit . . . that boyfriend. And then to quit smoking. But sometimes I still miss the smoking.

Jenifer Hixson is a senior producer at The Moth, where she is best known for launching and developing The Moth StorySLAM.

BRIAN FINKELSTEIN

Perfect Moments

So the standard commitment to work at the Humanitarian Suicide Hotline is six months. Most people work six months, and then they leave, quickly. A few make it a year. Nobody really goes beyond a year. I was a volunteer there for four years.

It started when I was twenty-two years old, and I was young, and I believed in things. I thought maybe I could help the world. I was that age.

And so I decided I wanted to be a clinical psychologist, but the problem was, I was a twenty-two-year-old freshman at Queens College, which is not a great school, and my GPA was a two point . . . zero.

And so I was gonna have some problems getting into a master's program, which is very competitive for clinical psychology, so I needed an internship—something to help me out, some leverage. I decided to volunteer at the Humanitarian Suicide Hotline.

So I show up one Saturday morning at 8 A.M., and I walk into this church on the Upper West Side of Manhattan. And there's a bunch of people milling about, but I see this guy that's clearly in charge. He's sitting on the desk. He's sort of an ex-hippie turned a little corporate. He's got a flannel shirt tucked into khaki pants, you know what I mean? He's dipping a chamomile tea bag into an NPR cup. I know who this guy is. I get it. He's a vegan who drives a BMW. I know it.

He tells us his name is Glen. He's like, "Hey, check it out, all right. My name's Glen." And then he thanks us all for coming and says, "Hey, even though we're in a church, you know, I just want you to know we're not affiliated with any sort of religion or God, so let me just tell you straight-out, if you're here for God, or any sort of politics or religion, you should leave now." And right then, some old dude in the back just goes, "See ya," and walks out the door.

And then Glen sits down, and even though he's got this corporate Jewish metrosexual hippie thing going on, he's also got a little bit of a Louis Gossett, Jr., drill sergeant thing going on, because as soon as he starts the training class, he's starting to weed people out. People start dropping.

There was this one guy who was sitting in the back of the class drinking a forty of beer. The class, I should remind you, was at 8 A.M. So he was gone.

There were these two teenage dudes from Queens who every time they talked were like, "Hey, douche bag," and then they'd high-five. They were gone.

There was a woman who did a mock phone call with Glen, 'cause in the two-week training class he did mock phone calls where he pretended to be callers. And Glen was pretending to be this seventy-year-old dude who was HIV positive and had just found out he had AIDS and was very upset. And he was talking to this potential volunteer, Nancy, who was doing the phone call.

And she said, "Well, I just want you to know that's very up-setting. I'm very sorry for you, but you did choose this lifestyle, so—"

Gone.

One of the most important things Glen weeded out was people who were there because they were either suicide survivors, meaning they'd lost somebody because of suicide, or because they themselves, the volunteer, had contemplated or tried to commit suicide.

And as Glen would say, "Yeah, check it out. You're really not a good fit." Gone.

At the end of two weeks of training, out of fifty-eight people who came to volunteer, there were only four of us left, because Glen was really good. But I will tell you right now, I was better.

Because what Glen didn't know about me was that about four years before this, I lived in San Diego, California, and I was dating this girl Tracy. Tracy was addicted to meth, and I was addicted to Tracy. So Tracy would try to do the meth, I would try to do her; neither one of us would ever be satisfied. That's addiction.

One day Tracy slept with my best friend, Baby Face, this guy who looked like Morrissey, 'cause she was into that.

I'd had it. And I bet you Glen didn't know that I then jumped in my five-speed puke-orange VW Fastback, an awesome car, and I drove up to my dad's house in Del Mar, California, 'cause my father's a retired cop, and I went into his garage, and I took his .38. And I bet you Glen has no idea that a .38 doesn't have one of those clips that you put in. You put the bullets in, then you snap it, and it's really easy, even if you don't know how to use guns.

I grabbed a bottle of tequila out of my father's liquor

cabinet, and I got in my car, and I drove to Torrey Pines Beach. I took the gun, and I drank about a half a bottle of tequila. And a gun like that is really easy, because if you pull the hammer back, it has a hairpin. You can just tap it, and it's gonna go off.

And I took the gun, and I stuck it in my mouth. And I'll bet you Glen has no idea how good it feels to stick a loaded gun in your mouth. It feels incredibly good. Things weren't going good for me, and I'm just pointing it out, just saying it right now in front of all of you—it felt good to have control. To say, *I'm gonna put a gun in my mouth, and I'm gonna have some control over something.*

And I sat there, and I was trying to contemplate doing it, and then . . .

Tequila makes me a little dramatic. And I threw up.

I'm not a good drinker. I want to be. I want to be the guy that drinks a bottle of tequila, but it's not me. I'm not Bukowski, I'm Dr. Phil. And I threw up all over the gun. And there's nothing that sort of snaps you out of a suicide impulse more than throwing up on a gun. It really clears your head.

And I took the gun out, and I thought to myself, *Well, at least I know I'm not the type of person that's gonna pull the trigger,* which is something I had to find out that way. It snapped me out of the suicide, and I felt really good, and I felt this moment of clarity. I wiped the throw up off me, and I got out of my car. I was at Torrey Pines—a beautiful beach—and I went into the water.

It was late at night. Beautiful full moon. And I went in the water, and it was perfect. I had what, for me, was the perfect life moment. I sat there under the full moon, in the water, just feeling really good, the waves sort of washing over me, and I realized that's what life is. There are these moments of beauty, like moons and oceans, and then there are moments of horror. And then it's good again. And then it's horrible and kicks you in the face. And then it's good again. And then it's horrible and a pig-sty, because that's what life is. But then for a moment it's good. And for me that was enough.

But I bet you Glen didn't know any of that, because I never told him.

So at the end of two weeks of training class we walk out of the training room, and there's the hotline room. There are three desks with phones and a couple of plants, and there's a list of phone numbers hanging on the wall. There's Glen's home number in case you need him. There's poison control, and then there's 911, in case you forget the number for 911.

And then there's a sign that hangs on the wall that says the motto of the hotline, which is SHUT UP AND LISTEN. Big block letters, SHUT UP AND LISTEN. And that is an amazing expression to me. That is exactly why I stayed there for four years. Because after six months, I got my certificate, I was free to leave. But I ended up staying for four years because it made me feel good to work there, for two reasons.

One, listening to people's problems on the phone, you start to think to yourself, *You know what, I don't have it so bad. These people have it a lot worse.* It's like if you go to the park, and you sit on a bench, and you look down, and you see a squirrel, and you think, *Well, at least I'm not a squirrel.* You know what I mean? It's something.

And two, seeing the sign, SHUT UP AND LISTEN, it's how you *do* prevent suicides—by listening to people.

We don't listen to each other. We have agendas. Whether it's somebody you love, or just casual, we all have agendas. We're all trying to get something, and we like to talk. I clearly like to talk a lot about myself. I'm up here. But the idea of sitting and listening to somebody else talk made me feel good. It made me feel like I was helping. And that's why I stayed for four years.

Now, the training basically says that what you do is you answer the call. You say, "Humanitarian Suicide Hotline. Thanks for calling." You then listen. You have to be an active listener. Glen said not to get scared of silence if there was silence on the phone because "Check it out . . . Silence is a form of communication. Right on." He also said that you can't get manipulated by silence, so if it lasts five minutes, you gotta hang up the phone. At the end of twelve minutes, end the call anyway, because that's the allotted time. But before you end the call, you have to evaluate the person's level of suicide. And the way you do that is you ask a series of four questions.

1. Do you feel so bad that you think about suicide?
2. Do you have a plan for how you would do it?
3. Have you set a time for when you're gonna do that?
4. Have you taken any steps today to kill yourself?

Now, in the four years I worked there, 99.9 percent of all calls were YES, NO, NO, NO. A lot of people think about suicide, but most people don't really go the next step.

Glen said the closest thing to a warning sign that you can have for suicide is if somebody says something like "I don't want to die. I just want the pain to stop." And if you hear somebody say that—that they want the pain to stop—a bell should go off. That's a person who's on the edge.

So four years later, I'm working at the hotline. It's just me and my shift partner, a guy named Adam. Adam's a communist. Not relevant at all to the story, just a little detail. You're welcome.

So me and Adam are working the overnight shift, from eleven o'clock at night to eight o'clock in the morning. You have to do one a month. And it's busy till like 4 A.M., till the bars close in New York, and then it gets slow.

And around four it was my turn to answer the phone, and the phone rings, and I pick it up.

"Hello, Humanitarians, can I help you?"

And this very young, cute, scared voice comes on the phone and says, "Hi. My name is Amy. I'd like to talk."

And I say, "What's up, Amy? What's going on?"

She says, "Oh, nothing. I was just, you know, calling because I was feeling a little sad."

And I was like, "Oh, what are you sad about?"

And she goes, "Ah, I don't know, things are pretty good. I have good grades at school, and my parents don't get it, but they love me, and, you know, I have a good friend back in Tennessee where I'm from, and NYU's good. I have good friends here."

She said she had two types of friends, which I thought was really funny. She had bar friends and then she had movie friends. I like that expression. I wish I had some movie friends, but so be it.

Right away I pictured her, the way you do when you talk to somebody on the phone. I pictured her in her dorm room, and I pictured a quilt, and I pictured her with long hair, sitting on her bed, and Rollerblades, and a Dr Pepper, you know what I mean? I got her figured out.

And so I said, "Well, that sounds good. But you said you were sad. What do you think about when that happens?"

She said, "I don't know. I don't understand what happens. I can't control it. Sometimes when I have a great day, what I do the next day is I try to duplicate it. I wake up at the same time,

I try to eat the same food, try to have the same pattern, so that I can control the day, so that I don't feel bad."

But then, out of nowhere, she said, she felt what she described as a hand coming from behind her and sort of pushing her down.

And I said, "Okay, well, what, what's going on when that happens? What are you thinking about?"

And she said, "Ah, everything, nothing, I don't know. I just feel so stupid." She started to sound uncomfortable. And then we started to flirt a little, not in an inappropriate way, but look, a lot of the callers I talked to over the years were crazy. This was different. She could have been a movie friend if I had met her in some other situation. I was talking to her, and we talked for a little while, and then she said she felt dumb because of depression.

She felt this crippling sadness, and that there *are* people who are clinically or socially or chemically depressed, but she thought maybe a lot of people overuse that word, or use it as an excuse, and she was worried she might be like that. And I could identify. I felt the same way.

I don't think I get depressed. I mean, sure there are times where I don't get out of bed for four days, but I'm not depressed, right?

So we were talking like that.

And then I noticed that it was about time to wrap it up, but Amy started telling me this story about going to some place with her family one day, and their father bought ice cream, and it was a great day.

I said, "Oh, that's great." And I looked at the clock.

But then Amy started to slur her speech a little bit.

I said, "Amy, what's going on? Are you okay?"

And she goes, "Yeah. Look, I know it's selfish, and I know it's stupid, but I can't do it anymore. I just want it to stop."

And I said, "What do you mean? What do you mean by 'it'?"

She goes, "I don't know. I just *can't*. I just want you to talk to me."

I was like, "Well, when you said 'it,' what did you mean?"

She said, "Look, I don't want to die. I just want the pain to stop."

And I woke up.

I said, "Amy, do you feel so bad that you think about suicide?"

And she said, "Yes."

I said, "Do you have a plan for how you would do it?"

"Yes."

"Have you set a time for when you're gonna do it?"

"Uh-huh."

"Amy, have you taken any steps today to kill yourself?"

And she said, "Yes."

And I said, "Amy, what have you done?" And she told me she took twenty high-strength painkillers, and I said, "What kind of painkillers?" because that's what you're supposed to ask, and she told me, and I wrote it down. And I threw a pencil at Adam who was nodding off, and I handed him the piece of paper so he could call poison control, and I could have some information about what would happen, so I could pass it on to her.

I tried to keep Amy talking. I was trying to ask her about other things, and she was again talking about that day her father bought her ice cream, and it was very confusing, and then Adam came back with the piece of paper.

He'd called poison control. I said, "Amy, given the fact that you took twenty high-strength painkillers, and that you drank, and that you haven't thrown up"—which she had told me—"do you understand that you could die, within an hour?"

And she started to cry.

And I was like, "Amy, look, do you want help? Do you want me to do something? I can do something, but I can only help you if you ask."

Our policy was not to intervene unless people asked us to.

I said, "If you want help, I can do something."

And she goes, "I do. I don't want to do this."

And I said, "Great, what's your address?" She gave me her address, I handed it to Adam, and he went to call 911.

And I kept Amy talking. I was like, "Uh, Amy, what kind of ice cream was it that your father bought you? You mentioned that your father bought you ice cream. What *kind* of ice cream was it?"

But it was silent. And it was silent for two minutes. And it was silent for five minutes. And I'm supposed to hang up the phone, but who the hell could hang up the phone? So I didn't.

And then around thirteen, fourteen minutes, I heard noises at the door, and I heard people knocking, and then I heard the door crash open. I heard footsteps, and then I heard the phone being picked up, and a voice said, "It's okay. We've got her."

Click.

I went home. I was supposed to go to class that day. I had classes at Queens College. But I didn't go back to Queens College. I never went back to Queens College. I never graduated.

I was supposed to go back to the hotline for a debriefing based on that phone call. I called Glen and told him I quit, that I wasn't coming back.

"Check it out . . ." *Click.*

And then I did all the things you're not supposed to do in

that situation. I obsessed about it. I stayed up, and I drank, and I smoked, and I drank coffee, and I searched. It was before the Internet, but I looked through the papers and listened to the radio, and finally, after three days, I found it. In the *Daily News*, page 23, a small paragraph that said that they had found the body of a nineteen-year-old NYU student named Amy Walters who had died of an accidental overdose.

And I know why they call it accidental. I get it. There's insurance reasons, religious reasons, family. They don't want an epidemic to start in a college. I get all that.

But what I didn't know until that moment was that she was dead, and I was the last person to talk to her. Not her mom in Tennessee, or her best friend, or some boy at NYU that probably had a crush on her but never talked to her.

Me.

And I wanted to call her family, and I wanted to try to go down to the funeral, but I knew it was inappropriate, and so I didn't.

And the thing of it is, I have had bigger personal tragedies over the years. I spoke to her for less than an hour twenty years ago. But I think about it every day. She's me, in that car. If I had pulled the trigger, that would be me. And she never got to find out what I got to find out, which is it's terrible sometimes, but there are these perfect life moments. And that's enough.

Brian Finkelstein (twitter.com/@bsfinkelstein) is a regular performer at the Upright Citizens Brigade Theatre and is also the host of the LA Moth StorySLAMs. Because he is über self-indulgent, he has performed way too many solo shows in a variety of venues, from the HBO/US Comedy Arts Festival in Aspen to the 2012 Summer Nights Festival in Perth, Australia. His solo show, *First Day Off in a Long Time* (about working at a suicide hot-line), was developed into a pilot script for Fox called *Blue*. Later he wrote for the *Ellen DeGeneres Show*. While at *Ellen*, Brian was nominated for two Emmys. Daytime Emmys . . . but still. Most recently, he has optioned (and reoptioned) his feature *Good Grief* with 72 Productions and has been working on his latest solo show, *Everything Is Everything*. Other than that, he watches a lot of TV and eats a lot of chocolate-mint-chip ice cream.

Fireworks from Above

What I always wanted as a little girl was to tell stories on the stage, because I wanted to be connected to something bigger than myself, and I wanted to be connected to other people.

And I believe that a really good performer takes a group of individuals and, through a shared emotional experience, turns it into a collective. For as long as I can remember, I've wanted to do this.

I've wanted to be a performer . . . slash STEWARDESS!

I grew up in my mama's beauty shop in Texas. It was this old A-frame house with big mirrors and swivel chairs in the front room and shampoo bowls in what had been the back bedroom.

My mama had this long line of hood dryers on one wall, and I would wait until all the ladies were held captive under the dryers and give mandatory concerts. That was my very first stage.

When I wasn't telling stories and doing shows for the ladies, I would play stewardess, and I would push this little manicure cart around the beauty shop.

[*with thick Southern drawl*] "Miss Helen, Miss Melba, would y'all like a magazine? Would y'all like a cocktail?"

And the ladies would say, "Baby, you just give great customer service."

I was *all about* customer service.

And sometimes I'd sit on the porch playing with my Barbie's Friend Ship airplane, and I would wear this long, silk scarf tied on the side (and it's *hot* in Texas in the summer). But I loved playing stewardess.

Well, about ten years ago, I was living in New York City, working as a performer, telling stories and singing songs on the stage. Bad pay, no job security, no benefits. I really needed a job. And I very randomly met this lovely girl with a long, silk scarf tied on the side, who said nine words that changed my life forever:

She said, "Have you ever thought about being a flight attendant?"

I had!

Three weeks later, I was in Miami training. Training was so exciting. It was a brand-new airline. They had seven airplanes, a handful of destinations, and a lot of great buzz. They had buzz around the fact that there was live TV at every seat. And they had blue potato chips and designer uniforms. But most of the buzz was around the fact that they had amazing customer service.

Perfect! I was all about customer service back at the beauty shop.

And when the founder and CEO of the airline came into our training class and gave this amazing, uplifting speech, I knew I was in the right place.

He said, "Every one of you is here for a reason, and that reason is your ability to smile and be kind. We can teach you how to evacuate an airplane. We can teach you how to handle a medical emergency. We can teach you how to serve. But we cannot teach you to smile and be kind. Your mother did that. Please thank her for me."

So beautiful. He said he saw this not as an airline, not as a corporation, but as a humanitarian experiment. He said his goal was to bring humanity back to air travel. I was right on board with this vision. I was so caught up in it. And when I graduated, they made me president of my class, and they even gave me this special certificate called the Spirit Award.

I couldn't wait to get out there on the line—to surprise people with kindness and, in the process of moving people from Point A to Point B, really, actually move people.

And then I graduated. And then I started the job. Maybe you see where this is going.

I had this epiphany almost right away: This job is hard, and *people are horrible*. Really horrible.

First of all, the job was physically exhausting. In the beginning I was on reserve, which meant that I was on call and had to be within two hours of Kennedy Airport at all times. So I was either running to get to the airport or waiting for the phone call to run to get to the airport, constantly on edge.

And then the actual commute to the airport was extremely hard. I had to take the subway to the bus to the shuttle to the terminal. Even before I got on the plane, I was exhausted. And then when I did get on the plane, there was a whole world of hurt.

My feet hurt. There's this thing that happens where you get bruises on the bottom of your feet from turbulence, and it was horrible. And new flight attendants are sick a lot, because it's kind of like being a kindergarten teacher—you're exposed to a lot of germs. At one point I had pinkeye in both eyes, a sinus infection, a double ear infection, and strep throat all at the same time. I couldn't see, I couldn't hear, I couldn't talk. And it was mainly because I was taking garbage from everyone all day. And saying "thank you" for it!

"Thank you. Thank you for your garbage. Thank you."

They actually made us stop calling it trash. We had to call it "service items," because some of the really bitter girls would say, "Sir . . . you('re) trash," "Ma'am . . . your whole family's trash."

But I understand why they were jaded, because I was kind of getting jaded too. I just couldn't believe how horrible people could be.

It's really hard to be mean when someone is smiling at you and handing you a cup of coffee and a cookie, but people are. Because a lot of times they don't see you—they just see a uniform.

And traveling is hard. It's stressful, and people get ugly. I tried really hard to keep that vision and to smile and be kind, even in the face of meanness.

But I hit bottom one day when I had a passenger who had a heart attack on my flight. He was lying in the aisle, and we had opened his shirt and had the pads of the defibrillator on him. I was holding an oxygen bottle.

And this woman in the row sitting next to me kept tugging on my blouse: "Excuse me. Excuse me!"

I was like, "Just a minute, please. We're trying to save this guy's life."

She kept tugging and tugging, and I said, "Just a minute! JUST A MINUTE!"

And then I thought: *Wait a minute. Maybe* she *has an emergency, or maybe she knows something.*

So I said, "What is it?"

And she held up her coffee cup and said, "This coffee is cold."

And I learned that *people* can be cold.

There's also something that happens to your psychology because you see the world from above when you fly a lot. And I saw a lot of really horrible things from the air, like devastating California forest fires, New Orleans under water, and most upsetting for me, lower Manhattan smoldering for weeks and weeks.

And in late September of 2001, I was working a flight, and a passenger came on with a garbage bag, which is kind of a flight attendant pet peeve, because, "Really, sir, a garbage bag? Fourteenth Street, $9.99. Get a roll-aboard." You know? But you see that. Sometimes people just throw things in a garbage bag and bring it on.

So he goes to row two, which is where he was seated, and he opened the overhead bin and put the garbage bag in.

And my next thought was: *What's in that garbage bag?* Because in late September of '01, we were all still a little edgy and paranoid, so I was kind of keeping my eye on him and the bag. And he put it in the overhead bin and closed the bin and stood there with his hand on it, guarding it.

Which is another flight attendant pet peeve. The overhead bins are shared space, okay? And if you hog up all the space, somebody's bag is gonna get checked. And by the way, if you're in row twelve, please don't leave your bag in row one. *It's not nice.* You're taking somebody's space.

So my instinct was to go up to this man and say, "Sir, please sit down."

But I thought: *Just let it go. Just smile and be kind, and if we need the space, I'll deal with it later.* So I didn't say anything.

I also didn't say anything when he got up while the seat belt sign was on and came and stood, waiting for the bathroom. If the seat belt sign is on, it's because the captain knows something we don't know, okay? And it might not feel bumpy, but he's probably heard from an airplane further out that there's turbulence ahead. I have a friend who broke his ankle on the ceiling on a smooth flight. So that's another flight attendant pet peeve.

He stood there, waiting for the bathroom, and I said, "Sir, the seat belt sign is on."

He said, "I know, I know, but I really need to go."

And again I thought: *Let it go. Just let it go.*

I was sitting on the jump seat, and it was kinda awkward because he was just standing there, and I felt like I should say something.

So I said, "Are you traveling for business or pleasure?"

And he said, "Neither. I live in California, but I came to New York because my son was a first responder at Ground Zero, and he died there. I came to pick up his uniform, which is all I have of him, and it's in a bag in the overhead bin."

And I remembered why I was there, and why I was hired and why I wanted that job. Because I remembered that everybody has a story, and I don't know what that story is. People fly for a reason. Maybe they're going to a funeral or to see someone who's sick, or maybe it's something joyful, like a wedding. I don't know what their story is, but for that little piece of time, I'm a part of it, and I have an impact on their experience.

And what I love about performing is taking a group of individuals and, through a shared emotional experience, turning it into a collective. But my job as a flight attendant is to take a *collective* and to turn it *back* into a group of individuals.

Flight attendants talk about "crowds" sometimes, like, "Avoid the Fort Lauderdale crowd. They're horrible," or "Avoid the Long Beach crowd."

But every crowd is a group of individuals, and every individual has a story. And yeah, I saw a lot of horrible things from the air. But I've also seen a lot of amazing, beautiful things from the air, like the Grand Canyon, the Northern Lights, fireworks *from above*.

And now when I go through the cabin with my garbage bag, saying "thank you" and smiling, I mean it, because I'm making a gratitude list in my head. And every time I say, "thank you," I think of something I'm grateful for:

"Thank you" (for my job). "Thank you" (for these comfy shoes). "Thank you" (for my life). Because my job enables me to be part of something bigger than me, and to be connected to other people, like this. So thank you.

Faye Lane is a writer and performer whose unique blending of story and song moved *New York Magazine* to gush, "She had them gobbling from the palm of her hand. They were howling, crying, falling in love with her." Her critically acclaimed solo show, *Faye Lane's Beauty Shop Stories*, a chronicle of her childhood in a Texas beauty salon, was born on the Moth stage and was the recipient of the 2010 Overall Excellence Award from the New York International Fringe Festival, the 2011 Bistro Award for Best Musical Comedy, and the 2011 MAC Award for Outstanding Special Production. The show has an ongoing residency at the legendary SoHo Playhouse in New York and has touched audiences across the country and around the world. Winner of The Moth StorySLAM in both New York and Los Angeles, Faye is a frequent contributor to *The Moth Radio Hour* and Mainstage. In addition to touring with her solo show, Faye uses storytelling as the basis for corporate motivational presentations and writing and performing workshops. For more information, please visit www.FayeLane.com.

Franny's Last Ride

When I was a kid, I wanted to get a Harley really bad. I was about seven, and I was in my dad's car in the back, and these dudes were driving by on these Harleys.

I remember looking at them, and thinking, *I want to do that, man, you know? I want to be free like those guys.*

And I then started doing heroin a few years later, so I couldn't really get a bike. I couldn't get toothpaste and shit, you know, let alone a $15,000 motorcycle.

When I was eighteen my parents found me in the house, overdosed, almost dead. They took me to a hospital, and then they took me to a detox, and then to a rehab.

When I was in the rehab, I met Fran. She was a beautiful, beautiful girl. The first time I saw her, I was just, like, wow—amazed. And we became really close, and we went through the rehab. She had been there a long time before me, and she was finishing up, and then I finished, and we started dating.

And life was pretty good, you know? It was hard to get off of heroin, but I was able to do it. I went to college, and Franny and I were together and dating and just having a good time.

One day she had a really bad fever. I took her to the hospital, and twelve hours later they said that she had pneumocystic pneumonia. I didn't know what it was. They said it was from AIDS. I didn't know what to do. I loved her, and I wanted to be with her.

New York got her sick a lot. She'd cough a lot and had bronchitis all the time, so we moved to Florida. Like when old people move down there. We went down to retire. I figured that we would live as much as we could. I just wanted to make her life the greatest life.

We got married. We used to go out for dinners and stuff. She wanted to go out, I would take her out. She'd have her oxygen tank with her, and I'd take her to a restaurant, and I'd look around and I'd see another couple with the husband taking care of the wife. But they were eighty, you know? We were twenty.

I thought the warm air down there would help her heal and feel better, but it didn't. She went into the hospital one night, and the next morning the doctor told me that she had pneumonia again, they couldn't really cure it, and she might have a few weeks to live.

I was devastated, and she was devastated. They put her in hospice. But two weeks later, they sent her out of the hospice because she started to get better.

She was thrown out of hospice for not dying.

Only she could have pulled that off. She was a young Italian girl, and she was not interested in suffering and dying. Like, who is? But she was extra not fucking into it.

A few weeks later, she got sick again. I took her back to the hospital. They put her in.

Doctor told me the same thing: "A few weeks, and she's gonna be gone."

So they put her back in hospice. A month and a half later, they sent her home again. Our families—my parents, her parents—were happy about it. *Oh, she's gonna be better.*

But I knew how the story was gonna end.

A few weeks later, she ends up back in the hospital. And on Thursday of that week, my motorcycle—my Harley-Davidson—was ready to be picked up. So I went that Thursday to get the bike. And it was beautiful. She was in the hospital, and I got a call that she went back to hospice. So I drove the bike over to the hospice, and I didn't know what to do. Should I show her the bike? What the fuck do you do?

I brought the bike out front, and I went into the room, and I said, "Franny, I want to show you something," and I brought her outside and showed her the bike.

And she was mad.

She was like, "What the fuck is that?" I brought it to her 'cause it was our dream together, and she was still very important to me, and I just thought that would make her happy. But it didn't.

So the social worker came over to me and said, "Mike, people are never dying. They *live* and then they *die*. And dying is in a moment. She feels that you're treating her as if she's dying, and you don't need her anymore. You don't love her anymore."

That wasn't the truth. I told her every day. But I went home, and I came back to the hospice, and I brought a few of my work shirts with me because she loved ironing for me.

I came back a couple hours later, and my shirts were all ironed, and she was walking around the hospice, dusting, like she would clean the place up. She was on a lot of morphine and—some of you that never did it—it's wonderful. It makes you feel excited about things.

So she saw me, and she's like, "Where's the bike?" Everything I wanted her to feel in the beginning, she now felt. Because I asked her to iron my clothes.

And I said, "It's outside. Let's go see," and I took her out.

She said, "Let me sit on it." So I put her on it.

And then she said, "Can you start it up?"

So I start the bike up, and it's rumbling. It was a loud bike. It was gorgeous.

And then she says, "Well, can you just take me for a little ride? Just around the parking lot here?"

And I'm like, *Fuck.*

I'm thinking she's gonna fall off the back, and I'm gonna have to tell her family, *Yeah, she almost died of AIDS. But then I killed her on my bike.*

So now we're riding around the hospice, and she's got the morphine pole dragging next to her.

And we're junkies, you know? We were different. We were fucking freaks. People crossed the street when they saw me. And her. She was a *prostitute*. She was a fucking drug addict. I mean all the shit that—you know what I'm talking about, some of you—I can tell.

So this was amazing, you know? We're riding around this hospice with this morphine pole fucking dangling. And all the staff comes out, and they're watching us, and they're cheering us on.

And then I hear the pole fall. And I think she fell off the back, but, no, she unhooked the morphine bag, which means, "I want to go out on the street a little bit."

So I take her out on the street a little bit. And then she just put her arm around my belly and started rubbing, and she said, "Can we go on the highway?"

And I thought of all that we'd been through and all the suffering.

And I said, "Yeah, we could do that."

So we got on I-95. And I had it up to eighty. And she was just screaming with happiness. Morphine bag was flapping over her head.

And that wind—I always imagined the wind on a bike making you feel free, you know? It's so powerful. And for ten minutes we were normal, and that wind just blew all the death off of us.

I promised her when she died that for the rest of my life I was gonna live for her. I mean, *really live*.

But nothing I'll ever do will ever be that grand again.

Mike DeStefano was a stand-up comic who overcame personal torment and drug addiction to become a regular at all the top clubs in New York City. He could be heard on Sirius Satellite Radio, and appeared on numerous television networks including Comedy Central, Showtime, and NBC. He was a featured comic at both HBO's U.S. Comedy Arts Festival in Aspen, and the Just for Laughs Comedy Festival in Montreal. *Time Out New York* called him a "Must-see . . . gruff, candid, and unflinching." His one-man show, *A Cherry Tree in the Bronx*, opened to critical acclaim. Mike died of a heart attack on May 6, 2011, at the age of forty-four. A documentary celebrating his life is in the works—about how Mike found the ability to rise from addiction, look himself in the mirror, and laugh at his pain in front of the whole world, and show those who are still suffering that they can always recover, and when they do, they can do great things. Learn more at www.mikedestefano movie.com.

Dates, Locations, and Directors of the Original Performances of the Stories

STORYTELLER	STORY TITLE	DIRECTOR	STORY PREMIERE
Janna Levin	Life on a Möbius Strip	Catherine Burns	June 4, 2011 Dark Night: Stories of Stars Aligned, Part of the World Science Festival @ The Players, New York, NY
George Lombardi	Mission to India	Meg Bowles	May 31, 2012 Too Close to the Sun: Stories of Flash Points, Part of the World Science Festival @ The Great Hall at Cooper Union, New York, NY
Andrew Solomon	Notes on an Exorcism	Catherine Burns	October 29, 2008 Guts: Stories from the Razor's Edge @ The Players, New York, NY
Alan Rabinowitz	Man and Beast	Catherine Burns	October 17, 2005 Hear Ye, Hear Ye? Lost in Translation Stories @ The New York Public Library, New York, NY
Jillian Lauren	The Prince and I	Meg Bowles	February 9, 2012 Heart of Darkness: Stories of Love and War @ The Great Hall at Cooper Union, New York, NY

(continued)

STORYTELLER	STORY TITLE	DIRECTOR	STORY PREMIERE
A. E. Hotchner	The Day I Became a Matador	Catherine Burns	March 16, 2012 Moved: Stories of Safe Passage @ The Players, New York, NY
Damien Echols	Life After Death	Meg Bowles	July 11, 2012 Eyewitness: Stories from the Front @ The Players, New York, NY
Ari Handel	Don't Fall in Love with Your Monkey	Catherine Burns	June 16, 2004 Blinded by Science: Stories of the Ologies @ The Players, New York, NY
Anoid Latipovna Rakhmatyllaeva	Tajik Sonata	Catherine Burns and Mike Daisey	August 12, 2008 When Worlds Collide @ Padida Theater, Dushanbe, Tajikistan
Joe Lockhart	Impeachment Day	Lea Thau	February 12, 2005 Out on a Limb: Stories from the Edge @ Wheeler Opera House, Aspen, CO
Wayne Reece	Easter in a Texas Roadhouse	Catherine Burns	October 21, 2010 OMG: Stories of the Sacred @ The New York Public Library, New York, NY
Richard Price	Bicycle Safety on Essex	Catherine Burns	January 22, 2008 Off the Map: Stories of Confabulated Geography @ The Players, New York, NY
Jon Levin	Elevator ER	Catherine Burns	June 21, 2006 Sick: Stories about Maladies and Medicine @ The Players, New York, NY
Annie Duke	The Big Things You Don't Do	Sarah Austin Jenness	September 12, 2013 Public Radio Program Directors Conference @ The Las Vegas Hotel Casino and Resort, Las Vegas, NV
Michael Massimino	A View of the Earth	Meg Bowles	November 14, 2012 Around the Bend: Stories of Coming Home, Part of the World Science Festival @ The Great Hall at Cooper Union, New York, NY

STORYTELLER	STORY TITLE	DIRECTOR	STORY PREMIERE
Kimberly Reed	Life Flight	Jenifer Hixson	March 16, 2011 Between Worlds: Stories of Passing @ The Players, New York, NY
Darryl "DMC" McDaniels	Angel	Catherine Burns and Lea Thau	April 13, 2007 Stories of Comedy and Calamity @ The Rose O'Neill Literary House at Washington College, Chestertown, MD
George Dawes Green	The House That Sherman Didn't Burn	Catherine Burns	January 23, 2009 In Harm's Way: Stories About Danger @ The Players, New York, NY
Sherman "O.T." Powell	Cocktails in Attica	Catherine Burns	June 28, 2011 Big Night: The Moth at Central Park SummerStage @ Rumsey Playfield, New York, NY
Ed Gavagan	Whatever Doesn't Kill Me	Catherine Burns and Maggie Cino	February 17, 2011 Building a Bridge: Stories from Both Sides @ Arlene Schnitzer Concert Hall, Portland, OR
Adam Gopnik	LOL	Catherine Burns	December 13, 2006 Feeding the Hand That Bites You: Stories About Parenthood @ The Players, New York, NY
Marvin Gelfand	Liberty Card	Lea Thau	October 23, 2002 American Myths: Stories of US @ The Players, New York, NY
Paul Nurse	Discussing Family Trees in School Can Be Dangerous	Catherine Burns	June 12, 2009 Matter: Stories of Atoms and Eves @ The Players, New York, NY
Steve Osborne	The Mug Shot	Catherine Burns	May 21, 2009 Crack Up: Stories about Comedies and Calamities @ Symphony Space, New York, NY
Erin Barker	Good News Versus Bad	Jenifer Hixson	February 9, 2012 Heart of Darkness: Stories of Love and War @ The Great Hall at Cooper Union, New York, NY

(continued)

STORYTELLER	STORY TITLE	DIRECTOR	STORY PREMIERE
Edgar Oliver	The Apron Strings of Savannah	Catherine Burns	January 25, 2006 Last Exit: Stories about Endings @ The Players, New York, NY
Ellie Lee	A Kind of Wisdom	Catherine Burns	December 11, 2008 It Takes Two to Tango @ Metabolic Studio, Los Angeles, CA
Carly Johnstone	A Perfect Circle	Jenifer Hixson	July 11, 2012 Eyewitness: Stories from the Front @ The Players, New York, NY
Sebastian Junger	War	Sarah Austin Jenness	July 11, 2012 Eyewitness: Stories from the Front @ The Players, New York, NY
Andy Christie	We'll Have to Stop Now	Catherine Burns	June 21, 2006 Sick: Stories about Maladies and Medicine @ The Players New York, NY
Malcolm Gladwell	Her Way	Catherine Burns	May 21, 2009 Crack Up: Stories of Comedies and Calamities @ Symphony Space, New York, NY
Cynthia Riggs	The Case of the Curious Codes	Sarah Austin Jenness	August 13, 2012 Big Night: The Moth on Martha's Vineyard @ Union Chapel, Martha's Vineyard, MA
Ophira Eisenberg	The Accident	Catherine Burns	December 13, 2006 Feeding the Hand That Bites You: Stories about Parenthood @ The Players, New York, NY
Ted Conover	Sing Sing Tattoo	Joey Xanders	June 28, 2000 On the Road Again: An Evening of Traveling Stories @ The Yankee Clipper, New York, NY
Matthew McGough	My First Day with the Yankees	Lea Thau	May 28, 2003 Wheeling and Dealing: Stories about the Business of Doing Business @ The Players, New York, NY

STORYTELLER	STORY TITLE	DIRECTOR	STORY PREMIERE
Jeffery Rudell	Under the Influence	Lea Thau	January 28, 2003 Under the Influence: The Powers That Shape and Shake Us @ The New York Public Library, New York, NY
Elna Baker	Yes Means Yes?	Catherine Burns	June 7, 2006 Cat Out of Bag: Stories about Confessions @ The Players, New York, NY
James Braly	One Last Family Photo	Catherine Burns	January 25, 2006 Last Exit: Stories about Endings @ The Players, New York, NY
Tristan Jimerson	A Dish Best Served Cold	Sarah Austin Jenness	November 11, 2011 When Worlds Collide: Stories from the Clash @ The Fitzgerald Theater, St. Paul, MN
Aimee Mullins	A Work in Progress	Sarah Austin Jenness	December 6, 2010 A More Perfect Union: Stories of Prejudice and Power @ The New York Public Library, New York, NY
Nathan Englander	Unhooked	Catherine Burns	September 21, 2012 Driven: Stories of Shifting Gears @ The Players, New York, NY
Wanda Bullard	The Small Town Prisoner	Joey Xanders	July 23, 2009 Coming Home @ The Telfair Museum, Savannah, GA
Kemp Powers	The Past Wasn't Done with Me	Meg Bowles	July 11, 2012 Eyewitness: Stories from the Front @ The Players, New York, NY
Jenny Allen	Hair Today Gone Tomorrow	Catherine Burns	April 30, 2011 The Moth at the PEN World Voices Festival: What Went Wrong? @ The Great Hall at Cooper Union, New York, NY
Joyce Maynard	The One Good Man	Catherine Burns and Joey Xanders	December 9, 2005: Under the Influence @ The Long Wharf Theatre, New Haven, CT

(continued)

STORYTELLER	STORY TITLE	DIRECTOR	STORY PREMIERE
Stephanie Summerville	Life Support	Catherine Burns	February 22, 2007 Save Me: Stories about Rescue and Redemption @ The Players, New York, NY
Jenifer Hixson	Where There's Smoke	Catherine Burns	October 22, 2003 Blue in the Face: Stories about Smoke @ The Players, New York, NY
Brian Finkelstein	Perfect Moments	Catherine Burns	March 1, 2012 Rush: Stories of Ticking Clocks @ Royce Hall at UCLA, Los Angeles, CA
Faye Lane	Fireworks from Above	Catherine Burns	February 17, 2011 Building a Bridge: Stories from Both Sides @ Arlene Schnitzer Concert Hall, Portland, OR
Mike DeStefano	Franny's Last Ride	Catherine Burns	March 3, 2007 When Worlds Collide @ The St. Regis Aspen Resort, Aspen, CO

Acknowledgments

THE MOTH WOULD LIKE TO THANK:

All of our storytellers. You are the heart and the soul of The Moth, and don't think we ever forget it for a second.

Our collaborators, friends, and partners: Ana Adlerstein, Peter Aguero, Jay Allison, Jenny Allen, Jonathan Ames, John Barth, Mike Birbiglia, Debbie Bisno, Deborah Blakeley, Andy Borowitz, Richard Brehm, Amy Brill, Todd Bush, Sandi Carroll, Angelica Compagno, Tracy Day and Brian Greene at the World Science Festival, Brooke Delaney, Mary Domowitz, Simon Doonan, Carla Hendra, Joanne Heyman, Lyndi Hirsch, Paul Holdengräber and the New York Public Library, Kerri Hoffman, Dan Kennedy, Bonnie Levison, Caro Llewellyn, John Martello and the Players Club, D. J. Martin, Viki Merrick, Michaela Murphy, the *New Yorker* Festival, John Newell, the *Paris Review*, the PEN World Voices Festival, Shelagh Ratner, Ray Blue, Paul Ruest, Rudy Rush, Joe Del Senno, Jake Shapiro, Tom Shillue, Israel Smith, Jayne Sosland, Jon Spurney, Mazz Swift, Susan Towers, Steve Zimmer, Adam Wade, Caleigh Waldman, Chris

THE MOTH

Wall, Katherine Wesling, and Alex Roy, who literally picked us up off the street and housed us, whisking us off to our future in his purple Porsche.

The hundreds of public radio stations around the country who air *The Moth Radio Hour* and all of our national partners for both the Mainstage and StorySLAM series, especially Mikel Ellcessor at WDET and Jennifer Ferro at KCRW and Steve Edwards (formerly of WBEZ) for being the first to take on the StorySLAM series; Andrew Proctor at Literary Arts for being the first to sponsor the MothSHOP program outside of New York City; and UCLA Live, whose offer to host us started the Moth Mainstage touring series. Kerry Armstrong, Gary Buchler, and all of our regional StorySLAM crews for their tireless dedication.

All of our funders who have been the wind beneath our Moth wings (and kept the lights on) for the last sixteen years. We are forever grateful. A special note of thanks to our lead donors: Amazon.com, Kim Bendheim and the Leon Lowenstein Foundation, the Educational Foundation of America, Charles Evans Jr., Maker's Mark, the National Endowment for the Arts, NBC Universal, the New York City Department of Cultural Affairs, the New York State Council on the Arts, Ogilvy & Mather, Alice S. Powers Irrevocable Living Trust, David Richenthal, and our deepest gratitude to the John D. and Catherine T. MacArthur Foundation and the Corporation for Public Broadcasting for helping The Moth's stories soar across the country on public radio.

Our gifted agent, Daniel Greenberg. Your consummate counsel, faith, and taste have been our guide, and we're forever grateful.

Editor extraordinaire Elisabeth Dyssegaard, who read hundreds of stories and taught us how to make a book from the ground up (it was like having Beethoven prepare us for a concert at Carnegie Hall when we'd never even played a scale).

Special thanks to The Moth StorySLAM, where each week, hundreds of five-minute true stories are shared across the nation. We provide a stage, a theme, and a host, and the general public surprises us with their stories. We owe a lot to the communities surrounding these special shows, which end up feeling like big extended families. Fourteen of the fifty stories in this book are from people we first met at The Moth StorySLAMs.

GEORGE DAWES GREEN WOULD LIKE TO THANK:

Our early curators and drivers and muses: Gaby Tana, who said just stop fussing and *do this thing*; Meg Bowles (the "Homecoming" Moth you curated is still my favorite); Ann Marlowe, the soul of Manhattan; Carolyn Marks Blackwood, our angel, seeing us through the dark.

Our Executive Directors: Katie Kerr, who was there at the conception and must share the blame; Joey Xanders, the irresistible force; Lea Thau, our architect, who built this house out of cobwebs and moonshine; Joan Firestone: you spent your life nurturing creators; how can we ever live up to the fierce pride you take in us all? And Sarah Haberman, who has to face down the terrifying future . . .

Our founding Board Members: Judy Stone, who won the brutal campaign to become our first president (coin-flip); Pegi Vail and her illuminated soul; Melvin Estrella (the right thing happens to the happy man); Sheri Holman, my deepest friend; my beloved editor, Jamie Raab (despising this obsession that stole my writing time, but signing on anyway to keep an eye on me).

My agent, Molly Friedrich, who gives everything, always and quietly.

Jenifer Hixson, Director of the Moth slam, fellow Marvin-lover, biting but tender wit, late late woozy nights at L'Express after the Players.

Sarah Austin Jenness (your laugh-out-in-the-dark audience, rescuing us on stage).

Former Board Members who took calls, many calls, at midnight: Mark Baltazar, Bliss Broyard (my partner-in-arms), Nell Casey, Margaret Braun, Nina Collins, Pamela Mitchell, Josh Shenk (our graceful philosopher), David Sarlin, Jeffery Rudell.

Alan Manevitz, who looks after us. Dan Kennedy, my brother rat. Our former timekeeper Katy Rose Cox McComb and her sweetly nagging fiddle. Alex Roy, whirlwind. Gary Lippman and Scott Asen with their wheels of gorgeous admirers at the Moth Balls.

Terri Galvin, our mad beautiful story connoisseur. Jenn Coonce (*Hmm*—are you really enough of a *celebrity* to be on this list?). Molly Greene, who found our name among the Moth-Seraphs. Rosalie Barnes (remember we cooked up the slam on a subway ride to Brooklyn?).

The powers behind our brand-new Moth High School slams: Anna Sweeney, Neil Gaiman, Catherine McCarthy, Micaela Blei . . .

Catherine will thank all the staff and the present board members, but may I say that our whole sprawling fly-by-night community has always been a dazzlement to me: you producers working endless hours, you curators and interns and donors and courageous raconteurs, and you hundreds of insanely time-generous volunteers: *Where in the world do you all come from?*

CATHERINE BURNS WOULD LIKE TO THANK:

My fellow Moth sisters and story directors: Sarah Austin Jenness, Jenifer Hixson, Meg Bowles, Maggie Cino, and Kate Tellers. Putting these shows together with the five of you is truly one of the great honors of my life. Your talent—only matched by your enormous hearts—inspires, humbles, and nourishes me daily.

Sarah Haberman, now officially my partner at The Moth: So lucky to stand beside you.

Our Board of Directors, who believed that the stories from the stage could have equal power and poetry on the page: Anne Maffei, Ari Handel, Serena Altschul, Lawrence C. Burstein, Deborah Dugan, Tony Hendra, Courtney Holt, Dr. Alan Manevitz, and Roger Skelton.

Joan Firestone, our captain, and my very first reader. You gave me faith that the baby had wings and was going to fly.

Lea Thau, whose strategic vision and bottomless determination brought the magic of The Moth to the national arena. For ten years she gave her blood, sweat, tears, and talent, and we are forever grateful.

Everyone who has ever worked, interned, or volunteered at The Moth and helped us achieve our goals. Particularly our talented and tireless full time staff: David Mutton, Anna Katrina Sacramento, Kirsty Bennett, Jenna Weiss-Berman, Laura Hadden, Terence Mickey, Robin Wachsberger, Larry Rosen, Brandon Echter, and Terence Mickey.

For panicked Sunday afternoon calls about correct tenses and the nuances of the publishing industry: Judy Stone, Joshua Wolf Shenk, Jonathan Talat Phillips, Sarah Porter, and Jennifer Echols.

For literally searching the Russian-speaking world for Anoid Rakhmatyllaeva: Michael Daisey, Muyassar Vakhobova, Shafoat Kobilova, Anne Benjaminson, and especially Anya Kuznetsova, forever our translator in every sense of the word.

Our staff's much-beleaguered spouses, particularly my husband, Joshua, without whose help and grace this book would not have gotten edited.

About The Moth

The Moth—hailed as "New York's hottest and hippest literary ticket" by the *Wall Street Journal*—is an acclaimed not-for-profit organization dedicated to the art and craft of storytelling. It was founded in 1997 by the novelist George Dawes Green, who wanted to recreate in New York the feeling of sultry summer evenings in his native Georgia, when moths were attracted to the light on the porch where he and his friends would gather to spin spellbinding tales. The first New York Moth event was held in George's living room, and the story events quickly spread to larger venues throughout the city. The Moth has presented more than three thousand stories, told live and without notes, by people from all walks of life, to standing-room-only crowds worldwide. Each show features simple, old-fashioned storytelling on thoroughly modern themes by wildly divergent raconteurs who develop and shape their stories with The Moth's directors.

Today, The Moth conducts six ongoing programs—The Moth Mainstage, which tours nationally, has featured stories by Malcolm Gladwell, Ethan Hawke, Margaret Cho, Annie

Proulx, Salman Rushdie, and an astronaut, a pickpocket, a hot-dog eating champion, and hundreds more; The Moth StorySLAM program, which conducts open-mic storytelling competitions in Ann Arbor, Boston, Los Angeles, Chicago, Detroit, Houston, Louisville, New York, Milwaukee, New Orleans, Pittsburgh, Portland, San Francisco, St. Paul, and Seattle; The MothSHOP Community Education Program, which brings storytelling workshops free of charge to underserved populations; The Moth High School StorySLAMs, which brings the thrill of competitive storytelling to high schools across the country; The Moth Podcast, which is downloaded more than a million times a month; MothSHOP Corporate, which offers industry-specific storytelling solutions; and the Peabody Award-winning *The Moth Radio Hour*, produced by Jay Allison at Atlantic Public Media and presented by PRX, the Public Radio Exchange, which was launched in 2009, airs weekly on public radio stations nationwide. Pitch us your own story at themoth.org.